PENGUIN BOOKS

A CASTLE IN SPAIN

Matthew Parris was born in Africa in 1949 and grew up in Cyprus, Rhodesia, Jamaica and Britain. He worked for the Foreign Office and in Margaret Thatcher's office before becoming a Conservative MP in 1979. Seven years later, he quit to present LWT's *Weekend World*, after which he became the regular parliamentary sketch-writer for *The Times* for thirteen years.

Matthew Parris's books include his autobiography *Chance Witness*, *Read My Lips*, *Scorn with Added Vitriol* and *Inca-Kola*, about his travels in Peru. He has also made a number of television documentaries. He is a regular travel writer, reviewer, broadcaster and columnist and divides his time between London, Derbyshire and Spain.

A plan of the house and a map of the GR II can now be found at www.avenc.com.

D1079704

A Castle in Spain

MATTHEW PARRIS

PENGUIN BOOKS

PENGUIN BOOKS

Published by the Penguin Group
Penguin Books Ltd, 80 Strand, London WC2R 0RL, England
Penguin Group (USA) Inc., 375 Hudson Street, New York, New York 10014, USA
Penguin Group (Canada), 90 Eglinton Avenue East, Suite 700, Toronto, Ontario, Canada M4P 2Y3
(a division of Pearson Penguin Canada Inc.)
Penguin Ireland, 25 St Stephen's Green, Dublin 2, Ireland (a division of Penguin Books Ltd)
Penguin Group (Australia), 250 Camberwell Road, Camberwell, Victoria 3124, Australia
(a division of Pearson Australia Group Pty Ltd)
Penguin Books India Pvt Ltd, 11 Community Centre, Panchsheel Park, New Delhi – 110 017, India
Penguin Group (NZ), cnr Airborne and Rosedale Roads, Albany, Auckland 1310, New Zealand
(a division of Pearson New Zealand Ltd)
Penguin Books (South Africa) (Pty) Ltd, 24 Sturdee Avenue, Rosebank, Johannesburg 2196, South Africa

Penguin Books Ltd, Registered Offices: 80 Strand, London WC2R 0RL, England

www.penguin.com

First published in Viking in 2005
Published in Penguin Books 2006
1

Copyright © Matthew Parris, 2005
All rights reserved

The moral right of the author has been asserted

Typeset by Palimpsest Book Production Limited, Polmont, Stirlingshire
Printed in England by Clays Ltd, St Ives plc

Except in the United States of America, this book is sold subject
to the condition that it shall not, by way of trade or otherwise, be lent,
re-sold, hired out, or otherwise circulated without the publisher's
prior consent in any form of binding or cover other than that in
which it is published and without a similar condition including this
condition being imposed on the subsequent purchaser

ISBN-13: 978-0-141-01943-7
ISBN-10: 0-141-01943-3

To my father, Leslie

Contents

Acknowledgements

All my family – the part each played becomes clear in the pages that follow – are owed more than thanks: the story told here would never have happened without them. Other heroes, too, deserve mention, but you will find out about them if you read on.

My sister Belinda and her husband, Quim, have an equal claim with me to the rescue of the house that we three own together, and Belinda has helped me at every stage in the writing of this book. So has Julian Glover, who has been a partner with me in the whole project.

Quim's brother, Francesc Abey i Palau, was at the outset one of the four owners, who became three when Francesc, having helped us get started, was confident we could manage alone; we will never forget his support.

We have been helped at l'Avenc by grants and subsidies, as well as professional help and advice, which I would not wish to go unacknowledged. We are grateful to the Direcció General del Patrimoni i Cultura at the Generalitat de Catalunya; to the Institut Català d'Energia for help with renewable energy; and to the Fundació Garrotxa Líder not only for a generous grant as part of their programme to encourage sustainable tourism, but for the faith in our project (and patient advice to Belinda on account-ancy) shown by Jordi Sucarrats and Manolo Sánchez.

The Oficina de Promoció Econòmica de Manlleu (and espe-cially Montse Rafart) helped and encouraged Belinda to go for and win the 'best business initiative' award from La Diputació de Barcelona, which so boosted her morale.

This is no work of scholarship and a bibliography would be pretentious, but among the many authors and experts I have consulted, relied upon and sometimes plagiarized, I should mention *Catalonia – Nation-building without a State* by Kenneth McRoberts and *The Diocese of Vic* by Professor Paul Freedman. Rafel Ginebra at the episcopal archive at Vic has been incredibly kind.

Colleagues at *The Times*, which published the first of what I wrote about l'Avenc, encouraged me to think readers would be interested. I have quoted freely from some of those early columns and am grateful to the editor for letting me do so. My editor at the *Spectator* magazine has been similarly kind.

Ed Victor has advised and exhorted as only Ed can, while at Penguin Tony Lacey and his assistant Zelda Turner have made all the difference. Bela Cunha's copy-editing has corrected a thousand silly little errors and a handful of silly big ones.

As the history of our project unfolds, I hope it becomes evident that the people of all the towns and villages around l'Avenc, but especially the villages of Tavertet and Rupit, have always supported our efforts and often joined them. I should like to thank this legion: unnamed but not unappreciated.

I cannot name here every builder, tradesman and craftsman whose labours have made the restored house what it is; I cannot list the occasions on which my mother, Theresa, would arrive after dawn with fresh croissants and sweet *coca* bread just purchased from the bakery in Rupit – and one day with a portable generator she bought us from her savings; I cannot count the hours friends and family have lit fires, patiently swept, cleaned and served food to keep us all going; I cannot convey in the detail they deserve the exquisite designs of each of Pep de la Torre's carved wooden panels which so delight visitors; I cannot begin to number and describe the efforts that add up to the collective achievement I must never claim as personal; but I am sheepishly aware that while I have swanned in and out, penning happy thoughts, others have been wielding hammers and chisels, drilling holes, laying pipes and carving wood and stone. To all of them, a heartfelt thank you.

*

The author and publishers are grateful to the following for permission to reproduce material. Every effort has been made to trace copyright holders. The publishers will be glad to rectify in future editions any errors or omissions brought to their attention.

Extract from *The Revolt of the Catalans* by J. H. Elliott (Cambridge University Press, 1963) reprinted by kind permission of Cambridge University Press.

Map of L'Avenc drawn by Andrew Farmer, copyright © Andrew Farmer, 2005.

Picture inset: Photographs reproduced by kind permission of Mercè Terricabras (5–9, 11–13, 23–4, 31–4, 36–7), Andrew Hubble (20, 21), Jason P. Howe (16 and 22), Rex Features (25), Adrian Glover (27), Episcopal Archive, Cathedral of Vic (28), Xavier Valls (30), Belinda Parris (29, 38), Mark Read (1–2, 39–40, 45, 50), Jordi Gumì (44, 49), Julian Glover (46–8).

L'Avenc
Catalunya

P

Sant Julià de Cabrera

Cantonigròs

L'Esquirol

← To Vic & Manlleu

Sant Pere de Casserres

Pantà de Sau

Riu Ter

Inside map:
FRANCE
L'Avenc
SPAIN
Catalunya

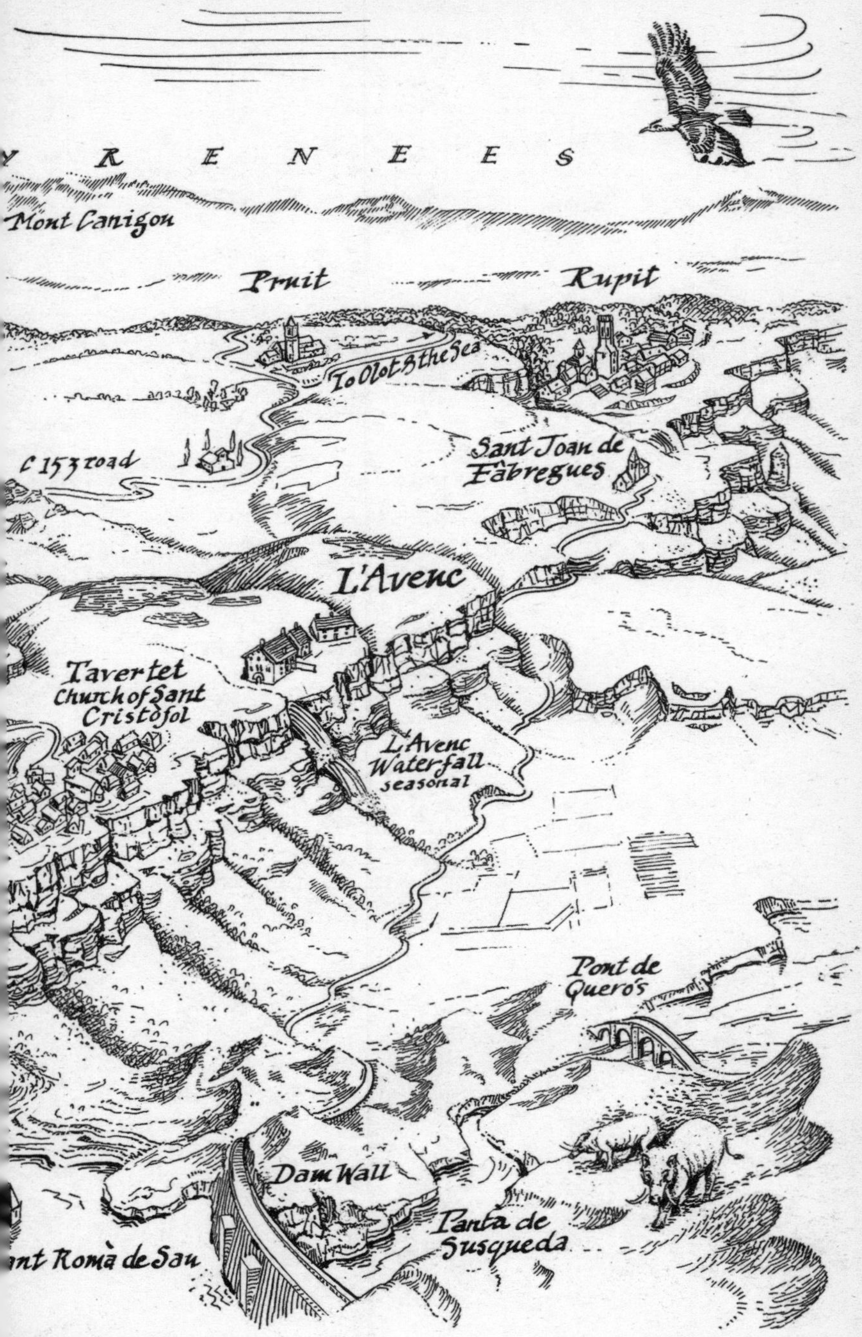

PYRENEES

Mont Canigou

Pruit

Rupit

To Olot & the Sea

C 153 road

Sant Joan de
Fàbregues

L'Avenc

Tavertet
Church of Sant
Cristòfol

L'Avenc
Waterfall
seasonal

Pont de
Queros

Dam Wall

Panta de
Susqueda

Sant Romà de Sau

Introduction

Why? Not 'Why restore a house in the mountains of Catalunya?' but 'Why write a book about it?'

Two reasons really, of which the first is obvious I suppose. I write for readers. Over the years I have written bits and pieces about the house for *The Times* and the *Spectator* magazine and been slightly surprised at my readers' interest and enthusiasm. I think it's a great story and, finding a willing audience, needed no further encouragement to tell it.

Except perhaps this. There is a market for books about quaint locals, funny foreign customs and the travails of Englishmen abroad, but, as I explain, this is not such a book. Others do that kind of thing better.

Nor am I trying to publicize the project in the sense of marketing it. L'Avenc will find its own place in the century ahead, and I believe we may have to turn people away in time. Please do not mistake my enthusiasm for the house and the region – though I hope to communicate it – for travel advice. Inland Catalunya might not be your cup of tea at all.

This is not a book about you or me. It is a book about a house. I have written it because I think the house matters. The very stones, their past and their future, are important beyond me, my co-owners, and our brush with their story. L'Avenc is the strong character in these pages. L'Avenc is the personality I want to introduce, the individual I hope you will remember.

The moment I saw this house I knew it was different and that its ruin must be averted. The story follows. If in reading it you begin to feel even a fraction of what I feel for the place, then it will have been worth telling.

L'Avenc, June 2005

1. A Meeting Between Strangers

From a mountainside at daybreak when it has rained in the night, you look out across land bathed in cloud. What is solid and dark swims in what is pale and insubstantial. An unremarkable heap of rocks emerging from the mists enjoys its moment of prominence as an Ararat after the Flood. A line of trees stands out as though it were alone, floating in unreal isolation between sea and sky. Rags of cloud fold themselves between the ridges, interleaving hard silhouettes with strips of soft white, layering the landscape. Each dark edge seems cut in cardboard, packed in cotton wool.

To a man walking alone in the bright morning air above this sea of vapours, every perspective is new. He pauses here above the swirl. Steam rises from the woods and flecks of fog are draped across lake and marsh below. He stares and stares in wonder. When it is time to walk on, he resolves to return.

L'Avenc was not ours when, on such a morning thirty years ago, I first stood at the great arched entrance to the ruined house. As yet unacquainted, l'Avenc and I looked out across the forested valleys and gorges of the River Ter 2,000 feet below.

To me it was new. I was twenty-five and just starting what was planned to be a career in the Foreign Office. My father's job had taken the family to Catalunya in north-eastern Spain, so for holidays I often stayed at the factory manager's house in the friendly but hard-bitten mill town of Manlleu, where my parents and younger brothers and sisters lived. But Catalunya had never been my home.

This Catalunya was now spread out at my feet. Twenty miles inland, under the fog across the plain of Vic, lay workaday Manlleu, where Dad's factory made electric cables, where my mother taught English, and where my younger brother and sister went to school. The plain of Vic is part of the inland area to the north of Barcelona, but short of the Pyrenees, which goes by the name of Osona.

These were the last days of General Franco's long rule, and though Spain was opening up and package holidays from Britain to the Costa Brava were getting into their swing, the shabby, grey industrial towns of inland Catalunya were little-visited places. To me the allure was always the countryside. Whenever I could I escaped to the hills and mountains, to explore.

The Pyrenees were not far away, and around their skirts hundreds of square miles of wild, wooded cliffs, gorges and flat-topped hills dropped away to the coast and the Mediterranean Sea. This strange and distinctive landscape is called the Collsacabra (mountain pass of the goat). It was made for walking.

The evening before I had been studying my collection of old-fashioned and inaccurate maps, hand-drawn and printed on rough paper, and noticed, on the brink of an immense cliff system in the Collsacabra, two villages. They were called Tavertet and Rupit, and they stood not far apart along the cliffs. Each lay at the dead-end of access roads which stopped at the cliff. From one to the other by road the long way round was about twenty miles, yet along the top of the cliffs, as the crow flies, they were hardly five miles apart. Surely, I thought, there would be a way on foot, tracing the cliff's edge, direct from Tavertet to Rupit? My map suggested a track of some kind.

And so it had proved. I had risen very early and parked in Tavertet. It was after Easter. The *alzines* (evergreen oaks) were fresh-leaved, the juniper bushes were pale grey-green, the sloe had come into leaf, and along the rocky edges of the cliffs tiny hyacinths and wild dwarf daffodils shone their purples and yellows up from the thin soil. Rising from an undergrowth of box bushes came a warm smell: savoury with just the hint of rankness about it. The fragrance was to become so familiar to me.

Where the track almost touched the edge of the cliff I stopped and, lying on my stomach, shuffled forward until I could peer over.

I lay in the morning sun. Far below, birds wheeled in the gentle upward draught. Into the cloud dropped the bare, sheer rock face, grey streaked with red. Through the cloud you could glimpse dense undergrowth at the cliff's feet. It was another country down there beneath the mists: here in the sun on this flowery shelf between the hills behind and the cliffs below, I could have been on a magic carpet.

Though unaware of this, I was within a few hundred yards of a mysterious, mildewed concrete circle, perhaps six feet in diameter, also near the cliff's edge. We do not know for how many years the deep vertical shaft it caps has protected cattle, sheep and the unaware from a fatal drop; nor do we know how deep is this *avenc* – an old word from the French Languedoc language of Oc, meaning 'natural shaft', 'vertical cave' or 'abyss'. But one day I will surely find out: for not a quarter of a mile away the house named after this *avenc* was to come close to taking over my life. I did not even know its proper pronunciation: *l'avenk*.

I walked on. The track was muddy and led gently uphill with no sign of other human hikers or of habitation. It seemed a secret world. A mile or two after leaving Tavertet, rounding a corner and resting under some oak trees, I looked up at a broad, shallow fold in the hillside across which my track would wind next, still climbing. And there at the top of a gentle rise, with the hills behind, stood l'Avenc.

I knew this was the house's name because, curiously and unlike most of the other isolated homesteads which dot rural Catalunya, it was marked on the map. Odd. Why would a particular house be shown and named? Even from this distance I could see that the place was derelict. Yet it had majesty. Something about the way that untypically tall, three-storey, stone façade dominated the sloping meadows around, marked it out as special: abandoned maybe, but with a kind of dignity, conscious of its position.

The shape was untypical too. Most farmhouses in the region had the characteristic rural Catalan outline: long and quite low beneath an off-centre roof with a longer slope to one side and a shorter one to the other. Charming as they are, they lack stature. L'Avenc's stature was what first struck you. Its back to the hillside, the house faced out, standing tall with a square-on symmetry.

I walked on and crossed a little stream; five minutes took me to the front door. Nobody who sees it ever forgets the massive stone arch above the doorway, fanning out wide and high, dwarfing what were really very sizeable wooden doors. They were shut, but broken and rotting.

I stood right beneath the stunning façade, craning my neck to look up at the stubs of gap-toothed eaves.

Big as the place was, I had seen in Catalunya mansions more massive, buildings ancient and modern which were every bit as fine. Isolated as this situation was, it was not the first isolated farmhouse my walks had taken me past. And grand as the view was, these were not the first wide mountains and green valleys I had seen: much of inland Catalunya is magnificent. But there was something different about this place: something enchanted. It hit you between the eyes. There was something striking in this solitude, too. Rounding that bend in the track, I had stumbled upon a sort of domain.

I swung round and looked where l'Avenc looks: southward, out over the Ter valley and Montseny mountains. You could see into the heart of Catalunya: to the east, where the river flowed out of the mountains and through the walled city of Girona, on its way to the Mediterranean. Was that the sea, fading into a horizon? To the west, past the small city of Vic, I recognized the mad silhouette of Montserrat, the holy mountain, all Gothic jagged rocks, the spiritual home of not just Catalan Catholicism but the Catalan identity itself.

Only the ridges and peaks of the Montseny mountains, breaking through the clouds, hid the city of Barcelona, hot and humid on the coast to the south. To the north the land behind me rose towards the snowy ridges of the Pyrenees and France. I could see as far as the mountains above Andorra.

And almost at my feet – just down the meadow which sloped away from where I stood – was the cliff's edge. The cliff over which the valley dropped away was sheer, brutal, magnificent. It looked like something from a science-fiction movie. Dark green Mediterranean oak forest frothed from the mist at the cliff's foot. A waterfall from the night's rain splashed over the rocks.

Cliff, mountain, lake and river; forests of oak and beech; Barcelona, the ski-slopes of the Pyrenees and – just out of sight – the Costa Brava: variously busy or serene, these worlds lay not far away, all around the points of our compass. L'Avenc was at the still, silent centre of this compass.

But of nobody's life. North-eastern Spain was one of southern Europe's most populated regions, yet here in its heart stood a ruined house in lonely majesty, empty; and the view from the carved windows at the front was pure wilderness. The picture was primeval.

How long had the house been here? Five hundred, 1,000 years? The view could hardly have been very different a millennium ago. There were no other dwellings around, no hikers, no fences, no roads, no sign at all of people. An old house in the middle of the Old World looked out at a savage mountainscape which could have been Bolivia.

I thought then, and have so often thought since, that in some curious sense this place was not *in* any country or continent at all, but ruled a kingdom of its own. I thought then, and have so often thought since, that l'Avenc did not quite belong where it was, and knew that it didn't. We regarded each other, the house and I, as might two expatriates meeting in a foreign land: hitherto unacquainted but joined by their strangeness to where they found themselves. We recognized each other.

Looking down at the clouds rolling around the valley, as you might from a jet, it was possible to imagine that l'Avenc was in the sky. This was a castle in the air; a castle in Spain. This could be my castle in Spain.

It was, at any rate, unreachable by road. One way along the cliffs, still an hour's walk away, was my original destination, the village of Rupit, its narrow stone streets and rustic houses tucked into a wooded gorge. In the other direction, from which I had come – half an hour's walk – stood remote Tavertet, at the dead-end of a tortuous road, in whose small, eleventh-century stone church of Sant Cristòfol I was later to find an old wooden pew carved with 'Avenc': a pew which had long been empty.

And in the middle — of nowhere, it seemed — stood l'Avenc in unobserved grandeur. Who had chiselled that stone arch around the great doorway, its curve a massive yet delicate construction? The windows — unglazed, rotting wooden shutters hanging askew to either side — had eyebrows of intricately carved stone screenwork, and there were arrow-slits beneath the eaves of the huge tiled roof.

Arrow-slits? Why? I knew at once that this house had never really needed them. They were a sort of caprice. The place was cocking a snook at fashion and functionality, unwilling to be bound to epoch or situation. Though the house was evidently very old, a rocket-launching pad would not have looked out of place.

A date was chiselled on a mysterious crest above one of these windows: it looked like 1557 or 1559. The back of the house seemed much older.

The workmanship breathed pride, taste — and wealth. The location was breathtaking. Yet though obviously once prized, this fortified stone mansion had been abandoned. Why? The question must have intrigued any passing traveller as he wondered at the splendour of the house, the beauty of its situation, and at its ruin.

This was not just another fine old rural Catalan mansion, of which there are scores in the region, all splendid, rightly prized, but typical: part of a set. The house I was staring at, the personality whose acquaintance I was making, was like one of those people who always stand out in a room, however large or fine the company. There is something about them. In the end what more can you say than that?

It intrigued me. I stood a long time, taking it all in, and wondering. 'I'll come back here,' I thought; and walked on. L'Avenc had stolen into my heart.

2. A Decision

Christmas Eve 1997. On the brink of a tremendous decision I hardly slept. I would doze off and within minutes be reawoken by another argument tugging at my sleeve: another argument about l'Avenc.

It is funny how the unconscious mind refuses to accept orders to close down discussion of what the unconscious considers unresolved. Deep down I must have known how big this leap was; and that if I took it I would take with me my sister Belinda and her husband and family too. We would be in this together, and it would be the biggest step any of us had taken since we were young, setting a course for the rest of our lives. I wonder whether unconsciously we knew that. That afternoon we had taken a decision which even now I was reconsidering.

More than twenty years had passed since first I saw l'Avenc. Times without number we had walked that way again, taking friends, younger sisters and brothers, and even my mother, Theresa. We piggy-backed her over ruts and gullies in the deteriorating track. Times without number we had fallen again beneath the spell of the house. Everyone always did. All who saw l'Avenc felt awestruck, mystified at its fate, and a little bit sad.

And still the place stood abandoned, the big doors now swinging loose in the wind, the roof a little more precarious. Never had we seen anyone around the place, taking care of it. Never had we seen the least sign of ownership. Villagers in Tavertet would shake their heads sadly when you asked.

For l'Avenc, we had learned, was neither unknown nor unappreciated. People locally said it was one of the finest old houses in the Collsacabra. Every farmstead, however isolated, looks to one or another village or town, and the people of Tavertet saw l'Avenc as in some way theirs, though miles away. In the days when the house had been inhabited, that is how its owners had seen things too.

'L'Avenc de Tavertet' was (and is) the house's full title. Its inhabitants would have walked to the village for Mass, to be wed and to be buried. The church, standing at the top of an ancient long-distance packhorse track up from the cliffs' feet – the track which then continued past l'Avenc – was well named after the patron saint of travellers.

Human links with Tavertet had been lost. Only a few of the oldest villagers could remember anyone living there. In another age the owners of l'Avenc had taken the name as their surname, but the family had died out long ago. The last people to live there, two brothers, Ramon and Bartalomeu, it was said, had left in the 1950s.

As the years went by we were to find out a great deal more about the house and its history, but from no single source. No one had made l'Avenc the object of their research, yet it had caught many people's attention and for centuries had been mentioned in passing; so though nobody had ever tried to piece together its story, the pieces – or some of them – were lying around.

That Christmas Eve, as I wrestled with the decision whether to turn away from what might amount to a staggering task, we knew only that the place was precious and important, that it had a history, and that its rescue was urgent. But why us? Anyone in Tavertet or Rupit would have sighed that something ought to be done, yet nobody had come forward. Why not? If we didn't know then, we were surely to find out.

Everybody regretted the fall of the House of l'Avenc, but all could see that the building's restoration would be a colossal undertaking. Tavertet was a modest village, rooted in farming but with a growing sprinkling of holiday homes. The problem with this house was its distance from proper roads and services. Restoration was beyond the ambitions of a small community, and nobody with both the sense of mission and the means had ever come forward. The house and its land were now part of an extensive agricultural estate stretching all the way along the cliffs, whose absentee owner either couldn't or wouldn't maintain the house at its centre.

One can see it from his point of view. Why should he? He was a farmer, not a custodian of historic buildings, and the house was of little use to his business. No modern labourer or manager would want to move in there with a family. What modern family would want to start married life or bring up children with no plumbing, telephone or electricity, all but inaccessible by road, under a roof that looked close to falling in?

So the owner had let it go. His cattle had invaded the ground floor of the house and were using it for shade and shelter. Cow-muck was everywhere. We had lamented the impending ruin of l'Avenc.

My brothers and sisters – just children when, newly arrived in Spain, we had first walked that way – had become almost Catalan now, all married to Catalans, all with children of their own. Belinda, a teenager then, had married a young man called Joaquim – Quim (pronounced kim) – whose family ran a builders' merchant's and home hardware business in the valley town of Manlleu. She had met him as his teacher trying to teach him English in our mother's school of languages. The attempt to teach him English failed, so she had married him instead. The young couple were soon as captivated by l'Avenc as I was.

And as our interest had deepened over the years, so had our curiosity. One bright morning in the early 1980s – before the cattle had broken into l'Avenc's ground floor – we had prised open the door and entered the house.

This time I was with my other sister, Deborah, who had married a Catalan farmer and still loved exploring the wild places in the Collsacabra with me. Before invading the house, she and I stood before it, and stared. This was no farmhouse at all. It was a stately home, a small château. Something about it was quite extraordinary: something in both the generality and the detail. To the detail in a moment; but it was the general impression which first arrested me as it has done countless visitors. It is hard to say why, for, though grand and shapely, it is hardly the finest house you ever saw.

I suspect it lies in the power of three. This is not the only Catalan farmhouse within which three floors will be found, but l'Avenc from the front declares itself a three-level building. And each upper floor had three windows at the front. It is also essentially a three-sided building, for, though the front and sides are square to each other and the world, it tails off like a snake at the back: there is no back to speak of.

Though no mystic or new-age visionary, I do think numbers matter and affect us. The number three – three of anything – very slightly jars, and very slightly thrills: perhaps because tidiness whispers that it ought to be two or four. Three is the ultimate odd number, and I doubt it is a coincidence that the word 'odd' has that other meaning. L'Avenc was odd.

It was dark inside (the rotting shutters were still on their hinges) and it took a while for our eyes to accustom. What we then saw astonished us.

We had expected dereliction, of course, and we found it. The two wooden floors had half rotted away and there were gaping holes in the woodwormed oak. Intruders – hikers, perhaps, taking shelter for the night – had built fires with fallen planks, and there was graffiti on the bare stone walls; but on the whole l'Avenc's uninvited visitors had respected the place. When we clambered up the remains of a staircase to the first floor, and picked our way around the walls where the floor was safest, we saw why.

The room we were in had obviously been the state room, about fifty feet long and half as wide. Its ceiling was three times as high as any modern building would allow, giving the whole space a cool, classical symmetry. At the room's end – the front façade of the house – the double-window, with a stone window-seat to each side, was crowned by an elaborately carved stone frame, very ornate. This and all the other features of the room, not least its scale, lent it an air of nobility.

The doorways were extraordinary, especially to an Englishman. On the whole we understate door-surrounds in British architecture. Even in grand houses they are usually of businesslike design: elegant or otherwise they are typically a series of moulded lines, modest frames to the main event: the door itself. What's around the door is rarely designed to draw the eye.

But these did. They were theatrical, like the squared proscenium arches of London theatres. All five doors to the room (one of which led nowhere) were framed by massive stone blocks, finely cut. To either side of one door was a sort of bas-relief pillar in decorated stone, topped by a carved stone head: a man's head, with a monk-like fringe. The other doors were bordered likewise in bas-relief carved stone, but in abstract not figurative designs. In each case the area covered by the surround was about twice the area of the door itself. L'Avenc's long-dead inhabitants would have to have had imposing figures indeed to make a grand entrance without being upstaged by the portals.

The ceiling too had been finely made, all its six big oak cross-beams, black with age, clad in finished oak panelling, now rotten and peeling back to reveal the beam beneath. The room cried out for a big, central chandelier.

None of this, however, was what first drew the eye. Most strik-ing of all was a minor mystery: an arched recess in the stone of one wall, raised about three feet from the floor and itself four feet by four, into which was set a wide, flat stone basin with a stone shelf to either side. The basin was backed by a sort of headstone.

In fact it was, literally, a headstone because into it was carved, in bas-relief and springing from the rock, a head: a man's, the size of a real human head, crowned in a full, high bishop's mitre. The stonework seemed badly eroded, perhaps by rain dripping through the ceiling: the mitre was broken; and a repair had been made in cement where a tap had been stuck in crudely. But a bishop this unmistakably was. His mouth made a round O, and this appeared to have been the orifice from which water had originally flowed, or been pumped, into the basin. The whole carved caprice some-how dominated the room which dwarfed it.

After wondering at this for a while, and taking care not to fall through the rotten floorboards, we had explored the two long rooms positioned like sleeves to either side of this state room, each with carved window-lintles and window-seats like the first. And in the room to the right there was something more: a massive fireplace, above its mantel a crest carved into the stone. The crest was the same as the one cut into the arch above l'Avenc's great doorway; the same as the one outside and above the lintel of a window bearing an inscription and date: IHS Maria 1559.

The crest above the fireplace bore no date but, like the others, was composed of a shield traversed by three vertical bars, and through these bars, woven in stone, the letter S. Think of the sign for a US dollar, but with three downstrokes instead of one or two. The top right-hand end of the S was carved into a tiny loop, like a piece of looped thread; and in the top left-hand quarter of the shield was a Templar cross.

Hardly speaking, we moved gingerly around, amazed. Then we pulled ourselves up to the next floor, the top floor, which was laid out in the same way, also with carved doorways and windows. Beside these windows, however, were the ornate stone arrow-slits carved in the shape of giant keyholes. Even without that dated crest we could guess that this part of the house at least was Renaissance. I reflected again that whoever commissioned these was not expecting to use them: the token fortification was a kind of boast, a rich man's folly.

Here on the top floor, in the big room immediately above the state room on the second floor, we saw the portent of a fatal turn in l'Avenc's fortunes. This hall was of identical size to the state room below but not so high. It lay under the roof, to whose underside one looked up from beneath, there being no false ceiling or attic. The ridge of a roof which was twice as long as it was broad was held up by a huge oak ridge beam spanning the length of this part of the house. Secondary beams, also oak, sloped down from the ridge beam to the eaves. And the ridge beam had cracked. Right in the middle it had split and, like a half-broken limb – a 'greenstick fracture' – begun to sag.

From outside the house this was not yet clear. L'Avenc is tiled in thick red-clay Mediterranean tiles, many of them (we later discovered) the originals, hand-made centuries ago, some at the house itself, which had had its own *teuleria* (tile factory) and used the clay we were later to curse for its super-glue powers of adhesion to the human shoe. Each tile had been shaped around a man's thigh – the traditional way of standardizing size. The roof's length and span were ambitious: there were tons of tiles up there. But though, from beneath, the fracture in the beam screamed danger, its deformation was not yet great and there was no obvious dip in the external line of the roof.

This was the first time we had climbed to the top floor, so for how long it had been like this we did not know, but somebody before us had spotted the impending disaster, and from beneath jammed a long pole (a rotten poplar trunk) into the underside of the split, to hold the ridge beam up. It looked like one of those wood poles people used to prop up a washing line in the middle when laden with wet clothes.

As a temporary measure this was all anyone could do, but it had one obvious weakness. The supporting prop was itself resting on the floorboards in the middle of the floor beneath. It could bear no more weight than the joist beneath it, on to which it was transferring the strain. Given that the massive ridge beam had failed, it could only be a matter of time before the more modest joist now indirectly supporting it would fail too.

When that happened, the roof and the second floor would collapse simultaneously on to the first floor. This would probably bring down the first floor too. The whole wing of the house – the Renaissance part – would collapse inwards. In a matter of minutes, this would be the end of l'Avenc. As surely as Samson's pulling down of one pillar levelled the Philistines' temple, the giving-way of that slender prop would doom the whole house. Exposed to the elements, the walls (and all the finely carved stonework within) would crumble and sag.

Once the roof goes, no building lasts. This split beam could have been there for a decade or a week, and might hold for a decade or a week to come. But sooner or later it would give. A heavy fall of snow would be the most likely final straw. Deborah and I could see at once what all this meant. The front, sixteenth-century end of l'Avenc looked unlikely to survive into the next generation.

The back was different, poorer, probably older – perhaps much older. Pokey, even darker, with small rooms and one window which looked Gothic, this was a higgledy-piggledy construction, dominated by a truly ancient-looking kitchen with bread oven and open fire, beneath a high stone arch. The immediate impression was of a big old farmhouse whose owners had come into serious money towards the end of the Middle Ages and refronted their property as a stately home in the new Renaissance style.

And here was another riddle. Someone, at some point in history, appeared to have lost confidence in the kitchen arch and built a twenty-foot-high stone column to support it in the middle – or, rather, not quite the middle, for it was offset to one side. At this too we wondered. We had yet to learn about the great earthquakes of 1427.

Blinking as we emerged back into the light outside, we had made our way home in excited speculation.

Home, my parents' home, was now (and by pure chance) much closer. A few years after I had seen the house for the very first time, my father, Leslie, had suffered a series of terrible heart-attacks at the age of fifty-eight, and been forced to retire. My mother's language school – 'Anglo-Català' – continued to thrive in Manlleu, where Dad had worked, but she and Dad had moved out of the factory manager's house in the town and, instead of retiring back to Britain, bought a small farmhouse in the Collsacabra called l'Hostalot. A welcoming place among woods and meadows, l'Hostalot had become the closest thing we had to a family home. And it was only about seven miles from l'Avenc.

Belinda and Quim lived not far away. They too, with their three children, had been drawn to the Collsacabra and bought and restored a farm cottage, Casalons, primitive but sweet, in the hills behind.

It was as though the Catalan side of my family was being drawn into a loose orbit around the house. This was accident, not design. But if you had asked any of us to name a spot which summed up for us the magic of the region, we would all have said l'Avenc.

And from faraway Britain where I still lived, I too had felt the pull. I never forgot that house. My sister remembers my saying to her, decades ago: 'If you ever hear of that house being up for sale, let me know.'

Since that summer of 1975 my life had spun wonderfully off into outer space. I had given up on a diplomat's career, taken a job working in Margaret Thatcher's office while she was leader of the Opposition, been elected to Parliament where I had served for seven years, and then left politics for broadcasting and writing. I had become an established columnist and parliamentary sketchwriter for *The Times*.

I had been lucky. I counted myself a success in my trade, worked hard, enjoyed it enormously, and was well paid for what I did. But it was a world with no outdoors. Words – my own and others' – commanded so much of my attention, and my stock-in-trade was the rancour and disputation of British politicians and the shock-horror of two decades of name-calling, scandal and so-called 'sleaze'. Puce faces, bold headlines, ridicule and anger, grey streets and grey skies . . . these occupied another universe from the blues and browns and soft greens of the Collsacabra. I had been living in that other universe for a long time, and perhaps that is why the house seemed to draw me. Standing clear, alone and apart on its clifftop in the sun, the house called.

For me, for Belinda and for her husband who shared my love of the house, that was, however, as far as it would have gone – a hankering – if in the autumn of 1997 news had not reached us which was completely unexpected. L'Avenc was for sale.

We heard it from a man who was to become very much part of the project and whom my family already knew as an inspired local master builder, and a friend. Joan Sarsanedas (Joan is Catalan for John, and pronounced jwan) was simply one of the best builders around but he was more than a builder. He understood the two elements – stone and oak – at the heart of traditional rural architecture in Catalunya. He knew how to work with them, how to design with them, and whom to call upon when craftsmen were needed.

Sarsanedas moved deftly in the world of restoration and refurbishment: he also had ideas, creative and original ideas, for building *upon* the past as well as rebuilding from the past. He knew his strengths and took pleasure from them. He could be obstinate, but only those who did not know him could call him mulish, for Sarsanedas was an imaginative man.

He had done well for himself – his services were not cheap –

and cut a figure locally as more than a builder. He has always reminded me of a less tragic version of Halvard Solness, the master builder in Ibsen's play of the same name. Joan Sarsanedas was a powerful visualizer, a big man with a strong will, bags of confidence, and a name to be reckoned with, which I think he enjoyed.

He told Quim that l'Avenc's proprietor, the pig-farmer and cattle-man who owned the clifftops and pastures almost all the way from the edges of Rupit to the edges of Tavertet, had sold l'Avenc to him: the house and thirty acres around it. Joan Sarsanedas's plan had been to restore the house himself: as an owner who was also a builder the idea made sense. But on reflection and closer inspection he had had to abandon the plan. He had too much on his plate to add what he had come to see would be a huge burden. Were we interested in buying l'Avenc from him?

I did not know then, and will probably never know, why the owner, another Joaquim, Joaquim Casals, had sold in the first place. The obvious explanation is the most likely: that he had no use for the house. Sr Casals was more an agri-businessman than a farmer. He did not live on his farm, which was named after the only other house along these cliffs, two miles further towards Rupit: Rajols was a fine stone dwelling now jostled almost from view by a gaggle of steel and wood sheds and piggeries. The business was run by hired farm managers whom he had installed in Rajols. A historic building in dire need of repair was the last thing he wanted and perhaps he too was sorry to see its impending fall. Though he had a reputation as a hard man, he may have felt uncomfortable about being the owner in whose hands, and after more than 800 years, such a notable house finally fell down.

L'Avenc looked in danger of being thrown from owner to owner like a game of pass-the-parcel, until in somebody's custody the roof fell in. Sarsanedas was ready to throw it on to us. Would we catch the unlucky house?

He was asking £160,000 for the house and twelve acres.

Sr Sarsanedas said he would be pleased to be our builder in the project. At the time I wondered whether this had always been his plan: to sell the house on. He was open from the start about his wish to be involved in the restoration, should we buy it. Experience since then makes me doubt there was any plan. The closer you looked at the challenges, the bigger they looked, and I think Sarsanedas bought the place on a whim then came to the conclusion he had bitten off more than he could chew. '*Les sabates massa grosses*' was his way of putting it: 'shoes too big for my feet'. Quim's father, Josep, was to remind his son and daughter-in-law almost daily that they also ended up dragging around bigger shoes than was dignified, as he saw Quim's car shrink from open-topped sports car to Renault Clio, and his seaside flat go up for sale. His mother, Maria, lovingly supports all his projects, as is the nature of mothers, including mine.

Whoever owned the house, Joan Sarsanedas would have been pleased to work on it for a variety of reasons: it would play to all his specialist skills in traditional Catalan building; l'Avenc was stuffed with the building and architectural challenges he most enjoyed. Were we to become the new owners, he knew he could count on being properly paid, and he knew we would want the work done to exacting standards. He could be as perfectionist as was his instinct, with no risk of being beaten down to a price. There would be no pressure from us to cut corners. Were the house his, the businessman and the craftsman in him might pull in opposite directions; were it ours, they would pull the same way.

Joan Sarsanedas was never short of work, but a man like that gets bored with building stone-faced boxes in newly allocated parcels of land outside rural villages, as second homes for jaded townies. He wanted a challenge. He wanted to give his imagination free rein. As we were never quite impertinent enough to remind Joan, his illustrious countryman Antonio Gaudí was always bankrupting his clients too.

But Joan, like me and all my family, and many in the area with a sense of its heritage, had been genuinely distressed to see so fine a local landmark, one which had stood there for so many centuries, heading – and in our own lifetimes – for its doom; and nobody coming forward to save it. This way, he could play his part, but with rather less risk.

Even in 1997 (and considering what we have spent since) £160,000 was not a huge sum, though it sounded more frightening in pesetas: 40,000,000. But we were under no illusion that this would be the end of it. The purchase price would be only the beginning of our expenses, and to rescue the house and bring it into modern use we would have to spend as much again – or more. We never doubted that.

Just how much more, we had little idea, but I think we all sensed the danger of any one of us trying to carry the project alone. Quim and Belinda were keen, but nervous. Quim thought his brother Francesc might join a consortium, but without wanting to get involved in an everyday way. My sister was no less beneath l'Avenc's spell than I was. But it would be a leap, and she was not certain how committed Quim would be; he was at the same time excited and doubtful. She did not want to push him.

I did not want to push her. Could we make a go of it? Had I the time? Had I the money? 'It will be,' warned my father, who always preferred Castilian Spanish to Catalan, '*un pozo sin fondo*' – a bottomless pit. How much could the others contribute? What part would I play in the project? My sister, I knew, would be asking herself the same questions. I think each of us was waiting for someone else to be surer than they were.

I was hesitant. But it's always been my role to be the one who seems sure, and you sometimes find yourself playing the part expected of you. You do this not so much out of confidence in the plot as out of obedience to the casting-director. I dare say that one of these days we'll all be 10,000 feet up in an aeroplane and someone will say, 'Apparently if you jump out without a parachute over an upward thermal by a sheer rock cliff and stick out your legs and arms, you can float gently down and land unharmed . . . Oh look – there's a cliff!' And we'll all look at each other, and nobody will utter a word until all eyes move to me, and I'll hear myself saying, 'OK, I'll give it a go.' I do sometimes try to remind myself that it isn't necessary to give things a go; but the reminder usually falls on deaf ears.

Besides, when everyone is staring at their feet I just get impatient. I once bought a pickup truck with a debit card because the salesman was rabbiting on about its merits and I was desperate for the loo. That was a whim – and, as it turned out, the best truck I ever bought.

If l'Avenc was a whim the whim was neither sudden nor new, but I shall not avoid the truth: the moment of choice was, finally, capricious. What else could so wild a project be? I had fallen for this idea. The house was on the edge of ruin. Nobody we knew of, or could imagine, would rescue it besides us. Now it was for sale. Heck, I thought, let's stop staring at our feet and give it a go. And if we bite off more than we can chew then we'll just have to chew harder.

All my life I've been biting off more than I can chew, and it's what has pushed me on to projects I hardly thought myself capable of. Of all those things which I've finished and now I'm proudest to have taken on, there's isn't one that I haven't at some point regretted ever starting.

Burying these early doubts, I had told Belinda I was sure we could do it; and wanted to be at the heart of any project we undertook; and would promise to stay there, come what may. I said this was a chance in a lifetime; that we had been offered the huge privilege of rescuing this wonderful house; and that we would be mad to pass it up. With her and her husband (and Francesc as an investor) that would make four and we could surely raise £40,000 apiece.

Strange to report, we hardly discussed what we would do with the house once we had restored it. That was never a big part of those early conversations. We thought, I suppose (so far as we thought at all), that what l'Avenc would be for would somehow just emerge. We would be joint owners, and take it from there. Why not? I said.

But do not suppose that it was I who was making all the running here. It was Quim and my sister who had found out from Sarsanedas that l'Avenc was for sale. I was in England and far from all this. It was my sister who approached me and asked my response to the idea that we would buy the house. And it was Joan Sarsanedas who convinced Quim, who was bedridden at the time with a temperature of 102° Fahrenheit, after at least half a dozen visits with the same objective: that the house had to be for us. Once he discovered I thought the same, there was no discouraging him. Without Sarsanedas, my sister and her feverish husband there would never have been a proposal in the first place.

The moving spirit – the germ of the idea – was Belinda's. She was a total enthusiast from the start. Much of the practical support, once we got going, was Quim's; and once he was fired-up he and his wife became backbones to the project. They have always led with new ideas. It is they who have done the most work.

So the dream belongs to all of us. Each of us, I suppose, thinks that what he or she did was what really swung it: each of us wants to believe we were pivotal. And in our way each of us was. I know only that in some strange and half-formed way I had the dream from the start, from when I was only twenty-five. And that at one particular moment, Christmas 1997, when we could have shied at the fence or taken the jump, nobody would have jumped if I had not wanted to jump. I think I did make the difference then.

I still have a postcard sent to me, dated Monday 16 February 1998, after we had bought l'Avenc. I remember my surprise when I saw it. It is of the front façade of the house, taken about the same time as we first walked that way. Someone else, too, must have been momentarily touched by the magic and thought the picture might sell as a postcard – though I have never seen another copy, before or since.

The postcard said:

Dear Matt,

You can imagine our surprise when we saw this postcard for sale! That terribly bumpy ride that we did at Christmas from the main road up to l'Avenc is being flattened into a civilised road . . . pity in a way . . .

I wonder if this is really only a dream.

xx Belinda xx

I too wondered as, filled with a mixture of excitement and dread, I drifted to sleep while that Christmas dawn in 1997 crept over the cold blue skies of Catalunya. Was it a kind of dream? I still wonder today.

3. A Sort of Goodbye

On a spring day in 1998 I joined Quim, Belinda and Francesc on the big, paved *plaça major* in the small city of Vic, forty minutes' drive down the mountains from l'Avenc. After Tavertet there is a narrow, lonely tar road for nine miles through a spectacular battery of cliffs, granite ramparts and steep woods where nobody lives, before you reach the main road to Vic. Early in the morning in the weak March sunshine this empty, Tolkienesque landscape felt like a frontier-land through which a traveller passes on his way down into the busy plain. I had with me my British passport, my sister had hers and the other two had brought their Spanish ID. We four prospective owners of l'Avenc had an appointment in the offices of a notary public: Sr Bendicho (Mr Well-Said, a good name for a notary). Under Spanish law the signature of important official documents needs to be notarized to be valid, and our assumption of ownership was of that kind. The procedure was a simple formality but a necessary one.

I had arrived in Vic in my old 1958 Land-Rover, driven over from England earlier in the year. Veteran of two election campaigns and many expeditions into the Sahara over sixteen years, the trusty old truck, its chassis now rusting badly, added (in my mind at least) a ceremonial touch to the occasion. Besides, though low-cost airlines like EasyJet and later Ryanair were beginning to bring down the price of flying to Barcelona, the fares were still not cheap. We often drove, belting through France on a 900-mile journey that could be done in twenty-four hours if you had a co-driver.

Journeys are a pleasure in themselves, but this time I had come to Catalunya for an important purpose: to assume my share of legal ownership of l'Avenc. I climbed the stairs to the notary's office and with the other three put my hand to a piece of paper dense with impenetrable Spanish legalese. I understood not one sentence in three. It struck me then, as it has so often since, that I was going to have to trust my Catalan partners at every important turn. I did. Then we trooped back down into the square. It was freezing: blue sky above, the crackling air without a breath of wind, the town just coming to life.

Vic was once a walled Roman city. Cut off from the warming Mediterranean by the massif of the Montseny mountains, it dominates the surrounding plain of Osona. Its history is bound up with that of l'Avenc. In its cathedral (rebuilt in the eighteenth century) a son of our house was once bishop, as I discovered later. It was in the marvellous episcopal archives that we were to trace much of the house's history. Vic has for 1,000 years been at the controlling centre of a prosperous and conservative rural hinterland.

It still feels like that. It is where we go to shop whenever we need more than everyday things. Vic is smart. The food is classier. Its restaurants feature in the *Michelin Guide*. The nineteenth-century avenues, plane trees, Old Quarter and city walls breathe confidence – even smugness.

The richest of the towns spread across the plain on which we look down from l'Avenc, Vic was a town which had bookshops before towns had bookshops in inland Spain; where women in cashmere or fur walked small dogs in tartan coats before women walked small dogs in coats anywhere in the Latin world outside Barcelona, Madrid or Buenos Aires; where you were never far from a lawyer or notary's offices; and where the decor of the coffee-bars was minimalist before that expression had been heard of in down-to-earth Manlleu, six miles up the ruler-straight Roman road towards the Pyrenees.

Here, then, on a morning that would point us in a new direction, we four walked, shivering, into a warm café. We had signed our names before the notary. We were quietly excited. The coffee was good and the brandy even better. It might be only 9 a.m., but glasses clinked. I headed the old Land-Rover back towards the hills, and l'Avenc. Mercifully the engine started, though I had brought the crank just in case.

What the hell had I done? Why had I bought this house? Why

had my sister and husband bought this house? None of us could have answered that question and we knew it. I had no plans to move to Catalunya: my life in England was all I wanted it to be. Belinda and her husband were busy, happy and successful in the lives and house they already had. Yet all three of us had been fired with an ambition to rescue a house, without knowing quite what for.

All we were sure of was that work must start soon. This trip to Catalunya had given me the chance to take a long hard look, with the new eyes of a cash-strapped owner rather than those of a starstruck rambler, at the property I was taking on.

It was a shambles. The roof, for instance: that split ridge beam had lasted a few years since we spotted it first – longer than we had feared it might – but there had been no unusually heavy snowfall in the intervening winters, and collapse was just a matter of time. Not only the ridge beam but many of the lateral beams sloping down from it to the eaves were in a dreadful state, rotten with woodworm or with damp where the tiles were broken and the rain had been pouring in.

The whole roof would have to be removed and replaced. It was a good deal bigger than the roof of an English town church, whose restoration would have involved endless appeals, coffee-mornings and applications for a Lottery grant. All this we would have to take on our own shoulders.

The steady drip of rainwater had done damage to more than the roof timbers. There were half a dozen large holes in the second and first floors where water had rotted the floorboards and, even where the boards were intact, about three-quarters of them were rotten. So were the joists supporting them, on both floors.

All the floors would have to be removed and replaced.

The great front door, and the side doors too, were in something close to shreds, hanging off their hinges and no longer possible to secure. If the windows had ever had wooden frames, these had long gone; and the shutters were rotten and loose, so the weather blew in through the windows as well as the roof.

All the doors and windows would have to be remade.

To the left side of the building as you stood facing the front façade, some owner (probably about eighty years ago) had tacked on a huge, stone-walled structure to form a barn-like addition to the ground floor: a sort of massive lean-to. It was ungainly, ran counter to the lines of the building, and seemed to lack foundations.

It would have to be demolished and removed.

Behind the house, fifty yards up the hill, stood the shell of another large house, also built in stone, but roofless and not solidly constructed. There were no foundations.

It would have to go; there was no point trying to save it.

Next to this ruin was the shell of a huge modern barn, its floor thick with decades of hardened cow-muck, its roof a canopy of rusting steel girders supporting a patchwork of broken or intact corrugated asbestos sheets.

The whole thing would have to be dismantled and demolished or removed.

The right side of the main house as you stood facing the front façade, but behind the sixteenth-century forward wing and forming the flank of the more Gothic section, was a bewildering array of old windows on different levels, some blanked off or filled in, a door from which stairs no longer led down, useless pipes and drains sticking out and going nowhere, and hundreds of square feet of rough external stonework. This side of the house had been so mucked about over so many centuries that any new owner would have to start again. At its feet was what must once have been a yard, with tumbledown stone columns which would have supported some kind of a roof or shelter. It all looked dreadful.

We would have to clear half of it away, redesign the side of the building, and start again.

Within, the Gothic part of l'Avenc was seriously confused. Stairs led nowhere, doors gave on to sheer drops, one floor seemed to have collapsed and filled what had once been a room beneath with rubble, now built over. The ancient kitchen, with its big stone arch supported eccentrically in the middle, its cavernous medieval fireplace and its enormous and still-intact bread oven, remained in one piece; and the minstrel-like gallery above it looked worth preserving, but its buckled and sagging floor of thick tiles laid over rotten wood appeared ready to drop into the storey below.

The entrails of this place would have to be pulled out and renewed.

Just behind the house and partially attached to the Gothic section was a string of what might have been cowsheds or stables: long, low, tumbledown stone buildings with tiny rooms, mostly roofless. These, I thought, could be rebuilt in stone in a traditional style in keeping with the rest of l'Avenc, as little cottages. We might one day let them, self-contained, to walkers or holidaymakers.

A complete reconstruction, almost from scratch, transforming fifty yards of outbuilding into three or four small houses, made sense: a tremendous task.

And that was just the structure: walls, floors and roof. What about services: water, plumbing, heating, telephone and light?

The property was without a telephone. There were the remains of an old line, with small wood poles. We heard they had been put in by an owner with an eye to a government grant – and later pulled down and chopped into sections to make a fence. To install a landline linking the house to Tavertet would call for hundreds of new poles and a couple of miles of overhead line, for which we would probably have to pay. There was, however, a reasonably adequate mobile phone signal: the nearest transmitters were twenty miles away across the plain, but l'Avenc's elevation allowed line-of-sight transmission, and the quality of the signal was (I supposed) likely to improve in the future. We decided to rely on mobile phones. The future might be, if not Orange, then wire-less, and l'Avenc could make the leap direct from a pre-land-line to a post-landline world.

There was no electrical power, and no sign that there ever had been – no wiring inside the house – even powered by generator. The closest approach to Spain's national grid was either the next farmstead, Rajols, or Tavertet. Both were miles along the cliffs. Each way, the empty slopes of meadow and wood were unscarred by any human mark beyond the track itself. And because of these slopes' elevation at the clifftop they are exposed: visible for up to forty miles in some directions.

I hate pylons. I hate poles and substations and overhead cables. I believe that in our day the cat's cradle of wires above our heads and the forests of steel and concrete poles erected to support them are one of the great unnoticed oppressors of our sense of clean space around us. Unnoticed, that is, only in the sense that we screen them out unconsciously, just as we screen out the sounds of traffic, the whirr of an extractor fan, the hiss of white noise on an audio-system, or the dirt on a window-pane through which we are looking. We may not have noticed it was there, but it's lovely when it's gone.

Poles, cables, girders and wires are part of the background noise of today's environment. We do not listen to it – we rarely look at them – but subliminally they degrade and clutter. If you doubt it, look at an English village where all the overhead services have been buried and the streetlights mounted on the sides of build-ings rather than on poles. You will be aware at once how good it looks, and this may strike you before you have realized why. Something tiresome is absent from the picture, though you are not sure what. Pylons, poles and wires – that's what.

Here, I thought, is one of the diminishing number of views in Europe where no overhead wire is visible. L'Avenc enjoys the rare privilege of having made it through the last half-century contin-uing to escape the ugly apparatus through which the intravenous drip of electric power is supplied. The house stands alone, unhooked up to anything or anywhere. This sixteenth-century building was not designed to have wires going into it above the eyeline. What a pity to spoil that and submit now.

Quixotic, perhaps. No, not 'perhaps'. Quixotic. But I set my face against bringing in power from the outside. It would be necessary, then, to build a 'green' system for generating our own electricity. The case for doing so was in part idealistic. The case for building our own domestic drainage and sewerage system was purely practical.

It looked as if l'Avenc had never had any plumbing beyond

some sort of a water pipe supplying the spout out of the bishop's mouth in that mysterious stone basin in the state room. There did not appear to have been any hot-water tank: presumably the house's inhabitants over the centuries had heated water to wash in, in pots and kettles on the kitchen fire.

And of course there had never been any kind of central heating. As is still the case in the old farmhouses of rural Catalunya, all the rooms are freezing in winter except the kitchen, where an oak-log fire (on the ground, not in a grate, so that the fire smokes and glows rather than flames up) is kept smouldering day and night.

As to the lavatory arrangements, these were clear: at the back of the building was an odd-looking little room, cantilevered out of the side of the house so that beneath its floor was a clear drop down to the ground where the muck heap would have been.

What would be needed, then, was the construction of a complete hot-and-cold-water system; a central-heating system (purists might object, but between November and April the temperatures up here in the Collsacabra plunge way below zero for weeks on end); and a waste-plumbing system internally, which would be served externally by septic tanks and what is euphemistically called 'soakaway'.

Perhaps you sense, as with growing alarm but a bit of a thrill too I was sensing, that as the euphoria which followed the purchase of a magic house subsided, our minds were moving onward from that first item on the agenda. *Owning* l'Avenc was not enough. Now we had a job on our hands.

One domestic need, however, did not look like posing any problem. Though immediately to one side of the house stood an ancient-looking brick-walled and stone-roofed well (if you peered down you could see a reservoir of water in a stone-lined chamber about twenty feet down), this was more a reservoir than a source: water seeped into the chamber during wet seasons, but only slowly. We knew this, so of course we had not in our excitement forgotten to make sure l'Avenc had guaranteed access to a more plentiful and secure supply of water.

The farmstead had always taken this from what was now the neighbouring property of Rajols, the farm and piggery in Joaquim

Casals's domain. The house and farm were supplied from a constant
and generous spring on the hillside just below the dwelling, by
the side of the track to Rupit. There was even a small shrine
erected to the Virgin Mary by what was now the pump. When
Joan Sarsanedas bought l'Avenc from Sr Casals, and we bought
l'Avenc from Sr Sarsanedas, the security of that supply was made
clear in the deeds. It was metered, naturally, and we would pay
for what we used, but it was our right.

A good pipe, underground, carried the water round the hill,
and from the pieces of old hose still hanging from the walls it
seemed that the last family to live at l'Avenc had brought the
water indoors: probably from a tap below ground level somewhere
outside the house.

There was one problem. We could not find it. It must once
have been clearly marked – perhaps it was sunk into a pit – but
wherever it was had presumably silted over. All of us had searched,
though without much sense of immediate need. One friend had
even tried to divine where the pipework ran, using willow-sticks.
To no avail. Dozens of exploratory holes were dug in adventitious
spirit, but we struck only rock.

One morning, soon after we had signed the deeds of ownership, I decided to spend a few hours on-site to solve the mystery.
My fifteen-year-old nephew Adam (my sister Deborah's son) came
with me to help. He and his sister Mima (Maria del Mar) were
to prove faithful helpers and friends to l'Avenc. Adam and I dug
here and we dug there. I went into the house and tried to follow
some of the old pieces of hose and guess where the system had
been sourced. I walked on to the Rajols property and followed
the mains which supplied cattle-troughs there – to which l'Avenc
was probably somehow linked. But as one approached the house
itself, the trail was lost. Joan Sarsanedas had not been interim owner
for long enough to bother with establishing a water supply; it was
enough that he knew there was water. Where precisely it was he
had not found out, though he had some ideas where to look.

We knew that the supply was likely to emerge near the top of
the property, where the main pipe would come round the shoulder

in the hills from behind, from the Rajols direction. We knew it was likely to be in front of the house as several broken hoses in the vicinity suggested they would once have been supplied there. But that only narrowed down the search to about half an acre and it was dispiriting work, scratching idly in the hard soil, without a clue.

I was close to giving up, as all the others had done, but decided to dig one final hole, and began a furious assault on a random piece of ground in front of the house, with an old pick and spade. I became aware that a man was standing nearby, watching me. He must have come down the track from behind the house – the Rupit direction past the nearest farm, Rajols, whose owner (Sr Casals) had sold l'Avenc. My bystander was an elderly man, perhaps in his late sixties, solidly built, dressed more like a farmer than a rambler or tourist, and impassive in manner and expression.

In Catalan, and rather roughly but not abusively, he asked what I was doing. Apologizing for my want of Catalan, I replied in Spanish that I was looking for the water pipe, and introduced myself as one of the new owners of l'Avenc.

He replied that he was Joaquim Casals, the former owner.

I had already guessed he might be. He had a peremptory way of speaking, devoid of the usual civilities. There was something angry about him, I thought, feeling myself to be in the presence of an unquiet spirit.

We shook hands. He was obviously completely uninterested in chit-chat and did not seem to want to talk about the house or our new ownership of it. But almost wordlessly he took me over to a patch of ground not too far from where I had been digging. To all appearances he might have chosen this spot randomly. 'Dig,' he said. 'Tap. Red.' With the most abrupt of goodbyes, Casals walked off. I was not to see him again for many years.

I had heard it said that Joaquim Casals was rough with people, but then again, farming is not an easy business and I did not myself feel ready to judge him, either before this incident or after. If I had sensed aggression, this had not been conveyed by anything he had said or done. Perhaps he was just a practical man whose directness some found hard to handle. Looked at in practical terms, his behaviour towards me had been nothing but helpful.

We started digging in the vicinity of where he had pointed. Nothing on the surface betrayed the presence beneath of a tap, and for a while we seemed to be getting nowhere, digging pointless holes here and there. Quim turned up on the scene and I told him about Casals and his advice. Surveying the area where I had been digging he pointed to a flat stone. 'Try that,' he said.

I got the point of the pick under it and lifted. Beneath was the top of a small brick-sided chamber, a couple of feet square. I excavated further. After ten minutes of scrabbling I had uncovered a junction in the pipe with a red-levered stopcock governing a short stub of upturned pipe, pointing at the sky. The stopcock was presumably turned off. I turned it on. A thirty-foot jet of water shot into the sky, drenching us. We didn't care.

The water ran rusty for a while, then sweet, and very cold. Never mind that our pipe led nowhere: we could still get water out of it for building, drinking and even washing. Of course I had never doubted that sooner or later we would find the supply, even if we had to track down Sr Casals to do so, but the finding of it still felt like a little triumph: a minor milestone. Now we had water. It was a start.

Before returning to England, though, there was something more I wanted to do. With me on that visit to Catalunya was Julian, already one of my best friends; the two of us were to become closer. He and I and another friend wanted to brave the cold and sleep a night at l'Avenc. Superstitious to say so, but after we went through with the transfer of ownership I wanted to make l'Avenc's acquaintance properly; and to know a place properly you must know it not just by day but in the dark. Sleeping somewhere makes a bond which cannot be made in any other way.

So we drove into the night with a bottle of wine, some sleeping bags, a boxer dog, Tana, candles and enough wood for a fire. The track had been roughly scraped by bulldozer and you could just about get a car across the mounds of rock and through the muddy holes, but it was tough going up the three-mile stretch from the main road above Rupit, through a beech forest on the hillside, past the Rajols piggery, then out to the cliffs, and along them to l'Avenc.

The house's elevation is above 3,000 feet and the climb from the tarmac road (up a track that shows no promise of going anywhere significant) is at first steep. News of the upgrading of the road had been over-optimistic. The effect of a bit of a scrape and a few tons of sand to fill in potholes does not last long, and besides the greater problem with this track lay in a handful of places where it was routed over bare and uneven rock, too uneven for the average low-slung modern car. My family were to lose more than one sump in the cause of getting to l'Avenc.

The beech forest the track soon enters as it climbs the hillside is dark, high and sepulchral, but by Rajols, after a final short but nail-biting one-in-three slope, you emerge into wide pastures, a flat shelf perched above Rupit.

This climbs gently for half a mile; then you are thrown into a steep bend to the right across an outcrop of rocks. You may not at first know it, but you are right on the cliff's edge. Get out of your vehicle and walk three yards to your left – but not too fast. There is a sheer 1,000-foot drop at your feet. Here it is always windy, and down to the left the whole city of Girona is visible 3,000 feet beneath on the plain, and behind it the Mediterranean. In summer you can see the aeroplanes landing and taking off from Girona airport, each loaded with its hundred-odd Costa Brava holidaymakers bound for the beach.

It is warmer down there even in winter – in summer you can see it shimmer – and I've often sat on those clifftop rocks in the cool breeze and wondered whether, as they emerge from their Boeing 737s, unbutton their shirts, gasp in the glare and cross their fingers that they remembered the swimsuits, they have the faintest notion that up in those mountains behind the runway – those strange angles of rock and geometric plateaus they may dimly have noticed after landing – lies another Catalunya, another Spain, from the one in which they plan to sink their San Miguels and top up their tans. 'I can see you,' I think, eagle-like on the clifftop, 'but can you see me?'

In winter it can be bitterly exposed here, and it was that evening in March. The sun had just set behind the eerie rock tentacles of the sacred mountain of Montserrat, tiny on the western horizon. To the east we saw the streetlights of Girona being switched on and twinkle orange as they warmed. We shivered and drove on.

Now the road crosses another rock shelf just inside the clifftop, tilted slightly downward like an inclined plate, the box bushes and evergreen oaks which cover it stunted by the thinnest of soil coverings and the solid stone beneath. This section of road is strewn with fist-sized rocks and if you try to creep gingerly over them your vehicle is likely to bump almost to a standstill; the only way to go is fast, and let the suspension take the punishment.

But not too fast, for at the bottom of the incline, after another half-mile or so, the track turns very sharply right in a right-angle bend. You may not realize this as you slew round, but if you overshoot you will go straight over a cliff, not ten feet away.

The track crosses a little gully, climbs a bit, rounds a badlands-like bare grey shale shoulder – and there in front of you is l'Avenc. You are behind and just above the house, looking down the sloped roofs from the Gothic end.

To get a picture of the lie of the buildings and place them in their setting, imagine yourself on the track coming diagonally down the steepish side of the hill which slopes uphill to your right (the north) to a sharp rocky peak, and away downhill to your left (the south) to the edge of cliff. The hillside is fairly open: small trees, sloe and box bushes and banks of wild thyme, but predominantly coarse tufted grass. Sometimes, where grey shale breaks the surface, there is a bald patch in the vegetation.

Were you able to soar out from the clifftop down to your left, you would be over a huge and wide valley through which threads the River Ter in a series of three very big man-made lakes, each quite narrow but many miles long, with gorges between them. The base of this valley is broken country: sharp hills and dales, for the most part densely wooded. The valley is about twenty miles long, and you can see most of it, running down from the plain (ahead and to your right) to where it breaks through foothills

L'Avenc's cliffs as I first saw them

How long had the house been here? Five hundred years, 1,000?

Cows had moved into the ground floor

This had once been
a noble place

Left to right: Matthew, Belinda and Quim

Joan Sarsanedas puts his hand to the chisel as a builder leans over and Quim's brother Francesc videos the moment, while his friend Denci looks on

I was proud of my steps

Belinda and I at
the carelessly
optimistic stage

The crest of 1559
and a new crest,
which we carved

Tom and
Jerry – the
real kings of
the castle

The chimneys were a caprice of our masterbuilder, Joan Sarsanedas

Often the windows were the best way in

A garage is constructed. I feared l'Avenc might fall into my brother-in-law's pit

Rupit

The sacred mountain of Montserrat

Mont Canigou (*below*) once surveyed a kingdom of Catalunya extending both to its north (now France) and south (now Spain). What remained of that kingdom finally fell at the Battle of Barcelona on 11 September 1714, pictured here in the eponymous painting, *L'Onze de Setembre del 1714* by Antoni Estruch. Reproduced by kind permission of la Fundació Caixa Sabadell

(behind and to your left) into the coastal plain where Girona sits.

The other side of the valley – two hours' walk but as the bird flies only a couple of miles – rises up into what become the Montseny mountains, a natural reserve rising to about 5,500 feet. If you look hard enough you may spot, hidden in the wooded slopes, the roof of a long stone house, totally isolated and far from any road. Here was born (it is said) one of the most notorious bandits of seventeenth-century Catalan history: Joan Serrallonga.

Raise your gaze up the slopes behind and you can see both the Montseny mountains' highest peaks: the sharply pointed Turo de l'Home (tower of the man) and the long, gentle slope of Matagalls (kill cockerels). They in turn look out across the city of Barcelona.

In front of you sits the settlement l'Avenc. *El casal de l'Avenc* as it was known, *casal* meaning 'great house' or 'fortified mansion'. You are looking down the line of a stone settlement which runs alongside the track, immediately above it, and, like the track, comes diagonally down the hillside heading south-west. Mediterranean houses have always followed roads and roads have always sought out houses. 'No one,' a historian and architect friend of the family's, Miquel Surinyach, told us outside the house one day 'would have wanted a house far from a road; roads twisted and turned to find houses and houses were built to stand beside roads.'

The settlement starts thin at the top where you stand – a terrace of four low and narrow stone barns – then thickens into the medieval part of the house proper. This in turn broadens further into the sixteenth-century end of the settlement: a big, high, wide three-storey house whose gable end you cannot see, at the bottom, facing (as you are) half towards the cliffs' edge and half towards the right-hand end of the big valley beneath them.

The façade of the house is its gable end which faces south-west, and you would have to walk right past it and down below it, then turn back and look up the hillside to see l'Avenc as it was designed to be seen first: from Tavertet. You have, as it were, sneaked down from behind and above.

When your track reaches the bottom end of the settlement it turns sharp right across the front of the Renaissance façade and contours along the hillside and gently down to a seasonal stream at the bottom of the property. The stream is heading straight for the edge of the cliff: in winter a spectacular waterfall.

Of all this we could see little by the time we got there that night. It was almost dark: just a glow of red above jagged Montserrat on the western horizon. And it was freezing. This would be a bitter night. At l'Avenc such nights are common in winter; and especially when the sky is clear the thermometer regularly plunges way below what you would expect on English winter evenings.

And we had forgotten to bring matches. Naturally. We spent an hour trying to light newspaper from a hired car's cigarette lighter (you can't), then tried to soak the paper in petrol by dipping it down into the fuel filler-tube (you can't), then stumbled with our sleeping bags up to the top floor.

It is scary trying to cross a rotten floor in the pitch black, though by now I knew roughly where the biggest holes lay in waiting, and how important it was not to kick away the prop holding up the ridge beam. We found a patch of sound floor-boarding and set out our bedding.

A bat flitted from the wall. The wind hissed in the rafters but there was never a creak all night. Urgently snuggled into our sleeping bags, we drank the wine then settled in, bags pulled up above over heads, icy noses alone peeking out. It was now very, very cold.

But we were not afraid. L'Avenc had a solid, sheltering feel, nothing bad. People can talk a deal of nonsense, I know, about the 'vibes' or aura of a house, but which of us has not, just sometimes, felt that a house was 'good' or 'bad'? L'Avenc was neither. It felt powerful, that's all; but I did not then, nor have I ever, sensed anything overbearing in the character of the house. L'Avenc feels proud and slightly secretive, keeping itself to itself; but there is nothing spooky or creepy about the place. Neither in the house's soul nor rising from its foundations is there damp or dankness of any kind. Its stone and its spirit are strong and dry.

We slept well, and when my mother and various nieces and nephews (I now had ten) arrived with coffee and warm bread from Rupit, and matches, and the dawn had crept past the boarded-up windows, bathing each floor with soft, dim light, and we had lit a fire of rotting oak planks in the cavernous old fireplace in the Gothic kitchen, thrown open the windows and watched the dawn breaking at the Mediterranean end of the valley below, and the streaks of cloud and mist rising from the woods and melting in the clear, dry morning, the long night behind us seemed a lifetime away.

We sat talking, the youngest nephews and nieces playing at being scared; but nobody was.

The moment of solitude had passed. The solitude had been earlier, in the dead of night, with a full moon outside. That was when I had awoken, as you do, for a while.

Have you ever lain in a building with holes in the stonework and gaps in the rotting wood, when there is a full moon outside? It is as if an unkind god were stalking the hillside, a palpable, luminous presence.

Without was moonlight and within – vague and unfocused – I could just discern the outlines of the room and see the chinks in the roof. Wind sighed outside, leaves rustled. Inside, old paper twitched in the draught.

Why do they speak of the *soft* light of the moon? Moonlight is hard, harder than sunlight, and crueller. Sun shines – moon stares. Solid things turn weightless. Shapes shift and melt. Our world in moonlight becomes shadowy, insubstantial – form without depth like scissored card; objects unreal; moonlight the reality. D. H. Lawrence speaks of 'the white whiplash of the moon'. Objects lose colour. '*Todos los gatos son pardos de noche,*' the Spanish saying goes: 'All cats are brown at night.'

The moon that night at l'Avenc shone through the wooden planks of the broken doors like a searchlight through black lace, wood skin flimsy against the glare, filigreed like a rotting leaf. Where the moon penetrated the holes in the stone, even the wall became a torn fabric, a skeleton of masonry pricked through with light. All around you what should be foreground became background in the presence of some great, unforgiving, celestial main beam. The light outside was close to breaking in.

I was seized with a sense of the ruination of this house, and of its beauty as a ruin.

A ruin is not the remnant of something else: it is a new thing, a thing in its own right. Its character is not the lingering remains of what was, but a living ghost. A ruin is lovely in itself. It has a personality of its own and the decay is part of the character. Decay has entered its spirit. The decay is beautiful, and delicate. There is magic in ruination.

When you restore a ruin you kill something fragile: a soul breaks free and flies away. All these years l'Avenc had had itself to itself, and now we were barging in with Caterpillar tractors. We thought to come as rescuers, and so we did; but we were also interlopers. We had come to interrupt a building's unhurried and passionate embrace with death; to break its solitude, to spoil its abandon. We had come to wreck the wreck.

Soon the diggers and the cement-mixers would be busy, and the air loud with labourers' oaths. Soon all the rotting wood would be stripped away and burned. Soon everything decrepit, frayed or crumbling would be carted away with the rubbish. Soon the walls would be solid, the roof secure, the windows glazed and shuttered, and the moon would no longer be able to see in.

I saw I had come to break a spell: I had come as a destroyer. Strange to report, but with the others asleep I felt that moment, in the still of the night, to be a sort of goodbye.

Soon a new chapter would start. The labour would be immense. There was everything to do. We had no electricity, we had no road, we had no plumbing. We had no idea what we were going to do with the house when we had finished restoring it. We had no heat; we had no windows; we had no doors; and the roof was falling in. But at least we had water.

4. A Nation without a State

Near a village called Mollò on a minor road over a high pass in the Pyrenees, there is an old customs post. This is the frontier between France and Spain. Now they are together in the European Union the small building has been abandoned and on a peeling wall someone has scrawled a piece of graffiti as telling as it is short. It confronts the traveller entering Spanish Catalunya from France. 'ESPAÑA – 173 kms', says the scrawl.

Catalunya is another country. I would call it a country within a country but many Catalan nationalists – *Catalanistas* – would find even that inadequate to describe the separateness of their nation. To them it is a nation, alone, in the fullest sense.

My sister Belinda raised her eyebrows at my proposed title for this book. She and my other younger brother and sister have become half-Catalan. 'Castle in Spain?' she said. 'But l'Avenc isn't a castle, and it's in Catalunya.'

I reminded her of the second meaning of the phrase; look it up in the dictionary, I said: '*castle in Spain*: impossible dream; wild ambition; castle in the air'. I pointed out that, as book titles go, 'Fortified Mansion in Catalunya' might lack the resonance of 'Castle in Spain'. She sighed. 'Don't expect Catalans to approve. You're misappropriating one of their finest houses.'

In some ways my sister was right, as I have learned in the thirty years since I first saw l'Avenc. In those earlier days I used to tell friends that my family lived in Spain, for at the time that is where we believed we had emigrated. We would think twice before saying that now. It is no political statement but a matter of human observation that if ever a people, their territory, their history and their culture deserved the name 'country' then Catalunya does.

A weekend break in Barcelona or a fortnight on a beach in the Costa Brava sends any observant tourist home with an inkling that this is not the Spain of straw donkeys, primitive plumbing, bare, baking hills, long siestas, wild dances and a *mañana* attitude to getting things done. The same tourist may notice that skins are not as olive, eyes are sometimes blue, hair sometimes brown; that gaits are brisker and life more bustling than down in the heat and dust of southern Spain.

Where are the delicate fans, the roses in clenched teeth, the castanets, the tight black trousers and sexual charge, the flamenco and the guitar – the languor and the passion of classical Spain? The missing Iberian stereotypes are easily called to mind; but what that is distinctive does modern Catalunya offer in their place?

Many, even among those who notice the difference, get the wrong end of the stick. There are at least four ways in which sympathetic visitors can go wrong. They may earnestly read George Orwell's *Homage to Catalonia*. They might as well ignore it. He pays no homage to a nation he hardly noticed in his quest to fight in the Spanish Civil War.

Or they may take their idea of Catalunya from Barcelona, city of culture, newly smart as a holiday destination, transformed by the 1992 Olympics into a world city. But Barcelona is really a city-state on its own, by no means the most Catalan of the country's big towns.

Or they may be persuaded that Catalunya is a kind of region, like the English North-East, and Catalan a kind of dialect, such as Geordie. *Dialect?* The very word will make a Catalan's colour rise to angry cheeks.

Or at the other extreme they may take Catalan nationalism to be a lesser-known equivalent of Basque separatism – only at the Mediterranean end of the Pyrenees. But this too is wrong. The Catalans are neither a violent nor a volatile race. Assassination is not their style. Catalans do deals.

Catalanism can seem quaint and cuddly, a kind of regional pride, whose principal product is an odd way of talking and a range of folkloric souvenirs such as little crimson pointy-floppy hats worn mostly ceremonially these days. With them goes a fondness for one of the world's most boring folk dances, the *sardana*, in which everyone holds hands in a ring and bounces gently up and down to a caterwauling of muted trumpets – every now and again, at a signal, bouncing more violently for a few seconds.

But on top of this romantic affection for field, farm and village and a sentimental attachment to the artsy-craftsy side of their cultural identity, Catalans have a clear-eyed picture of where they want to go, as well as something amounting almost to worship for where they've come from.

The dream is of nothing less than formal, internationally recognized nationhood. The difference is that Catalans are not given to blowing each other, or others, up. They do not care for the destruction of property and they do not like a mess – that's all. Patiently they plan to carve out their autonomy by negotiation and cunning.

Negotiation and cunning have always been the Catalan way, but they have not always worked. Catalunya – so often the victim and so rarely the victor – has a sort of doggedness to its history, a series of failed heroics and lost revolts on the part of a bold nation that has found itself trapped between the brawling bullies of Spain and France.

'For provinces as free as Catalunya, the proper medicine is severity,' the Archbishop of Tarragona wrote to the King of Spain in 1612. 'When I arrive in Barcelona I shall put the entire principality in the galleys,' wrote another royal governor four years later. To this day there are Spaniards who, when they hear the Catalan language spoken, snigger to each other, '*Porqué no hablan Cristiano?*' – 'Why don't they speak Christian?'

So if today's flaunting of Catalan nationalism can at times seem childish, with its flags and costumes, its country-dancing and tuneless music, and inbred disdain for all things Castilian, however cultured, this is only a reaction to the repression that came before.

The Catalans have survived and that survival has produced bombastic and at times comic claims to glory that none the less deserve some respect. Catalan nationalism is not like some mitteleuropean invention of the nineteenth century; it is arguably less invented (and indisputably more ancient) than Britishness; it is older – much older – than 'Spanish' nationhood. It is real and rooted and today's rich, plump, sunny, commercial land has grown out of the nation's medieval origins. There is something characteristic about the story of two galleys, sent from Barcelona to defend the sea route to North Africa but which were captured by the Moors in 1623 because they were too overladen with cargo to escape.

Given a choice between commerce and fighting, Catalans will always choose commerce. It is the autocratic French and Spanish interruptions that today look out of place. Maybe the Catalan spirit is better suited to a globalized twenty-first century than the French instinct to subordinate economics to politics.

Catalunya's geography defines its history. It was not just the Pyrenean mountains, halting the French advance, or the bleak, freezing, baking high desert of Aragón, cutting the nation off from the rest of Iberia, but the sea, bringing civilization in the first place. Catalan prehistory begins on the coast; its first sophisticated cultures, the Phoenicians and then the Greeks, arrived and traded by ship. So did the Romans who followed. At a time when the New World was unknown and northern Europe barbaric, the Mediterranean meant order and prosperity.

The coastal towns and cities – Perpignan, Figueres, Girona and Barcelona – shaped the nation. Like the guild system of Germany, medieval Catalunya was dominated by a balance between traders and nobles, not kings and princes. Progress was hardly interrupted by the Moorish conquest of Spain, which began in 711. Though the Turkish baths in Girona, with stars cut into their domed roof, bear witness to occupation, the Moors never really ruled this far north. The absence of Arab words in Catalan (Spanish is riddled with Arabic) proves it.

By 1137 the Moors had gone for good and Catalunya and Aragón were free and united under one ruler.

Though the name of this new land was commonly abbreviated to 'Aragón' it was Catalan industry that dominated. From Barcelona, traders roamed the Mediterranean, settling in Greece, Sardinia and Sicily. Even today Catalan is spoken in parts of Sardinia. An economy based on textiles bred a sophisticated political culture. The quantity and quality of documents still surviving in Catalan archives from this period – some of the finest being housed in Vic and some relating to l'Avenc – are testament to a system in which, as one historian writes, 'the conflicting necessities of liberty and order are uniquely harmonized'.

In 1293 – just seventy-eight years after England's Magna Carta and perhaps the very year in which the l'Avenc bishop Galcerán Sacosta was born – Catalunya too agreed that no law could be changed without the consent of both the King and the Corts, or parliament. By the fourteenth century the phrase '*la nació Català*' was in use. A civil government, the Generalitat, emerged, funded by a tax on textiles. It was all way ahead of the rest of Spain and most of the rest of Europe. And it was too good to last. The next 700 years of Catalan history are the story of what went wrong: today Catalunya is a nation in recovery.

In 1333 plague hit for the first time and returned often in the years that followed. The population collapsed, towns starved and banks failed. Nor did the earthquakes of 1427 help, shaking to the ground towns and villages around l'Avenc and as far afield as Girona. Ordered, prosperous Catalunya became bandit country.

That decline might still have been overcome had it not been for three great and almost simultaneous events. The first was the marriage of Ferdinand, the most famous of Aragón's kings, to Isabella, the monarch of Castile. For the first time Spain was united as a territorial whole and even though Aragón's identity was preserved within the dual monarchy its independence was gone.

The second event to shake Catalunya was the completion of the reconquest of Spain from the Moors, with the fall of Granada in 1492. Suddenly the focus of Castilian energy was shifted north and Catalunya lost the benefit of a weakened neighbour.

But it was the discovery of the New World in 1492 that hit the nation the hardest. Catalans were excluded from the new Atlantic trade and the great inland sea, the Mediterranean, which had provided their wealth, became a backwater, a lagoon.

As Spain built an empire, Catalans could only watch, though as individuals many played their part in trade and in battle, even after that empire was gone. On the shores of Lake Titicaca in Peru, I once smiled to see the monument to Admiral Grau, commander of the Bolivian fleet in the nineteenth century when that country lost the remainder of its coastline to Peru. Grau is a potently Catalan surname – the very sound declares it. Not far from l'Avenc is a fine old house, Grau, where bandits were hanged; perhaps that is where the admiral's family came from.

And recently in Colombia my taxi-driver told me his surname was Rupit. I was able to tell him (he had had no idea) about his family's ancestral Catalan home.

Those families emigrated because their home was in crisis. In 1516 King Ferdinand, 'the old Catalan', was gone, and with him his country's last royal protector. His successor, Charles V, spoke no Catalan and brought with him a desire to dominate bred in the fight against Protestantism in the Hapsburg's Dutch territories.

Philip II, who replaced Charles in 1556, saw mercantile, educated Catalunya as a problem and treated it as such. By 1600 the economy was struggling while Castile flourished on the back of untold South American riches. Up the hills, l'Avenc's owners began to rebuild – but left their project unfinished.

With its autonomy all but gone, Catalunya was in anarchy. The French invasion in 1637 offered the merely temporary protection provided by any foreign power trying to exploit dissent within its enemy's territory. The Catalan revolt of the 1640s led only to the bloody siege of Barcelona and its eventual fall in 1652. The country was ruined and divided: Roussillon and Perpignan went to French control, never to return.

Catalans are fond of reminding each other (in a somewhat inaccurate approximation of the historical facts) that the Treaties of Utrecht in 1714, in which Spain ceded Gibraltar to the British, also confirmed Spain's renunciation of Roussillon and Perpignan. If Madrid now wants Gibraltar back from Britain (Catalans chuckle), then shouldn't Madrid also demand 'French' Catalunya back from France? Unlikely.

And still the Catalan story gets darker. Under Louis XIV France invaded again in the 1690s and captured Barcelona. Attacked from all sides, Catalans sought help from the Austrians and the English. It was a terrible error. Spain returned in 1707 and though Barcelona held out heroically it finally fell on 11 September 1714. That day, now (Al-Qaeda notwithstanding) Catalunya's national day, forms the centrepiece of a national identity that comes close to celebrating failure. It is the same spirit that traces the origins of the Catalan flag to the bloody marks left by a Catalan king's fingers as they dragged down the yellow of his shield. Catalans will tell you, with a trace of sardonic humour, that their country has lost every battle it has fought in its history.

The result of the fall of Barcelona was the end of Catalan autonomy: the 1716 Decree of Nova Planta is now remembered as 'the death certificate of Catalan nationhood'.

As Spain ossified in the eighteenth and nineteenth centuries, Catalunya did too. Subsumed under a veneer of Castilian rule, Catalan identity persisted and found new outlets. The nineteenth century brought industrialization: English merchants built textile mills modelled on those of Lancashire – some of them along the River Ter, which runs through Manlleu and into the lakes below l'Avenc – and railways broke the grip of geography. With it a new urban culture developed; Barcelona grew from its medieval core to include elegant planned streets and squares, a southern challenge to Haussmann's Paris. Gaudí's sugar-sticky neo-Gothic and Dalí's shockart surrealism were products of returning prosperity and confidence.

This cultural awakening was not, however, matched by political freedom. The early twentieth century saw hesitant moves towards democracy, climaxing in the Spanish republic and the return of Catalan autonomy. But its roots were shallow and when the head of the army, Francisco Franco, led a rebellion in 1936 the state was too weak to defy him.

For the next three years Madrid, the Basque country and Catalunya resisted, until in 1939, with nationalist forces closing in, the Catalan parliament met for the last time as up to a million refugees fled to France, many of them past l'Avenc, through the Collsacabra and over the Pyrenees.

It is too soon, even now, for anyone to provide a balanced account of Catalunya's role in the war years. Certainly many Catalans resisted fascism and there were heroes such as Luis Companys, the socialist president of Catalunya, who persisted in his search for unity until

he was driven from Spain in 1939, only to be returned from France
by the Gestapo in 1940 and executed on Franco's orders. But many
communist factions, recorded by Orwell, had their own agenda. So
did many other Catalans, l'Avenc's owners among them, who as
Nationalist sympathizers provided shelter for local people seeking
refuge from compulsory military service under the Republicans.

Today many Catalans would rather forget (and some have) that
the Nationalists had much support in some quarters in Catalunya.
They can be forgiven for preferring to forget this: Franco certainly
did. That not all Catalans had been Republican counted for little
when the General took over. The 1950s may have seen the first
stirrings of tourism on the Costa Brava but for most people it
was a time of near famine and repression. In May 2005 I stood
at the door of the ancient parish church in Pruit, near our house,
and surveyed the departing congregation. 'How tall younger
Catalans are!' I thought. 'How much taller than their parents' –
then realized that this was because so many of their parents and
grandparents were malnourished as children.

How, then, did George Orwell, writing only some seventy years
ago, so overlook the slumbering Catalunya which has now awoken?

In choosing the title *Homage to Catalonia* Orwell coined the only
famous reference to Catalunya in the English language. Catalans
themselves are proud of the book's fame and buy it for their book-
shelves. Hopefully few ever read it. If they did they would feel hurt.
Homage to Catalonia has little to do with the place from which the
book takes its name. Catalans as Catalans get only a handful of
mentions in Orwell's narrative. His mind is on war, the tedium as
well as the horror of it, and the sense of being bogged down. He
writes wonderfully about short periods of intense terror and long
weeks of cold, hungry boredom. He describes the scrappy hills of
Aragón well. His chillingly calm report of what it is like to be shot
is one of the best short passages of English journalism I have read.

What, amid all this, though, of the Catalonia to which the book
is supposed to be paying homage? A key to Orwell's curious deaf-
ness to the Catalan sub-plot to his story of war lies in the name
he chooses. It is true that 'Catalonia' was and remains the official

English name for the place, but it is not the Catalans' own name for their country nor is it used by their Spanish neighbours. Everyone who lives, works or stays in the country for long discards the English name for the Catalan one – Catalunya.

As a cool tourist destination, Barcelona has sold itself more successfully than any European city I know. Hard to put your finger on when and why, but it has become stylish to enthuse about it. Tourists tell each other, so Catalans tell themselves, that Barcelona is a happening place. The city has acquired a buzz. The clubs are open late and crowded with the young and smart. The pickpockets are non-pareil: devastatingly ingenious and sudden. The Rambles – a tree-lined promenade packed with parrot shops, cafés, craft stalls, florists, yucca salesmen, street entertainers and pavement artists, and thronged with the curious, the amorous and the idle – is worth an hour's ramble.

Nearby, the genuinely Gothic quarter of the city, with its thread-narrow streets between ancient, lofty and stylishly shabby stone tenements, filled in summer with the sound of canary song, does make a powerful impression, and the dark cathedral at its centre is still, cold, calm and real.

Then there is Antonio Gaudí, the Catalan architect whose name has become synonymous with Barcelona. I have always thought Gaudí-ism an intelligent joke rendered in masonry, a brand of architectural wit. Certainly his apartment blocks are droll and are worth seeing, while his still-unfinished putative cathedral, the Sagrada Familia – sci-fi-meets-Disney-meets-neo-Gothic – is extraordinary, though that in 2004 visitor numbers to the place actually overtook those for the serene and beautiful Alhambra in Granada is as grotesque as the Sagrada Familia itself.

This modernity is an important strand in the fabric of Catalan culture, and one to which ambitious, cosmopolitan Catalans are naturally attached. They have heard the jokes elsewhere in Spain and they do not like them. They do not recognize caricatures of themselves as a nation of money-grabbing sausage manufacturers, small businessmen and mud-booted agriculturalists with an ugly accent and a strange guttural tongue of their own. They resent the implication that Catalans lack the grace, style and refinement that characterize Castile, the pride of Aragón, or the warmth and *joie de vivre* of Andalucia. They know they have one set of qualities which none of the rest of Spain can deny: hard work, obstinacy and a talent for making money; but they want us to know that Catalunya is also a sophisticated and culturally daring place. And without doubt Barcelona is.

But how deep and how wide does this go? My family and I belong to the hillbilly side of Catalunya. Barcelona is Barcelona: it is not Catalunya. More than in any city you will find Catalunya in the countryside: the towns and villages, the rural homesteads and little stone churches, the rhythm of life across that great swath of valleys, mountains, plains and forests.

My own impressions are those of an outsider. Catalans are solid, earthbound people. They set no great store by delicacy, mystery or grace. They are unceremonious and direct. They are deeply materialistic – but not so much (as some other Spaniards imagine) in the sense of being greedy or grasping, as in the sense of attaching importance to ownership and stewardship, and to the security which comes from property.

The security which comes from family, too, matters more to them than it does to us British. They are overwhelmingly Catholic without being remotely overwhelmed by Catholicism. Ostentatious displays of religious devotion are rare, church attendance is nothing like what you will find in the poorer south of Spain, and the Catalan matron arriving in the incense-tinged dark of an ancient chapel, though she will cross herself perfunctorily, is more likely to light a candle to being kindly remembered in an uncle's will than to throw herself weeping upon the altar in prayer for the uncle's health.

That, anyway, would be Madrid's caricature of the Catalan character. Catalans fight back: defiance, even dislike, of 'Spanish' Spain runs deep among many, deeper than I find comfortable – there being a danger that the people, like some Scots, get into the habit of defining their identity through a sense of shared dislike of another people. The talk can sound dangerously close to racism, the Catalan caricature of their Spanish neighbours having something in common with the British version: the waiter Manuel, and his infernal '*Qué?*' in *Fawlty Towers*.

Many in Britain will have noticed, as a bumper sticker, the big C on the vertically striped red-and-yellow background which is the Catalan flag. Some of our countrymen return from a happy holiday on the Costa Brava with these placed beside their GB stickers. They've been around for years. But in 2004–5 there was a new flowering of the art. Catalan car stickers started appearing which depicted just a donkey (the Catalan *Guarà Català* is a special breed of which the nation is proud). This was in some ways an answer to the black bullfighting bull which across the rest of Spain features in Osborne Brandy advertisements.

Some Spaniards answered the Catalan donkey sticker with a simple, equally wordless, black-bull sticker. Spanish nationalists found it highly amusing that a people would want to be identi-fied by a donkey, and there was a good deal of ridicule expressed. Others, the conciliators, started displaying a bull-plus-donkey sticker ('I am both Catalan and Spanish'). Provocative Spanish motorists then sported a bull mounting a donkey. *Catalanistas* retaliated with a donkey mounting a bull. After this, some people from the Collsacabra (named after its wild goats) started to display goat stick-ers. Finally, an idea occurred to some living in the nearest town to Tavertet, where (as I explain later) a long battle has been in progress to replace the old Spanish name of Santa Maria de Corcó with the town's informal Catalan name of l'Esquirol (squirrel). You will guess what sticker they chose. Enraged Spanish traditionalists in l'Esquirol (obviously unwilling to involve the Virgin Mary in anything unpleasant on a bumper sticker) have yet to produce an image of a bull mounting a squirrel, but, count on it, they will.

Nose-thumbing, however, is (or ought to be) a very small part of what constitutes modern Catalunya. Industry, in the modern as well as the old-fashioned sense of that word, is what character-izes the country.

Catalan entrepreneurialism (though it has grown into big busi-ness as well as small, and sustains what is economically the most flourishing corner of the Iberian peninsula) is rooted in a small-business and family-business ethos. But a Catalan will buy on price, not on friendship, and they are not susceptible to Sicilian-style blood networks or the sort of mateship which bedevils some southern European business.

A pension, a savings account (or two), a plot of land: these are stars in their firmament. And family, always family, which will usually consist of two children not too far apart in age. Their lives are rooted in what they have and hold; what they can count; what they can measure; what they can use; what they can inherit; and what they can pass on.

To a degree I find uncomfortable, Catalan national identity is rooted in blood and soil: and if you don't have the blood, or have not inherited a few hectares of the soil, you may be seen by some as a second-class citizen. Like the British, Catalans are great grumblers. They bark but they hardly ever bite.

Catalans do not, on the whole, make displays of their wealth, but they do not admire poverty. A typical Catalan would not see the point of letting go of material possessions. He would find difficulty – in the New Testament's imagery – in passing through the eye of the needle.

I think Catalan culture is the most egalitarian I have encountered. By that I do not mean that people think incomes should be equalized, or that they do not admire those who struggle from modest beginnings to raise their earnings or status. 'Poor boy made good' is considered as heroic a tale in Catalunya as it is in America.

But 'class' and class distinction hardly exist as they do in Britain. There is no 'working class' in Catalunya: there are people who labour with their hands and those who labour in offices. Nor have Catalans much interest in aristocracy, 'good' families, or what we British call breeding. Catalans are very familiar with that mindset – they get it in spades from the Spain of Castile and Aragón – but they dislike it. You could almost say that the whole Catalan race, from peasant farmer to business director, is one big petit bourgeoisie, but with this difference: achievers in Catalunya need to take care not to show off. Bank balances and land holdings are respected, but even the rich try not to be too different. There is a sort of cultural uniformism about the place, and birds of brighter plumage than the brown-feathered generality risk wagging tongues and popular suspicion. They are much more communitarian than the British or the Americans.

Catalans are dreadfully gossipy, love a good chin-wag, and speak at a volume a couple of notches above what we are used to. When not discussing the subject that is their national favourite – illness and its remedies, particularly colds and flu, are the Catalan equivalent of the English obsession with the weather – they are not averse to poking a stick at the reputations of those whose separateness from the herd is (to their way of thinking) arrogant or sinister. 'Who does she think she is?' (*Qui s'ha cregut que és ella?*) is as common a cry in Catalunya as it is in England; and even the cadences of Catalan seem to lend themselves to a sort of sing-song, 'well-I-never', 'whatever-will-they-get-up-to-next' undertone.

That said, this is a civil nation, though not a mannered one. Catalans hate airs and graces and show neither the taste nor the talent for what we might call *politesse*. It is quite alien to them to make a show of manners, and the rest of Spain is wont to throw up its well-manicured hands in horror at their rough-and-ready lack of etiquette; people are direct, with a lack of pleases and thank yous. But in all practical things they will lend a hand, make time to advise or direct you, sympathize with your woes or take pleasure in your own pleasure. There is a great deal of kindness in Catalunya, but of a gruff rather than showy sort, a sort of hobbit way of dealing with things.

And there is a great deal of pride. There can be no people on earth who are prouder of their country, their language and their culture than Catalans. You hardly ever hear a Catalan talking down or deriding their nationhood. There is simply no room for dissent. And for Catalans, language is the key.

Catalan is not a dialect of Castilian Spanish. As old as or older than Spanish, it is a little older than English, but not much. It has entirely its own vocabulary and grammatical system. Some of the words look like their Spanish equivalents, but many do not, and few sound like any other language. Spoken Catalan sounds nothing like Spanish and reads as much like French as Spanish. If anything,

Catalan is closer to French, but it has not come *from* French,
Spanish or any other living tongue.

Like other Romance languages, Catalan was born in the fusion
of Latin with the vernacular spoken before the Roman conquerors
arrived. In fact Catalan is more like Latin than most other Romance
languages; some say it is the closest living language to Latin. It is
spoken today by about seven million people (as many, for instance,
as any of the Scandinavian languages) and understood by about
ten million.

In sound the Catalan language is, not unlike its people, earthbound. It is unmelodic and lacks grace – you could call it a little
ugly – but it is more brusque than brutal. Words and phrases are
short, and tend to be delivered in a loud, definite voice. With its
clipped 'au', 'eu' and 'ou' endings it is not in the least lilting or
feminine, like French; to me the rough, abrupt words seem redol-
ent of the land: the odd, solid, angular hills, the bald patches of
grey shale and the flat-topped mountains and sudden cliffs. It
would be quite hard to sound hesitant, tentative, wispy, whimsical or fey in Catalan. Should you wish to convey gaiety you would
do best to pick another language.

'To really integrate,' writes my Catalan-speaking mother, possibly with the hint of an admonition aimed at me, 'one must know
the language of the people. Catalan not only projects earthiness,
but age. Over more than a thousand years of its known existence,
it has absorbed some French from over the Pyrenees, much Castilian
Spanish through trade with and eventually subjection to Spain,
overcoming many vicissitudes in its struggle to survive. Perhaps
that's why I like it so much – the Catalan language is a survivor!'

My parents were surprised to find Catalan, not Spanish, was the
language spoken in Catalunya. 'We came to Manlleu,' my mother recalls,
'to a semi-industrial-agricultural town in Catalunya, with four weeks'
instruction in Spanish, given by a Peruvian teacher in Manchester.'

Catalan has its own way of telling the time: 'two quarters of
five' means 'half-past four'; and the language, rather like the people,
tends to look on the sombre side: where we would say that time
is 'passing', Catalan says that time 'is being lost'.

And I still get muddled with the Catalan way of surnaming people. Look at a message my sister sent me after she saw that this book planned to attribute photographs taken by her to 'Belinda Abey Parris' (Abey is her husband's surname):

Dear Matt,
My name is Belinda Parris by the way. Abey is only Quim's name and our children's 1st surname by way of his contribution to their existence! Women have never forfeited their surnames to their husbands', but the clever thing is that the children take on the father's surname first (call it 1) and the mother's second (2). So two cousins will know they are cousins because they will have surname 1 or 2 in common. It also makes it easy to track down family trees and relationships. Only sometimes people do cheat: our Bishop, Galcerán Sacosta, did.

Clear? I have on many occasions succeeded in getting it clear in my own mind – but then forget again. A particular oddity occurs when a man marries a woman whose maiden name is the same as his. Some years ago a well-known Catalan politician whose father and mother were both born with the surname Colom took the surname Colom-Colom. As his parents christened the boy Àngel, and as *colom* means 'pigeon' in Catalan, Mr Angel Pigeon-Pigeon was quickly dubbed 'Six-Wings' by Catalan wags, and the nickname stuck.

Perhaps the best measure of the love the Catalan people have for their language is the total failure of the Spanish authority's various and systematic attempts to eradicate it. In the seventeenth century the Bourbons tried hard to suppress Catalan; Franco's campaign against its very being was remorseless and he made it illegal to speak the language in public, so that in a restaurant diners could talk to each other in Catalan but to hail the waiter in Catalan was illegal. The rest of Spain has always shown a curiously nervy, irritable reaction to the existence of the tongue, as though it were profanity – some sort of virus which might get out of hand.

In some ways the tables have been turned in Catalunya since Franco's death, and Catalan speakers tend to be the top-dogs, while the majority of native Castilian speakers are poorer 'immigrants' from the south of Spain. Catalan is now the language of the bosses, spoken loud and confidently in classroom voices, and Spanish the workers' idiom, its hinted context the canteen or playground. But let a Castilian company chairman, or judge, or professor stride into the room, and you may encounter a sudden collapse in the Catalans' assertiveness about their tongue.

I reprint below a short passage a student of my mother's wrote when she asked her to express in Catalan what her language meant to her. As you may have gathered from the previous exchange, to read it aloud pronounce every syllable more or less as lettered – the 'x', however, being pronounced 'sh':

Estimo, respecto i admiro el Català amb la mateixa força que un ciutadà anglès, francès, italià o espanyol ho fa amb la seva llengua. Per sort o per desgràcia, tots som fills dels nacionalismes europeus, dels que han estat modelant en els últims segles identitats pròpies i ben diferenciades les unes de les altres. Des d'aquest punt de vista, no crec que ens puguem plantejar perquè ens agrada o no la nostra llengua: simplement és la nostra. 'És la meva llengua' significa que és la llengua que m'uneix socialment, històricament i culturalment a una comunitat que m'ha fet de bressol, que és casa meva i que m'ha ensenyat quasi tot el que sé. La meva llengua m'identifica amb un territori del món i així puc dir d'on sóc.

Cristina Molas Casacuberta, 3 març 2005

(I love, respect and admire Catalan with the same force that an English, French, Italian or Spanish person feels for his language. By luck or misfortune, all are children of European nationalisms which have forged their own identities in recent centuries, well differentiated one from another. From this viewpoint I don't believe anyone should take the position of liking, or disliking, our language: simply, it's ours. 'It's my language' means it's the language which unites me socially, historically and culturally with a community that has been my cradle, which is my house, and which has taught me almost everything I know. My language identifies me with a part of the world, and thus I am able to say where I come from.)

Note that fascinating association between Cristina's language and her 'house': the very roof over her head. She assumes that people of every European nationality would feel that same almost quivering passion for their own language, and the same deep sense of personal identification with their native tongue. I think the French might, but I am not so sure about the English or the Spanish. Perhaps it is because we have never felt linguistically beleaguered.

Should you doubt this, look up at the statue of Christopher Columbus on his pedestal near the dockside in Barcelona. Columbus (in Spanish Colón), Catalans hold, was Catalan, and they would spell the surname Colom. But the evidence of the great discoverer's Catalan nationality is sketchy at best. Barcelona's city fathers have him pointing an imperious finger out to sea from the Catalan coast . . . in the direction of Italy. I protested to one Catalan friend that on his voyage of discovery Columbus did not depart from Barcelona. A mere detail, replied my acquaintance. This was the way he would have left port if he had.

Or look beyond the statue, into the hills behind. There, over-looking the city, stands Mount Tibidabo, with a funicular railway up to the top, where there is a church, and a funfair. From here the whole of Barcelona is spread out at your feet.

So why that curious name 'Tibidabo'? Because, Catalans will tell you, it means in Latin 'I will give to you'. As everyone knows, the Devil took Christ up to the top of a high mountain to show him the world, in exchange for which he invited Jesus to bow down and worship him. 'I will give you this,' said Satan. And as everyone also knows, Jesus was sorely tempted.

Well (the story continues), this temptation obviously cannot have taken place in Palestine because Palestine is dry and stony; Jesus would hardly have been sorely tempted by a waste of rock and scrub. So there is an unanswered question.

The answer is now known. It must have been Catalunya that Jesus was shown. Beautiful, rich, verdant, ordered Catalunya. Now that really would have been a temptation.

5. A Birth at the House of Avench

Towards the end of the thirteenth century, perhaps in the old kitchen, a young expectant father looked out from l'Avenc over the valley below, waiting for news of the birth of his second son. By then the house was probably about 150 years old.

Of neither the exact date nor the place of this child's birth can we be absolutely certain, but we know that his father, Guillem, and his mother, Bondia, were married in 1292; that their house was l'Avenc; that they already had one son, also Guillem, their firstborn. We know too that by 1310 Guillem's younger brother would be training as a canon (still a teenager, but that was common) in Urgell, on the edge of nearby Andorra.

The boy was almost certainly born between 1293 and 1295. Nine hundred miles away the English King Edward I was on the throne. Oliver Cromwell and the English Civil War lay as far ahead as now they lie behind us, and it would be 400 years until 'Britain' – the United Kingdom – would take shape. London was a rising walled city beginning at Holborn and ending at Tower Hill. The Strand was a bog. Westminster was a marsh. The ascendancy of the British empire was still more than five centuries into the future – and even the Spanish empire was an epoch still undreamed of. It would be 200 years before Christopher Columbus (Catalan or otherwise) sailed off over the western horizon in search of the New World.

In 1294 fifteen full lives, laid end-to-end, would have taken you back to the birth of Christ. Since then the Moorish followers of an even more recent religion, Islam, had advanced as far as Vic and further, and been driven back. Granada was still in contention between Christians and Muslims, but the reconquest of Spain from the Moors had been almost completed. A small Moorish fort called Majirit had fallen to the Christians. It was to become Madrid. As a political map, Europe, as it then was, is almost unrecognizable to the modern eye.

Though the view from the kitchen window at l'Avenc on a thirteenth-century dawn would at first glance have been much as it is now, life there will have been very different: harsh, bare and cold. The young mother, wife of l'Avenc's son and heir but last in the pecking order of her mother-in-law's house, would have faced an uncomfortable quarantine. That is probably why records suggest that for the birth Guillem sent his wife to her parents' home, twenty miles away in Les Planes, down on the plain near Olot. They were rich and high-born, and life down there was easier.

Perhaps, too, there lurked a desire to associate the boy, as far as possible, with his mother's side of the family. True, Guillem Avench (an h was inserted in those days) was the heir to the substantial fortified house in the Collsacabra whose name he had taken; but however much it stood out within its region, this was a hill-farm and these were hill-people.

In marrying a daughter of the minor nobility, Guillem had married up. As the careers of both his sons were to demonstrate, his was an aspirational family. 'Social climbers' might not be too harsh a phrase, for something rather curious was to emerge. The boys appear never to have used their father's name (which, as we have seen, in the Catalan style that survives to this day, couples the father's with the mother's surname, in that order) but only their mother's.

The baby was christened Galcerán. His full and legal name was therefore to be Galcerán Avench Sacosta, abbreviated in everyday use (as Catalans often do) to Galcerán Avench – dropping the mother's name. The family did abbreviate, but they dropped the father's name instead. Little Galcerán Sacosta's parents plainly had high hopes for him.

So for this birth there was probably a midwife, who will have come from a nearby house in the valley of Hostalets d'en Bas. News of the birth will have been sent up on the *camí reial* (royal way), past my parents' house, l'Hostalot (probably a wooden shack by the river), to l'Avenc and to an expectant father.

Looking out for the arrival of the messenger with news of the birth, the young father will have had his spirits lifted by the same vast, green and quiet mountainscape as lifts my spirits today. But on closer examination there will have been key differences between what we see now and the scene upon which a child born then would, forty days later, be learning to focus his eyes. Down below in the valley of the Ter there was probably more sign of humanity than there is now – we have evidence that in the Middle Ages, before the tremendous earthquakes which pulverized whole cities, the Collsacabra supported a larger population than in modern times – and woodcutters and charcoal-burners will have been busy among the evergreen oaks which carpet the valley.

The castles at Rupit, Tavertet, Fornils and Cabrera are all ruined today. What an era of earthquakes did not fell was reduced to rubble by King Felip V when he subjugated Catalunya 500 years later. Just over the cliffs from l'Avenc, the wonderful little church of Sant Joan de Fàbregues still stands, but empty, alone and hardly visited. Then it was the centre of a thriving community. Down in the valley of the Ter the monastery of Sant Pere (Peter) de Casserres, later ruined, now restored, protected and prayed for a scattered population of self-sufficient smallholdings. Now you push through forest to Sant Pere.

Most houses huddled around these strongholdings for security against raiders. Others, more isolated, fortified themselves as l'Avenc did, arrow-slits making the show that burglar-alarm boxes do today. By day, smoke from crude hearths rose from the trees; at night, where now you see only black, the darkness will have been pricked by the glow of fires and the occasional tallow lamp.

Tavertet was already there, its Romanesque Church of Sant Cristòfol, much of which survives today, more than a century old even then; and so was Rupit, which had a castle; their inhabitants little knowing that a century and a half later both villages and hundreds of surrounding settlements and towns were to be shaken to the ground by two devastating earthquakes in the spring of 1427.

Down in the valley where now there is not a single hamlet, at least two villages – Sau with its church spire, and Querós with its high, slender medieval stone bridge over the river – will have been visible. Both now lie beneath lakes created for storage and hydro-electric power in Franco's time, the spire and the bridge emerging only during droughts when the water is low: a bleached skeleton from the depths. There will have been a better, busy road along the valley than the rocky track above the lakes which is all there is today.

Nobody goes there now; then it will have been a thoroughfare. The Sau and Susqueda valleys fed Rupit's Sunday market with home produce that the more exposed Collsacabra's thinner soils and shorter growing seasons made harder to grow up there. Tavertet and Rupit exchanged charcoal, ironware and textiles from their mills.

Charcoal was a huge local industry: with rainfall better than in most of the rest of the Iberian peninsula, the high, dry central plains of Spain critically short of fuel, the great port of Barcelona not far away, and thousands of square miles of the slow-growing, dense-wooded *alzina* (evergreen oak) tree within easy reach, woodcutting and charcoal-making were highly profitable. This part of Catalunya has never been so heavily forested as it is today, when the woodcutter's axe has fallen silent. Then, the hills around and below l'Avenc will have rung with its sound.

To carry all this busy traffic horses, mules and riders will have passed up and down the steep, stone-stepped climb between rock cliffs where an ancient packhorse route still ascends from the valley, emerging near Tavertet. Now only the occasional rambler goes that way.

To muleteers en route to Rupit from Tavertet passing right beneath l'Avenc's kitchen window – and unaware that into that big house had just been born a boy with a strange, famous and angry future – how will l'Avenc have appeared?

The biggest difference will have been the façade. It would be 300 years before the front of the house was demolished and rebuilt in the Renaissance style of the day, and gained its present aspect. We have found no account of what the front looked like before then, though there may well have been a tower of some sort where our staircase now stands. But it seems likely that the front of the building will have been in keeping with the back: less elegant and probably more ramshackle, added to slowly over the previous century, with rooms tacked on as the need arose and the family grew wealthier, but according to no grand design.

An inventory of 1486, which survives, gives us a feel for the place as it will have looked nearly sixty years after those terrible earthquakes. The Widow Constança, then the proprietress, had the document compiled by the local scribe, to record the state of the house and all its possessions, on the death of her oldest son. His death left her second son to hold l'Avenc in trust until her deceased first son's oldest boy reached the age of majority and could take possession. Real estate in Catalunya always went in its entirety to the oldest: a seemingly harsh custom with the practical advantage that properties were not divided; a *finca* (a house with agricultural land attached) needed to remain large enough to be sustainable. L'Avenc used to be about 250 acres.

Rafel Ginebra i Molins, archivist at the episcopal museum at Vic, where these records are kept, has provided me with this introduction to the parochial records of the village of Tavertet, from which the inventory is taken:

On 4 April 1486, Constança, the widow of Martí Avench, taking account of the death of the heir to Avench, her son Francesc, leaving small children, temporarily cedes the administration of the estate of Avench to her other son, Pere Avench. To back up this responsibility all goods and chattels in the house, movable or otherwise, are inventorized as at 5 April.

Four years later, on 5 May 1490, Constança formally acknowledges that her son Pere Avench has satisfactorily discharged his responsibilities for looking after and administering the property, and taken proper account of everything. The same day, partly in recognition of his caretaking of the property and partly as a dowry upon his marriage to Isabel Bach de dos Munts [Isabel will have come from Can Bach, which remains to this day a homestead nearby], he is awarded one hundred pounds.

The same day, Pere Avench acknowledges that the sum has been duly paid according to his rights, and transfers it to the estate of l'Avench, reserving the right to be maintained at the house, in sickness or in health.

Finally, on Wednesday 6 April [a year later] Pere Avench makes a new inventory of all the property that had been his responsibility.

For those like me who have tended to imagine the Middle Ages as a ragged and disordered era, lacking regard (or system) for what has come to be known as due process, documents like this come as a surprising reminder of formality and order – and of humanity's age-old hankering to make lists of things.

The inventory itself is in Old Catalan, with the occasional Latin word or phrase thrown in, usually in a declaratory context, to add stature to the document. It is a curious mixture of formality and informality, with occasional flashes of pathos and plain-speaking, such as might be penned (with help from a scribe) by someone of limited education attempting a little grandiosity to suit the occasion.

It amused us that the whole exercise had been triggered by the death of an heir to the house whose name was Francesc. That was not only the name of the latest co-owner, Quim's brother Francesc, but my middle name (Francis) too. L'Avenc, we smiled wearily as we wrote out the cheques, seemed to be taking its toll on the Francescs of this world.

A IIII del mes debril de LXXX^ta VI°

In Dei nomine. Noverint universi et cetera. *Cum jo, na Costansa, muller den Mertí Avench, quondam, hereva universal he dona útil del mas Avench de paròquia de Sant Cristòfol de Tavertet del bisbat de Vich, vahent jo dita Costansa que per mort natural den Fransech fil meu . . .*

When intent on legal business, it seems, draftsmen were as prone 600 ago as they are today to compose sentences of infinite length and an indeterminate verbal structure . . .

I, Constança, wife of Martí Avench, deceased, inheritor of the whole estate and housekeeper of l'Avenc in the parish of Saint Christopher in Tavertet, in the Diocese of Vich, now that my son Francesc has died, and being in the difficult position of lacking any faithful or useful person to care for or till the land, or to supervise payments and debts, or to defend and maintain the house, or to provide for me and the offspring of Francesc, my late son, and all the family whom these deaths have greatly burdened; and being fearful of what is to come, therefore, because of what is stated below; and wanting to look after our possessions and to make provision for the future of this house, and your brothers, my sons, and other friends of mine, and for the tutoring of said children; and trusting your loyalty and industriousness, Pere Avench, my son and son of my late husband Martí, I give, in the form of a pure and simple gift, declared in the presence of the living, all the fruits that can be gathered in the said House of Avench, both of the land and of the animals and of honours [rents] and possessions of said house, for as long as myself, Constança and you, Pere, should please, according to the agreement and conditions and retainers stated below:

Phew.

Firstly, that you, Pere, will have to work and till the land of said house and provide me and the household with the fruits of the land, as long as you are responsible for this inheritance, and pay the ordinary outgoings and customary expenses, et cetera . . .

If our experience is anything to go by, poor Pere was in for a shock.

Further that you, said Pere, will have to take charge of the inventory of all the immobile property of the said house et cetera.

Further that you, Pere, will begin to keep, administer and provision said household and to reap the benefits and pay the outgoings the day you receive the inventory.

Further that this year you will become the owner of all the benefits to be enjoyed by the aforesaid children, which are: 2 pounds and 4 salaries, without small change, to be invested in whatever will be most useful and profitable for the said children.

Further that I require that henceforward, for me and for my kin, you will take charge of the inventory.

Further that we have agreed between us that if you, Pere, while managing l'Avench's inheritance, have to pay any old or pre-existing or future debts, and if while having the use of the house you have to improve it, incur building expenses, then as long as you demonstrate that you have incurred these expenses or had to work hours, that you are fully repaid in the presence of our friends, et cetera.

Sadly it is too late for us to do the same. Pere and his successors left a lot still to be done.

On the fifth day of April of 1486 in the presence of my notary and Barthomeu Crosos and Andreu de Novellas witnesses, etc, and according to the instructions of our lady Constança, wife of the late Martí Avench and inheritor of the whole estate and usage of the House of Avench of the parish of Saint Christopher of Tavertet, Diocese of Vich, and the tutors of the late Francesc Avench, and with the consent of the Honourable Barthomeu Joffre, mayor of Tavertet, the present inventory was taken of the movable possessions of Avench, furniture and animals and similar objects, so that said property is described in a true and complete record, and so that an honest track can be kept of what happens to this property. What follows is what is found to be there, etc:

The et ceteras are not my work but the medieval draftsman's. He keeps chucking them in for no apparent purpose, as though, like a shyster lawyer, to impress his clients that their inclusion will somehow remedy any possible oversight on the inventory-makers' part.

First: we come to the main doorway where there are some reasonable doors and iron hinges without a lock. It looks as if there has once been one, but it is no longer on the door.

We too found we kept losing locks, or when we found them

forgetting where we had put the keys. L'Avenc seems to eat locks and keys . . .

Further: we go into the kitchen and we find an earthenware drinking vessel.

A dozen and a half soup bowls, half a dozen plates and a couple of cutting boards.

A copper mortar and its pestle, in quite good condition, and complete.

An earthenware cooking vessel and one salt cellar.

Poor-quality fire irons, medium-sized.

A poor-quality iron frying pan and some iron levers (for leverage) and some fire chains and hooks (to hang the pots on) and their fine decorative extras.

Further: we come to the oven which is in good condition; we find two oven spades to bake bread, of between good and poor quality.

Further: in the room in front of the dining room, we find middle-sized doors; and, in a room with two middle-sized beds, cotton sheets, a blanket on one bed, two sheets of three different pieces of material that are about 10 hands long, and a new blanket which is white with black and white lines about 26 hands long, and an old straw mattress. On the other bed is 1 sheet and a straw mattress and a new blanket about 29 hands long.

Further: there is a shepherd's chest, middle-sized, white and red; and there are 2 implements to reap wheat.

There is a room above this dining room, with middle-sized doors without locks. In this room we find two beds, one good, one bad and old, one straw mattress and 2 sheets that are nearly 9 hands and middle-sized, made of three pieces of material; the other sheet is one and a half sizes, and half a new black blanket, 20 hands long; and another good bed with a middle-sized feather mattress and two medium sheets of three pieces of material that are near to 10 hands long, and two bad-quality black and white blankets with black and white stripes about 20 hands long.

Further: we find a stake and 1 good sheet of three pieces of material that is 10 hands long.

Moreover we find a good-quality tablecloth with stripes which are about two yards and a half long, and two medium-sized tablecloths, about three yards all together; and more bad-quality tablecloths that measure about 9 hands.

Further: 1 spinning wheel and its necessaries in good condition, and 2 pairs of carders to card the wool, in poor condition, and 2 iron files to file down the hooves of the animals before being shod.

And we find 30 pounds of spun thread, 15 pounds of canem material and 15 pounds of rough canem material.

Moreover two reasonable saddles, one for a mule, one for a steed. It's true that the saddle belonging to the mule is without stirrups.

2 old iron poor-quality chandeliers: one is all right and the other bad quality, with many supports for candles made of black tallow or wax, and one glass barrel covered in basketware, about one measure in capacity.

And we also find 1 long lance and 1 medium shield and a good sword.

Moreover, 1 long box, bad, with lock; and also another box with a lid but no bottom.

And 10 measures of oil, and 2 bad-quality buckets and 3 baskets (neither big nor small) and 1 big bucket, and a bread-basket and 1 poor-quality sieve; and a poor-quality tree-pruner.

Moreover another room off this dining room, facing east, which is all destroyed and without beams across the ceilings. In truth it does have beams on the roof, but it is not covered. It is true that all the walls of this room are new. But there are no doors.

Further: 1 new shed with lime-covered walls on the outside facing South, to keep big or small animals. In truth it is all open and without doors.

Further we found 3 cats and 4 dogs, some small, some big.

We also find all the house in reasonable order, except the two rooms above the aforesaid, covered and with beams ready. It is true that the archway of the kitchen made of stone is held up in the middle.

Moreover we also find all the fields of the aforesaid house, and ditches, in good state, swept, and the roads are also in a similar state.

And also we find wheat seeds for 11 quarters [about 1 acre], rye seed [for] 4 quarters, black oat seed for 3 quarters and broad bean seed for a quarter of a quarter which all together adds up to 18 quarters and one eighth of broad beans.

And also we find a dozen hens and a cock. Also two outhouses built on the threshing yard, one without a roof and one with a roof, and half a hay-stack in the threshing yard.

Also an oak trough for pigs to drink from, next to the wall of the threshing yard, in a reasonable state.

And a vineyard growing under the cliff which belongs to the Avenc, on the way to the Surroca house when you go from the church in Tavertet.

And we also find a rat-skin-coloured middle-aged female donkey with a year-old foal of the same colour. There are also the panniers and all the rather old implements for the donkey to pull in the fields. Also two old ropes and one new one.

And three used ploughs and one new one. And two yokes for ploughing.

And also two ploughs. And also we find among all the animals half a dozen bells, large and small.

We also find a heifer and a very small year-old calf, worth very little, owned by the rentee called Master Fransí Sabater, citizen from Vic.

Curious how this inventory, like the house we found half a millennium later, seems to revolve around bread-making. The old bread oven is still at the heart of the Gothic part of the house. I suppose that if Tavertet had a bread shop in those days (it does now), the walk to and from the village just for your morning toast would have been impractical.

We come to a ruined room that adjoins the kitchen in the mountain-ward direction [north], and the direction of the sunset [west], in ruins.

1 sideboard in reasonable condition to keep bread and cheese.

In said kitchen we find a poor-quality table and 1 bench and 1 settle and benches around the oven, all of poor quality.

A large and good-quality Girona stoneware mortar, and another broken one, made of boxwood.

Further: a copper saucepan that must weigh about 10 or 12 pounds. It appears that it has one hole. And another small copper pan.

The place was evidently full of pots and pans. What did they cook in them? Mostly stew, social historians of the era tell me.

Further: 2 oil lamps and a broken iron grid and a reasonable iron spit.

A poor quality kneading table with its decorations and bolts, and a small, broken laundry vessel below the kneading table.

Half a dozen handspindles and 2 drop-spindles and a dozen whorls and a distaff to spindle.

We find 4 axes, one good, two bad and one broken. [Added in pencil] It appears that the broken one is missing.

I have the impression that Constança was quite a stickler for total accuracy.

4 hoes, one good and three bad. One razor-knife to shave beards, and a poor quality cutting instrument.

One small chisel and another big one, and a one-handed flat-iron (to use with one hand).

As Constança grew older (we have no idea of her age), it will have been Pere's wife who took over the more humdrum household tasks, such as ironing, while her mother-in-law sat in the upstairs room, spinning, sewing, and complaining that daughters-in-law in 1486 were not as dutiful or respectful as had been the case when she was a girl. A sort of shiver of recognition that humans change so little goes down my spine, to think that this family, miles from anywhere and surely in no sense needing to keep up appearances, should have spent time and fuel laboriously heating a ruddy great lump of flat iron, in order to remove the creases from their clothes. Heavens, if the item here inventorized was a 'one-handed' flat-iron, what did a two-handed iron look like – and weigh?

Further: 2 reasonable baskets to carry dung, and 1 middle-sized and 1 medium-sized iron crowbar and one pickaxe to make basins and a small folding beechwood chair and a poor-quality box to keep bran, near the kneading table, and a poor-quality mortar-like instrument to crush salt for the animals.

We find 1 sack of breadwheat containing near to 3 measures.

We find 21 sacks of one-and-a-half measures (more or less) of breadwheat. [A 'measure' is equivalent to the harvest of 1 *quartera* – as much land as can be tilled by one man in one day.]

2 poor-quality sacks.

Imagine today including in an inventory a couple of tattered sacks. Was Constança obsessive – or was a sack a much more expensive and prized possession then than it is now?

Further: we enter the dining room where there are poor-quality doors as well as a poor-quality large table and 2 poor-quality benches in said dining room.

A large walnut chest, lockable but with no key.

There we go again. The curse of l'Avenc strikes. Maybe it's still under the floorboards somewhere?

A great chest and a bread cupboard and wooden scales.

3 sides of bacon, and a half-side, weighing about 30 pounds per side.

Further: a bottle and a salt cellar and 2 glasses and two glass salt cellars and one tin, and 2 earthenware basins neither large nor small.

We enter the cellar where there are some vertical poor-quality doorposts at the doorway, and we find a large barrel, 2 of whose wooden segments are full of holes, [bound by] 5 rings of poor quality.

Moreover we find 1 poor-quality barrel to keep wheat, decircled [presumably with broken metal hoops] as well as 2 poor quality.

Other barrels to hold wine, 1 of which is good quality, containing about 5 measures, the other medium-sized, with about 3 measures; it appears that the larger barrel contains about 12 bottles-worth of reasonable wine, as well as half a barrel and a couple of middle-sized vessels and 1 large tub/container to hold wool, with a narrow bottle-neck, which we find in said cellar.

The inventory then turns to the living creatures which were part of the smallholding. The differences from a modern farm are striking:

The animals at l'Avenc:
First, 115 sheep were found,
Further, 80 reasonable lambs.
10 castrated oldish sheep (for mutton), 9 youngish castrated ones, 23 male donkeys and 38 females.

Consider that. More than sixty donkeys. In a modern farm these would be substituted by machines: cars, vans, tractors and harvesters . . .

3 sows and 6 young pigs and 7 middle-sized castrated pigs.

25 middle-sized goats, 10 male yearling kids and 3 female yearling kids.

2 oxen for ploughing, which are 8 years old, one being reddish, the other white, reasonable beasts for this type of land.

An old ox, white in colour, only able to work another year; and can be seen to be wearing a bell around its neck.

A black bull nearing 7 years of age. And also 2 black bulls of 2 years old and another three-year-old. Also a red bull nearing 3 years old.

2 medium-aged reasonable cows, one with a three-year-old male calf, the other one-year-old female calf, very small. The cow with the male calf is black, the other has a red coat.

Another cow with only one horn, with a year-old calf. It is true that said cow is nearly nine years old and not worth much, and very small. It has a black coat.

Another red cow without a horn and not worth much, with a male calf that was born nearly half a month ago; said cow is nearly 8 years in age.

Another red cow of 5, with a female calf half a month old and is nothing. Said cow is very small.

A small three-year-old heifer worth very little. All the aforesaid cattle, except for the ploughing oxen, are very small and of a bad breed; and what are listed next are also worth little.

A grey mare and her bad-quality saddles and irons, must be nearing 10 years old, middle-sized.

Another black-coated mare with a white muzzle, 3 years old and middle-sized.

A three-year-old grey-coloured beast, middle-sized.

A smallish one-year-old mule, son of the old mare.

This was not a household at the peak of prosperity. One has the impression that the estate – or *masia* as the Catalan word (which means something closer to 'homestead' than to 'house') has it – was at that time in a rather precarious position. Precarious or not, however, it will have been an imposing place: big and sprawling and almost certainly among the finest in the area. How else, ninety years earlier, could such an isolated place have provided an education for the little baby born to be a bishop?

Reading *The Revolt of the Catalans* by the twentieth-century historian of Spain John Elliott, I was struck by the following passage about the ancient role of the *masia* in rural Catalan life. It expresses well the centrality of the homestead to the culture:

The [way of life of the] *masovers* [yeomen-farmers who would often hold a secure lease rather than the freehold; we do not know the status of the owners of l'Avenc] . . . reveals something of the attitude of Catalan society as a whole to land, the house and the family. The home, *masia*, is the typical Catalan house, the one that has most helped to shape the pattern of Catalan life over the centuries. The *masia* was generally set alone, on a hillside or in a clearing, where corn would be grown and perhaps also vines and olives. Built of stone, it served originally as a stronghold as well as a farmstead. *Masies* constructed during the Middle Ages, and even later when situated in dangerous coastal regions, often had a fortified tower adjoining them.

There were naturally several types of *masia*, but from the end of the fifteenth century perhaps the most common consisted of two storeys and was covered by a sloping roof. On the ground floor would be the entrance hall running the full length of the house, to the left of the hall would be the stable and cellar and, to the right, the kitchen, the most frequented room in the house. At the back of the hall a staircase led to the main floor, which consisted of a large room known as the *sala*, occupying the area immediately above the entrance hall, together with bedrooms leading from it. Sometimes there would be attics above, but there was always ample storage-space, as every *masia* had its outhouses, where the crops would be dried and stored.

The compact building was well suited to the needs of an agrarian society. It housed the farm animals and the farm produce as well as the family. The very distribution of rooms within the *masia*, in particular the presence of a stable and a main hall devoted to carts and tools, again emphasized the close ties linking the *masia* to the land on which it stood.

In a sense the *masia*, the solid symbol of the family's property and status, was more important than any of its occupants. One generation of *masovers* succeeded another but the *masia* remained, solid and immutable, an entity in its own right. In the last resort, all personal considerations were sacrificed to the interests of the *masia*. The *masia* was the family – the family to which it had often given its own name. . . . The kitchen . . . was the centre of family life. Here it would congregate after the day's work. At the long, narrow table it would eat its supper of bread, wine and the traditional *olla*, a stew of boiled meat and soup, and then sit by the fire with its great sloping chimney, possibly passing the time weaving, for [as one peasant wrote in his diary] 'in winter when the nights are long' the peasants 'occupy themselves in weaving as many cloths as they can'.

It is only by chance that half of that old thirteenth-century house whose contents Constança listed remains today. Three centuries later new owners would complete the first phase of a demolition planned to remove and replace the whole building. We know this because the obviously temporary join made between the new, sixteenth-century end of the house and the more ancient part betrays it. Stones resembling teeth jut out in preparation for the continuing Renaissance plan which was never put into effect.

Why did they stop half-way? Maybe the family ran out of money – we do not know – but the renewal was never completed. Our thirteenth-century muleteer passing beneath l'Avenc will have seen a different façade, but, jutting into the hill behind, a roofline little changed today. He might have noticed smoke rising from the same old fireplace and the same bread oven, in the same kitchen, as stand there now.

The day of this birth was no ordinary day, though. It was to prove momentous in the life of the house and of the family who owned it. It was to carve itself into the history of another town, far away, and into the very stones of twenty-first-century l'Avenc.

The key to all this could be discerned, tiny, on the horizon. When that small boy was old enough, did his father point to the grotesque shapes of holy Montserrat on the skyline, and tell him about the town at its feet: Manresa? These were to be his downfall.

The boy's name was Galcerán or Galzaran, or Galzeran, or Galcerandus, or even (in one version) Galleran. Spelling was haphazard in those days, and along the borderline between Castilian Spanish and local Catalan (with random infusions of Church Latin) names appear in many guises. Catalan names from the Middle Ages have just the same gruff, elfin, pagan oddness as old Celtic and Anglo-Saxon names do. Like our Beowulfs and Ethelreds, those old Catalan names have almost died out today.

Here, for instance, are the names of some of the first bishops of Vic, taking into account that their spelling has been *castellanizado* (Castilianized) some time after the beginning of the eighteenth century, when Catalan was declared to be vulgar, and every Bernat became a Bernardo, every Guillem a Guillermo. Who can imagine meeting a Wisefredo, or dining with an Atón?

Cindio (AD 516)
Aquilino (589–99)
Teodoro (610)
Esteban (614–33)
Domnino (mentioned in 638)
Guerico (643–53)
Wisefredo (mentioned in 683)
Godmaro (886–99)
Idalcario (902–14)
Jorge (914–47)
Radulfo (948)
Wadamiro (before 949–57)
Atón (957–71)
Frugífero (972–92)
Arnulfo (993–1010)
Borrell (1010–17)
Oliba (1017–46) . . .

Did they all have vast, wild beards? Let's skip to 1302 . . .

Poncio de Vilaró (1302–6)
Ramón de Anglesola (1306)
Berenguer de Guardia (1306–28) . . .

. . . And the thirty-second would be that boy whose childhood at l'Avenc lay ahead: Galcerán. From the grass mound where he will have taken his first steps he could already see Vic far away across the plain, and the cathedral of his future diocese. If he looked further he will have seen the sacred mountain of Montserrat on the horizon, at its feet a sprawling town called Manresa.

Vic, Montserrat, Manresa . . . these names will have meant nothing to him, high on the hill above them all. Yet had he but known it, in one sweep of the eye, little Galcerán Sacosta could see all the way from innocence, to hubris, to nemesis.

I did not know about Galcerán when we bought l'Avenc. All we knew was that there was that curious stone washstand built into the wall in the grand reception room called La Sala (on account of its being the place where 'salaries' were paid weekly to labourers in the currency of salt) on the second floor – the one with a carved bishop's head in his mitre, in bas-relief, with the water-spout coming from the mouth. Later someone told us they thought a bishop had been born at l'Avenc. This was the beginning of research which led us finally to many sources, but first, and most importantly, to the diligently kept episcopal archive at Vic.

Perhaps Galcerán was consumed by ambition, for he was to become a driven man. He cannot have been more than seventeen when in 1310 he became a canon in the beautiful cathedral at La Seu d'Urgell, looking up into the valleys of Andorra, so he must have been bright and numerate. In 1328, in his mid-thirties, Galcerán Sacosta became the thirty-second Bishop of Vic, in the See of La Seu d'Urgell.

To show the upward mobility of this family, here's a bit of Old Catalan which I reproduce not only to amuse you but to swell the rather small body of Old Catalan appearing in any English publication. It charts the prominences of both Galcerán and his brother, Guillem:

Fonch dit bisbe natural de les Planes del bisbat de Girona y cavaller, germà de Guillem Çacosta, cavallerís major del rey de Aregó y criat de dona Maria, reyna

de Mallorca. Lo qual Guillem fundà dos beneficis, lo primer en lo altar de nostra Señora en la igléisa parrochial de St Christòphol de les Planes, bisbat de Girona, y vol que sia patró lo hereu de la casa del Avench de Tavertet . . . públiqeus de Vich a 12 de las calendas de janer del any 1346.

(Thus the said Bishop, born in Les Planes, of the Diocese of Girona, and knight, [was] brother of Guillem Çacosta, senior knight to the King of Aragón and courtier of Dona Maria, Queen of Majorca. Guillem founded two benefices, one at the altar of Our Lady in the Parish Church of St Christopher of Les Planes in the Diocese of Girona, and wants the patron to inherit the house of L'Avench of Tavertet . . . Recorded in the public deeds of Vich this 12th day of the calendar of January 1346.)

The Pope was not so far away as today: in Avignon in the south of France; but journeys were slow and dangerous and communications poor, and before an age when even the most distant outposts of Catholicism would bow the knee to a strong and centralizing papacy, the Church locally enjoyed a hefty measure of autonomy. Some bishops did almost as they pleased. Galcerán was to be one of them.

That he had put his unpopular nephew into a plum job in church bookkeeping may not have been unusual by the standards of the age; that he had begun a purge of all the parishes for moral backsliding as well as heresy was distinctly odd. Sacosta would visit, or send representatives to, each parish, and invite clergy and laity there to testify against each other. He was a *visitator*, a visitor of the unwelcome kind and hailed in church accounts as a *persiguidor de falsos clèrics* – a persecutor of false clergymen. Priests whose personal or sexual behaviour failed to come up to scratch found themselves denounced and punished.

There are even accounts of the attempt by one poor woman (we don't know of what heresy she was accused) to have her excommunication lifted the moment Galcerán died. She was small beer. On another occasion (it is said) Galcerán was to excommunicate an entire town. The town was Manresa, thirty miles to the west of Vic, over the plain and over the hills. Through Galcerán Sacosta, the story of this town is inextricably tangled with the history of l'Avenc.

Manresa sits at the foot of saw-toothed Montserrat. Seen from l'Avenc, Montserrat is a tiny yet strangely intense squiggle on the horizon. Seen from Manresa, the spine-tingling outline of that rock mountain is so unreal that were it to be painted by computer-graphics into the backdrop of a Disney fairyland you would think it too fantastic. Montserrat shoots vertiginous fingers of rock in impossible pillars high into the sky. No dragon's back was ever as spiked; no rooster's comb as careless of gravity. As stunning to me as Ayer's Rock, famous in Catalunya, Montserrat is (like Manresa itself) hardly known outside north-eastern Spain, except to the devout. For here is found the Holy Grotto. Even in the thirteenth century, a devout child like Galcerán will have been taught all about this story.

In the year 880, says the legend, on a Saturday night when the sun was going down over Montserrat, boy-shepherds saw a bright light coming down from the sky, accompanied by beautiful music. The following Saturday they returned with their parents. Again the vision came. Everyone who went saw it.

The bishop arranged a visit from Manresa. A grotto was discovered, and in it a black wood carving of the Virgin Mary. The bishop suggested the image be taken to Manresa, but whenever anyone tried to lift it it became too heavy to move. So a chapel was built to Mary, around the carving.

Or so runs the legend. The carving is there to this day. Since then all kinds of stories have surrounded Montserrat: that St Peter carved the statue and St Luke left it there; that Ignatius Loyola prayed there; that the legend of Parsifal was born there; that Richard Wagner visited it for inspiration for the opera. In the nineteenth century the Virgin was made the patron saint of Catalunya. At the end of the twentieth it was found, when the virgin was rescued from a ferocious fire, that she was not black all the way through after all but had been painted black some years after being carved.

The site has since become a place of pilgrimage, a sort of mini-Lourdes. Montserrat (affectionately abbreviated to Montse) is now one of the most popular of all Catalan girls' names. When Galcerán Sacosta got on the wrong side of the Virgin of Montserrat, he made a terrible mistake.

Legendary in Manresa's history, his is a name you will seldom hear spoken there. In Tavertet a main street bears his name; in Vic a major road is called after him; but in Manresa no street, avenue or park carries the name Galcerán Sacosta, no statue is raised in his honour, and no plaque or monument commemorates him in the vast, ancient Basilica de Santa Maria de la Seu. The horror inflicted by Galcerán upon Manresa is the reason why. The tale has entered local folklore and appears in different versions, but all agree that something very odd happened to Manresa in the first part of the fourteenth century; relations between an obstinate bishop and a desperate town broke down with devastating results. This, so far as we can gather, is the story.

In a dry epoch when water was chronically short, Manresa's expansion had been throttled by drought. Farmland lay sterile and disease became rife. This drove the townspeople of Manresa to desperate measures. Finally Manresa's councillors agreed a tremendous and difficult project: to build a 25-mile canal to the town from higher up the River Llobregat, through atrocious terrain of mountain and rock. It was a brave plan. The secular authorities were in favour: King Pere III signed a royal authorization. The Church did not dissent – Manresa was in the Diocese of Vic and our friend Bishop Galcerán raised no objection.

In October of that year, 1339, able-bodied townsmen enlisted to dig, and the work began. It proved hard going indeed. Workmen died. But slowly the canal advanced towards Manresa, until it reached the edge of lands in the possession of the Diocese of Vic.

Then – to the shock of all Manresa – the bishop blocked its way. Nobody had expected this. Refusing permission for the canal to cross his land, Galcerán began a bitter five-year stand-off with the whole town. Why? No one really knows. A story runs that he preached that God had sent the drought on account of the sinfulness of the townspeople: the remedy lay in prayer and virtue, not civil engineering. It is also said that the bishopric owned several water-mills downstream of the canal's entrance, and Galcerán was unwilling to see them robbed of power.

He hated Manresa and Manresa hated him. Whether this was among the causes of Galcerán's mulish obstruction of the town's welfare, it was certainly among the results. One story has him being jeered and spat at on a visit to the town, and departing, cursing Manresa and swearing never to enter its walls again.

Galcerán then appears to have gone mad – at least as regards poor Manresa – and cut off the town not only from water, but from divine grace. He placed the whole population, clergy and laity, under a kind of suspension from the Church itself, closing its churches and prohibiting the hearing of confessions or the celebration of Mass there. One account refers to this as a collective excommunication, though it was perhaps more in the nature of a personal curse. Another account says he excommunicated the members of the town council. The canal-builders tried to ignore his interdiction and continue over his land as trespassers, provoking pitched battles between Manresans and mobs sent by the Bishop of Vic.

Poverty-stricken Manresans emigrated in despair from their benighted and thirsty town.

A kind of paralysis followed in which none among a range of rival powers seemed able to command enough authority to break the impasse. The Pope was appealed to, without apparent result.

The King, Pere III (known as 'El Ceremoniòs' on account of his weakness, vacillation and love of show), who had approved the project, received a delegation begging him to act, but he would or could not cross swords with his over-mighty cleric. Contemporary Manresan pageants show Pere III prancing around, drunk.

The townspeople prayed for relief, but the drought did not break and nor did Galcerán's resolution. The bishop would not budge. The town's churches stayed closed and dark. The canal project had ground to a halt. Manresans made pilgrimages to the shrine of the Black Virgin at Montserrat. Who would save them and their canal? In the late winter of 1345, the answer came – and it came from Montserrat.

What happened? Word of mouth is all we have to rely on, and the tale has no doubt changed and grown in the telling and retelling. But what everyone at the time seemed to agree on was that some kind of mysterious light (it was ever thereafter called 'La Misteriosa Llum') appeared to emanate from Montserrat and travel across the sky to Manresa, diving into the Church of Carme on a hill in the town, dancing around the altar, and returning to Montserrat.

'It was like a star, it came through the window and rose softly to illuminate the archway above the altar,' said one witness. When the Prior of Carme asked for more evidence 300 people came forward, all certain that they had seen a miracle.

'All saw the marvellous light appear brighter than the sun itself, directly from Our Lady of Montserrat . . . it passed over half the

city between two districts, outshining the sun's rays and following along the road of the Virgin Mary of the Mountain of El Carme, which is in the city on a hill near the wall . . .'

In one subsequent version of the legend, the Mysterious Light enters the nave, splits into a trinity of rays before the altar, reunites and departs by the same route as it arrived by – headed back to Montserrat. From accounts I have read and engravings I have seen, there is at least one central confusion. Was the *Misteriosa Llum* a ball of light or a ray of light? The many suggestions that it somehow 'travelled' from (and returned to) Monserrat are more consistent with the ball theory. But others speak of (and artists have drawn) a sort of beam; or sometimes a comet.

We shall never know. What we do know is that Galcerán then died and the town was rid of his curse.

Some say the arrival of the Light marked the very moment of Galcerán's death. One account I have says news of the event was carried to him; in horror he tried to repent of his earlier obstinacy and begged for absolution, but death struck him down before he could put things right. Anyway, repentant or otherwise, Galcerán died. The obstinate and angry old man who would not budge had come a long way from l'Avenc.

That the problem had been purely personal and that the vendetta against Manresa had been Sacosta's alone is confirmed by the speed with which, once he was gone, everything was sorted out. A new bishop was quickly appointed, who in turn appointed a subordinate to resolve the dispute over the canal. Work was restarted almost at once, and the great canal was finally completed in 1383. It is still in use today.

Manresa never looked back. The town went on to become a big and thriving place – twice the size now of Vic, though never as fashionable. But a certain tension between the two, not entirely good-humoured, seems to have persisted down the centuries, and Galcerán is the cause: quite an achievement for one man.

The town still celebrates his death and the mysterious Light that heralded it, and has made it the centrepiece of its major annual fiesta: a ten-day affair called the *Fira de l'Aixada* (Fair of the Pickaxe) – the axes, that is, that were used to dig the canal.

A pageant is re-enacted every year before admiring crowds, many of whom these days hardly know what it is all about. Nor did we when first we saw that elaborate joke in stone: the carved bishop's head serving as a water spout in the state room at l'Avenc.

On 21 February 2005 Belinda, her husband and I drove down from l'Avenc to Manresa to join the crowds, staying in the town's only major hotel (a pleasant enough but rather seventies Franco-era monolith, the Pere III) and attending the medieval fair.

There was music and dancing, jousting, horses and carriages, and stalls selling olives, cheeses, oils and wine. All the shops were festooned with leaves; many of the shopkeepers had dressed themselves in old sacks; and walking down the streets were people in medieval costume, decorated horses and pantomime carts.

'It seems strange,' Belinda said as we stood among an outdoor audience booing the on-stage figure representing Sacosta, 'that we're the only people here who are on his side.'

As for the Light, the Church does not seem to have made any move to declare this an official miracle. It is treated almost sheepishly as a piece of folklore into which one does not delve too deeply. God (one supposes) would not lightly strike down one of

His own anointed bishops, nor take the mob's or the laity's side against him. Galcerán was an embarrassment, to be sure – but maybe we who do not know the whole story do best to leave it at that?

For yes – disgracefully, I know – I feel a sneaking pride that he was ours. Modern politicians love to prattle about 'making a difference'. Our Galcerán certainly did. Curious how, as the owner of l'Avenc more than seven centuries after Galcerán's birth there, I find myself searching for ways to excuse his behaviour. I keep thinking of that kitchen, that newborn baby boy, and the beauty outside. And perhaps rather than try to excuse or condemn, we should accept that we do not know Galcerán Sacosta, and never will.

What power and position, what misery and disorder, what Mysterious Light and what mysterious dark lay ahead of that boy playing at l'Avenc. Infamy beyond a child's imagining awaited this scornful, driven, restless medieval spirit. To be booed in civic pageants more than six centuries later; to be written about, as today he is, in another country, by another owner of his house, in another millennium . . . what a twist!

It is not the final twist. Manresa has had its revenge. A son of l'Avenc had blocked their canal and cut the town off from water. Now another obstinate and angry old man, who would not budge, was to do the same to l'Avenc.

6. An Enemy

It happened like this. Belinda and her husband often used to walk along the cliffs' top – not too close, but close enough to peer down from time to time at the hills and woods and water of the valley below. In the spring of 2002 Belinda detected a faint but unpleasant odour: the smell of death.

She looked around but could see nothing: no cow's or sheep's carcass lay anywhere within sight. And, strangely, the smell seemed to be rising from the cliff's edge. Yet this seemed unlikely. It was at least 1,000 feet down to the thick wooded country at its base. She did think, however, that she could pick out something mangled at the base – something suspiciously unlike trees. It could be a carcass or carcasses – of what, she could not discern and did not especially want to.

There was no way down to this lonely place, short of a long journey by road around a gap in the cliffs beyond Rupit, plus a lengthy walk – or an even longer journey on foot, all the way by the packhorse route down from Tavertet. She told the police.

She asked both her husband and me whether we thought she had been right. Of course she had. We had no doubt of it. None of us had any way of knowing whether the practice had been abandoned or whether animals were still being thrown over. Swine fever is a scourge in Catalunya, and Osona and the Collsacabra are at the centre of a pig-farming and sausage-manufacturing industry for which this part of Europe has long been famous. Leaving diseased carcasses out in the open air to rot – and not far from water courses – was irresponsible as well as grisly.

The countryside, the landscape, belongs to everyone. When people see something wrong in the countryside they should be open about what bothers them, not surrender to the timid notion that only those directly concerned have a right to act. Those directly concerned often speak for nobody but themselves; and those indirectly concerned often long for somebody outside to barge in and make a fuss. I'm all for barging in.

I had experience of this when I was a Member of Parliament for a rural constituency in the Peak District of England. Even locals – people born and bred in a village or valley – would often defer to one or two bullying landowners or big cheeses against whom nobody would raise their voice. These bullies used to cultivate me as the local MP, and give me to understand that they knew their neighbourhood, its people and its problems backwards; that they were respected by all, and spoke for all. My experience was that this often did appear to be the case – until they died. I would then discover that they had been feared, not respected, and that I had missed an opportunity as an 'outsider' to speak up for insiders who did not dare to.

My sister did not know when she made the complaint who had thrown the animals over the cliff but of course she guessed it would be likely to be someone local – no stranger could take a truckload of dead animals through Tavertet (from the one side) or past the farmstead at Rajols (from the other) without being noticed. So if we'd thought much about it we would have realized that the culprit might well be Joaquim Casals, our neighbour, the old man from the nearest house, Rajols. Sr Casals was the man who had first pointed me to the water pipe supplying our house.

The fact that it was from Casals that l'Avenc had been bought was to cause no end of trouble. But my sister's reaction – to report what she had seen – was instinctive, and right. It was not directed against any individual. I am still glad that she did not stay silent, and if we had our time over again, I would encourage her, again, to do what she did. She was not alone. The builders at l'Avenc had also noticed the smell on their way home in the evening, word got around and the mayor of Rupit decided to report it to the police too.

The police investigated. And the long and the short of it was that there were many rotting carcasses down there, mostly of pigs but also of cattle, some fresh and some which had been there a long time, as well as piles of rubbish, old toys, medicines and rubble. They were traced to the ownership of Joaquim Casals. It seems he or his labourers had been pushing animals – dead or alive, we did not know – over the cliffs for some time.

We have never wasted our time trying to find out exactly why this was done. It was none of our business. Maybe it was a way of dealing with wounded or diseased animals, or maybe just a cheap way of disposing of fallen stock. And what was done was done. But it was obviously wrong, obviously unlawful and obviously had to stop. Casals was prosecuted, found guilty, and it is said fined €60,000 as well as charged the fee to hire a crane and specialized team of cleaners to clear the whole area.

A word here in Joaquim Casals's defence. He had had a hard life. He was from another era. His approach to farming came from another era. There was a time in rural Spain, and not so long ago, when a farmer's methods were nobody's business but his own, when the police did not poke their noses into environmental or agricultural matters, and when those on the land made their living as best they could.

Nobody ever went down to the bottom of those cliffs, nobody's interests were obviously damaged in any serious way by throwing objects over them, and if those objects were dead animals, well, that might seem to a certain cast of mind an efficient and trouble-free way of getting rid of something useless. The consequences would rot away fast enough and would even have contributed to the livelihood of a fox, vulture or stray cat. Farmers always used to dispose of dead animals in this way; rubbish collection was unheard of until the 1960s in rural Catalunya. It was second nature to farmers to pile up natural waste to rot. There was a time when Casals's approach would simply have been approved as self-sufficient.

Modern attitudes to farming and the environment have come later to rural Spain than to rural England and much of Europe. Casals, who started from nowhere, had made his way from poverty to security by work, a hard-nosed attitude, a driving will and a ruthless streak. He was born and raised in Franco's time, when the European Union and Brussels directives were not even dreamed of.

I heard a sad story about Joaquim Casals, a story which is almost certainly true, and perhaps shows something about his lonely defiance. When he was a small boy his family, who were very poor, lived by the back-track on the other side of Tavertet. He was sent out, as small boys were, to tend the cattle, and one day was with his cows when along the track came a motor car (itself a rarity then) whose driver was lost and asked for directions. The boy directed the driver, who by way of a thank you gave him a sweet.

It seems nobody had ever given him a sweet before. Apparently the child returned day after day to the same place by the road, at the same hour, in case the man should come back and give him another. Which of course he never did. It caused some local amusement.

Today the old man is not alone among his generation in having carried on as though nothing in farming was changing, only dimly aware that things must, and with an attitude of resistance to change – of which our arrival will have been a notable example. It will have come as a terrific shock to such a man to discover that how a farmer treated a carcass was no longer just a matter for himself alone.

And when he discovered that those who had become (unintendingly) his accusers were the English and Anglo-Catalan family who had (via Joan Sarsanedas) bought l'Avenc from him at what now looked like a knock-down price – urban sophisticates who were (as it will have appeared to him) tarting the place up into some sort of minor Pyrenean palace, and who depended for their water supply on the spring on his own land . . . well, I can almost understand his reaction.

Almost but not quite.

Ten days later we went up to l'Avenc in the morning to be told by the builders that the mains tap had run dry and they could no longer mix cement. Someone had cut off our water. It did not take us long to work out where that had been done. Somewhere not on our land but on Casals's, where our water pipe crossed, the supply had been cut. We were pretty sure who the culprit must be: Joaquim Casals.

It's a strange feeling to be targeted in this way and with such obvious malice. To all three of us it was new: nobody had ever done anything like this in our lives. Nobody had ever hated any of us that much. And it was somehow all the more shocking that this had happened at l'Avenc, a place which breathed serenity and beauty. None of us had the least idea how to react. We suspected immediately that the water had been cut as a simple act of revenge for my sister's report of the animal carcasses, and we quickly learned that this was true.

Casals had never doubted that my own family were to blame for all his tribulations. He was concentrating all his hatred on the new owners of l'Avenc and left Rupit's complaints out of it. Belinda was a foreign *mala puta* (evil whore) and his hatred was so strong she says she felt physically aware of the vibrations of rage whenever his white Mercedes cruised by.

Her husband went to talk to Casals, but to no avail. He shook his fist and wagged his finger and called us names.

It was the beginning of a kind of drought, the tribulation which Manresa had known. It was more than a shortage of water because it was all done in anger, and the feeling of anger infused the whole affair. This was more than an absence of water, it was a modern version of a Biblical curse.

I should dearly love to make light of the episode – to describe it as a silly fuss, a rollicking chapter for my book, caused by a colourful local character, a hoot in its way, all part of life's rich tapestry, 'Aren't they rum creatures, these grumpy old foreigners' . . . etc. But it was never for a moment amusing, and we were quite unable to rise above it. It made us miserable. It spoiled the atmosphere of renewal, friendship and local support in which the whole project had been born and grown. And hung in the air, clinging to us, and clinging around l'Avenc. And even when it is solved, as it will be, and the water is turned back on, as will happen, I shall not say that all's well that ends well. It casts a cloud of anger and sadness over a long chapter in the story of the restoration of l'Avenc. Somebody out there – somebody not far away – really hated us, hated us enough to want to destroy us and everything we were doing. It hurt.

Beyond the hurt, there were also tremendous and continuing practical difficulties. Through all this period – three years at the time of writing – we were forced to ship in water in tanks on lorries. This was expensive, but we kept receipts, so that in the end we could claim our costs back from Casals. For the first of those years nobody was living permanently at l'Avenc and water was needed only for building. The old brick well supplied a few score gallons, but replenished itself only after rain, from a fissure in the rock, and only in a trickle. This was not enough, particularly during the dry summer months.

One summer I determined to go down to the bottom of the well (nobody ever had, apart from me, briefly, once before, for a photograph for *The Times*). I wanted to find out for myself what was there and what we might hope for from it.

A bright searchlight showed it was not enormously deep, perhaps about twenty feet. The top of the well was protected by a round housing of old red brick with a stone roof, but there was a small iron door and through this we managed to lower a short length of ladder on a rope. Settling it on the bottom I then climbed down the rope until my feet touched the ladder and descent became easy.

I found myself standing in about three feet of very cold, clean water. I shone my torch around. The well was formed of a round brick superstructure, then about twelve feet of stone-lined shaft, also round, at the bottom of which the shaft opened out into a sort of natural bulb within the rock – like that of a mercury thermometer. Into this sphere water was slowly dripping from the solid rock all around. There was no spring. The wetter the subsoil and rock, the faster the pit filled. Really this was no more than a reservoir: useful, but hardly a boon during summer droughts.

Still, I cleaned out a few centuries' worth of old bricks, stones, rocks, jars and tins, making space for more water; and the well has been a boon to the builders during days when the tanks have run dry. It was not, however, the answer to our prayers.

Once in frustration my brother-in-law went on to Casals's land, found the stopcock which had been turned off, and turned it on. Water flowed. We refilled a big plastic storage tank near the road. Maybe, we thought, this is what we should have done all along, and Casals, having made his point, would give up his siege. Our confidence was shortlived. The next morning someone had opened the tap on our storage tank, and drained its entire contents away.

The stupid thing was that Casals was cutting off his nose to spite his face. At least one of the drinking troughs he kept for cattle on those parts of his lands adjacent to l'Avenc's was supplied from the same main as ours. Now he was denied its use for his own stock. He was also losing the payments we had made, per litre, and according to the agreement under which we had bought the property, for the Rajols water we used.

So how should we handle this conflict? Catalan friends locally, and villagers in Tavertet, were full of sympathy, but a number of people pointed out that Casals was known for his anger and his intransigence. My instinct was to keep the temperature down, carry on shipping in water by tanker for the time being, try to open some line of communication with him, and hope that he would cool off and let bygones be bygones.

No doubt that was Quim's instinct too: my sister's husband is a good-natured man who has no taste for disputation. But once engaged on a project he does not like to hang around, as you will see. Work on l'Avenc began almost the moment we bought it, never stopped for long, and intensified with every passing year. For months we tried to play the stand-off down, carrying on in a rather English way as though our neighbour had not declared a virtual war on us, but it was embarrassing as well as highly incon-venient: we felt like fools.

Speaking for myself, I felt like a naïve foreigner who had blundered in, offended local sensibilities and ended up with a property on which half my earnings were being spent but where I could not get my right to a water supply respected; still, I was for letting matters lie.

My brother-in-law, in the end, was not, and he was right. His patience had limits. It was becoming ridiculous, he said, and we could not carry on like this. We took legal advice and were recommended to report Joaquim Casals for depriving us of water – a criminal offence, apparently, in Spanish law. This we did in 2003. We had no thought of punishing Casals, simply of forcing him to turn our water back on. Our first lawyer believed it was worth trying to secure a criminal conviction for the cutting off of water as it was clearly not a case of negligence. Casals had a lawyer, Pep Rovira, a drummer in his spare time, who had been playing only days before at our midsummer eve party.

It was, with the benefit of hindsight, a mistake to take the route of criminal proceedings, and I do not now think we were well advised. The case failed, and we should have seen that it would.

As in England, a criminal charge needs to be proved beyond reasonable doubt. That we had no water we could fairly easily demonstrate, but we needed also to show it had been deliberately turned off, and that this had been done by Casals himself, or on his instructions.

Before we pressed charges, Pep Rovira had recommended Belinda to talk to Casals. Pep felt sorry for us. He said Casals was now convinced that my brother-in-law was innocent and (like himself) a victim of his evil and manipulating foreign wife, who was totally to blame. 'Ask Casals out for a tonic water,' Pep had said to her, 'say sorry, and he's sure to forgive you.'

So Francesc together with Belinda and Quim's eighteen-year-old son Rodger telephoned, arranged an interview, and arrived at Casals's house in Manlleu at ten one morning. Casals – face creased with a frown – received them in his downstairs office. Never for one moment did he look Rodger or his mother in the eye. Instead he directed a string of insults about her at her brother-in-law Francesc. 'Is there nothing we can do to fix things?' Francesc asked. 'Pay me half the fine . . . after all, it is of her doing not mine and you will have your water back . . . Otherwise you will never again have water at l'Avenc.'

After that we decided to press ahead with our doomed court case. But, perhaps because we had been so confidently advised to

lay this criminal charge, we never focused realistically on the
difficulties of making it stick; we assumed our lawyers would somehow square the circle. We knew we were in the right; we felt a
sense of righteous indignation about the affair; and as the date of
the trial approached, we were looking forward to our day in court,
and to being vindicated at last. I had returned to Britain quietly
(and unthinkingly) confident that the case would go well for us.

It did not. When Belinda rang I could tell at once from the
catch in her throat that something had gone wrong. The case had
been thrown out. Casals had denied all knowledge of any cut to
our water supplies. Obviously we had no witness to his having
turned off the tap himself (indeed we did not know who had
actually done it) and, faced in court with an absolute denial of
any complicity, we had nowhere to turn and no witness to call,
to prove otherwise.

My immediate reaction, like my sister's and brother-in-law's,
was to think, 'Well, telephone the judge at once and tell him to
come and see for himself that the water's off now, whatever Casals
may have told the police' – but of course in Spanish law, no less
than in English, you cannot reopen a case which has failed to be
proved at the time it was heard.

Should we, then, get back into the queue for the hearing of a
new criminal charge? Or should we face the prospect of being
the perpetual owners of a dry house in a dry property: a shell,
fascinating historically but uninhabitable? Or should we just sell?

We decided to fight it. Spanish justice must surely be able to
do more for us than had appeared so far to be the case. This time
we were better advised: to take civil proceedings for the restitu-
tion of our water, and for damages. It took time to set this up but
within a year and with careful research and much to-ing and
fro-ing with our lawyers the case was prepared. What we would
have to show (but on the balance of probabilities, not beyond all
reasonable doubt) was that we had a right to the water, and that
it was being denied us by Casals.

My sister and her husband set to work lining up the witnesses
we would need. They were: Joan Sarsanedas, to testify to the fact

that Casals had never challenged or questioned l'Avenc's right to water when the property was sold to him, and that he had sold it to us on the same basis; Toni, Tavertet's mayor, who had tried to get Casals to turn the water on and had heard that only the payment of money would achieve this; two of Molina's workers, David and Lluís, who could testify to being thrown off his land when trying to repair the pipe. And finally myself. I would testify to the occasion on which Casals had actually shown me where to find the water main to establish our supply as new owners.

Though on friendly terms with all our witnesses we were not close to all of them, and the only thing we were asking of them was to tell the truth. But sticking your neck out is not always easy or comfortable, and were they to do so, they must have known it would infuriate Sr Casals. Nevertheless all these potential witnesses assured us they would come to the court hearing, to testify. But Belinda, her husband and I felt nervous. It is one thing to promise to swear on oath and publicly what you have assured someone privately to be the truth; and quite another to do it.

The case was to be heard at 9.15 on a winter's morning, 27 January 2003, in Vic. Come that chilly dawn, would our Catalan friends or acquaintances, some of whom might have to rub shoulders with Casals in the years ahead or work for him, actually make the journey to Vic to stand with us against this vengeful and by no means powerless man? I must honestly say I doubted most of them would. Belinda was more hopeful. Her husband, as so often, kept his own counsel.

We three were there in good time. It would be my first experience of Spanish justice. I climbed the stairs to find the usual gaggle of lawyers, defendants and witnesses in a range of cases, hanging around in a corridor. It was not unlike an English court scene, except that nobody was dressed up in wigs or gowns, and there was a somewhat lower-key and more businesslike atmosphere about the place. One feature I could not explain, however, was what looked like a DVD machine, standing by the wall.

We glanced at our watches. Our case had been slightly delayed (no surprise there) but still there was no sign of our friends. Then

Joaquim Casals came up the stairs, looking grey-faced and angry, but exchanging the minimum, at least, of civilities with us: a nod and a *bon dia*. He moved away to talk to his lawyer. It was Pep Rovira again.

But where were Joan, Toni, David and Lluís? I had by now more or less given up much hope of their appearing. My sister looked tense. My brother-in-law is always hard to read. I cared less about the case than about how hurt and let down Belinda would feel if people she had trusted did not support her.

Then Joan Sarsanedas came up the stairs. A great relief, but he, I had thought, had always been the most likely to attend, as he would recognize it as an obligation. He was, after all, our builder, and he had sold us the house. Anyway, none of us could now feel that nobody had supported us.

Then Toni came up the stairs. He could have been forgiven for staying in bed. He was mayor of Tavertet, he had done some building work for us, it is true, but he had also worked for Casals and did not like taking sides. He needed to be on the best terms he could with as many as he could, and I should have understood if he had preferred not to testify.

Then David and Lluís appeared together. All they had to say was that Casals had seen them on his land, asked them what they were doing and on learning that they were trying to reestablish the connection shouted at them to leave immediately.

All our witnesses had come, and I had been wrong to doubt it.

Sometimes one reads reports in newspapers, or books by English people living abroad, where 'the locals' are written about either comically as strange natives – objects of amusement – or as a potentially hostile force. Locals feature as though they were a tribe, all on the same side, all understanding each other at a deeper level than that on which they can understand the English *arriviste*, or he them. The English writer's attitude is that these people are friendly enough when it suits them, but liable to close ranks against the foreigner when the going gets rough.

That approach is understandable, and makes for a good story; but it represents a mild form of paranoia. The temptation to succumb to the affliction is strong if you come from another country and do not (as I do not) speak the language properly and cannot always understand what people are saying; or if you are fluent like my two sisters, but still always feel a little different from the others. When tired, perplexed or frustrated, the Us *vs* Them attitude is easily slipped into as a kind of explanation.

But it is not our experience in Catalunya. It distorts reality. Catalan people do not all know each other and understand each other and confide in each other, any more than English people do. By no means are they all on the same wavelength, any more than we are. Quim was perhaps more baffled by the behaviour of his namesake (Casals) than I was. It was not the case that everyone was on Casals's side. Catalans who were our friends or with whom we had worked shared our outrage. And now four people who might have found an excuse not to stick their necks out and tell the court what they knew had all turned up to support us.

The hearing seemed to go well, from what we could tell. There were procedural similarities with English civil law, and some differences. The courtroom was small and tidily decorated, but without any ceremonial flourish. There was no jury, and the judge looked thirty-something at the most. In Spain, legal adjudication is a career in itself, on a separate path from advocacy, but apart from a plain grey gown our judge was not set on the kind of pedestal English judges enjoy, and there was no bowing and scraping, no flummery and no elaborate forms of address – so far as I could make out. But, as in an English trial, each side was represented by counsel, who were given the opportunity to question both their client's and their opponent's witnesses.

The judge, however, Judge José Luís Gómez Arbona, took a more active part in the questioning, his manner cool, businesslike and disinterested. He betrayed none of the eccentricities or outward impatience of an English judge. Witnesses and counsel were allowed to speak in either Catalan or Spanish, while I (although I found I could understand most of what was being said in both languages) was given an interpreter. The truth is I would have been hard put even to pronounce the name of the legal partnership whose clients we were: Advocats Puigdecanet.

We were the plaintiffs, Casals the defendant. Our counsel, Marta Rovira (no relation to Pep), was a young woman advocate. She was brisk, clipped and untheatrical of manner. Sr Casals's counsel was an older man who conformed more to the stereotype of an English barrister, not least because the harder his client made things for him, the more florid became his behaviour. He was putting on a bold face, making the best of a difficult case and an even more difficult client.

For a former Member of Parliament, I felt surprisingly nervous. My sister, too, seemed nervous. Her husband was matter-of-fact. Quim, Belinda and I each gave evidence, mine very brief.

My brother-in-law told the court how he tried on three occasions to get Casals to see some sense and to turn on the water; how he had had to buy water and how this was making the reconstruction of l'Avenc slower and more expensive. He reminded the judge why the water had been turned off in the first place.

My sister recounted the same situation and told the judge of the frustration of watching Casals's cows drink the little water we had in a big and useful puddle beside the house. She told the judge she had tried to get the water reestablished by talking to Casals but that she had been asked for money in exchange and felt she shouldn't have to pay for something to which the house had a right.

I recounted the story you have read: of the day Casals showed me where to find the water pipe.

Counsel for the defendant was in some difficulty because his client, monosyllabic to the point of being delphic, appeared for much of the time to be denying that there ever had been any right to water from his spring. I was unclear whether he was denying cutting the water off, or having had to supply it in the first case. I think he was unclear too.

Toni Molina told of his meeting at Rajols with Casals and the tenant farmer and how Casals had said he had no intention of reconnecting the pipe and had suggested we pay him half the fine to put things right.

The two workers described how they were shouted at and had given up trying to mend the pipe, which had obviously been intentionally cut and stopped up.

Joan Sarsanedas was a compelling witness. Persuasively, he explained the understanding on which he had both bought and sold l'Avenc.

Not unnaturally, Casals's counsel tried a couple of times in his questioning to discredit our witnesses by suggesting that they would offer evidence in our support simply because we knew or had employed them. Toni and my sister, the lawyer said, were in the same political party as mayor and town councillor, Toni had worked for us. 'And also for Casals, I take it,' said the judge, to which Toni replied, '*Sí, senyor.*' 'But Sr Molina buys his materials from Quim's builders' merchant's shop in Manlleu; he is not neutral.' '*No, senyor,*' said Toni endearingly, 'I use another builders' merchant and always have done.' Both my brother-in-law and Joan pointed out that in small places like Tavertet or Rupit, few were complete strangers to each other, and many had worked for each other.

The questions and evidence tended this way and that, not assisted by Casals's somewhat cryptic approach to the nature of his defence. I think the court was left unsure which part, if any, of the plaintiff's case was being contested by the defendant. The defendant just looked grey-faced, angry and defiant.

After about an hour of questioning, the judge dismissed the court. His verdict, in written form, would come later. As we left, I realized what the DVD-vending machines were for. Legal counsel were able to obtain video-recordings of their cases, for later reference. It seemed, on reflection, an obvious innovation. I expect we shall adopt it in England in about sixty years.

Leaving Vic, we felt hesitantly encouraged by the way the hearing had gone, and greatly encouraged by the way Toni, David, Lluís and Joan had supported us. We had not, however, been left with much idea of when we could expect the verdict. I guess I thought it might be a few days.

Our judge, we learned, had been taken away on a more urgent case, and the delivery of his verdict on ours must wait. I returned to England. In the event we heard nothing until November 2004 – ten seemingly interminable months later.

When my sister's call came, this time I could hear in her voice that it was different. The judge had ruled in our favour and awarded us our costs too, including our continuing expenses in tankering in our water. I was delighted but I never feel euphoric in victory: it only tempts fate. And fate, as it turned out, was to prolong our torment. Casals simply ignored the ruling.

This fast became clear. By now we had been without a proper water supply at l'Avenc for nearly as long as the drought suffered by Manresa at the hands of Bishop Galcerán Sacosta.

Crudely scrawled signs had appeared on the way to Rupit calling Casals a pig. They were a mystery; nothing to do with us or anyone we knew. Belinda phoned to tell Casals not to suppose she had written them. 'It is not my way,' she said. 'Someone, somewhere is enjoying our conflict.'

'I have no other enemies except you,' Casals replied, and hung up.

A week later, a new sign: '*Belinda torera, Quim cornut*' (Belinda man-eater, Quim cuckold) appeared on a rock on the way to Tavertet in big clear lettering which my nephew Adam and my sister Debs chipped off a few days later. My sister has many qualities, huge enthusiasms and one or two eccentricities; she is also, in an understated way, rather chic for a Parris. But a man-hungry vamp she most emphatically is not. Her enemy, whoever he was, lacked information.

Wearily we went back to the court with an application for enforcement proceedings.

In the meantime the three of us decided to try one last throw. We arranged a meeting with our lawyer, Casals, his banker and Quim. We had an offer to extend. If Casals would restore our water supply without further ado, then we would suspend indefinitely our demand for the damages, so long as Casals would sign papers binding him to maintain our supply on pain of a reimposition of our demand for damages. We would give Casals a week to respond to this offer, and if he failed we would withdraw it.

Silence and then, after the deadline had expired, Casals finally met up with our lawyers and shouted, swore and thumped the table. 'And tell them to take down the sign showing people the way to La Roca Llarga. That's on my land, how dare they show people the way into my land!' We had put up a sign for hikers, who were losing the footpath in the huge building site l'Avenc had turned into. Even this had been interpreted as an act of aggression.

Meanwhile we waited. The judge was busy, very busy; and our lawyer Marta Rovira tirelessly knocked at his secretary's door to check if the sentence was to be enforced, only to be told, over and again, 'not yet'. Days, weeks, months went by and we still had to buy water. At times we almost felt l'Avenc was cursed to remain dry.

There was nothing to be gained from despair. We decided to try getting a borehole dug near the house. The work would be expensive, we knew, but it seemed worth a try.

I was away when the boreholing company arrived with their mechanical drilling monster. Quim and his wife watched tensely as the drill bit went in, and down, and down . . . And down. After fifty feet the machine came to the limit of the the drill's reach. It was withdrawn. A small exploratory pump was lowered . . . and switched on.

Water came gushing to the surface in a temporary pipe. Everybody cheered. Belinda filled a cup and began to drink it – only to be told to spit it out at once because an initial dose of disinfectant had been introduced. But still she and her husband rejoiced. All our troubles over, perhaps?

It was not to be. The pump yielded about sixty litres then dried up. Like the old well I had plumbed, holes in the ground at l'Avenc act only to drain water held in suspension in the rocks and subsoil. There was no source.

Well then: no water from the direction of Rajols, little water beneath us, not enough from the sky. So what about water from the other direction: the village of Tavertet? For while all this had been happening, the road from Tavertet, through l'Avenc, to the highway near Rupit – the rough track which passes right beneath

Rajols — was being graded in preparation (we hoped) for being given a concrete surface, albeit narrow.

Before this was done and after years without water, we decided to bury a pipe from Tavertet to l'Avenc and pipe the municipal water to the house. Toni, as local mayor, gave us the permission and the task was done — at considerable expense and even greater effort, for much of the road was almost solid rock.

Pumping, too, would be a problem: the pipe had to gain 600 feet in height in less than two miles — no easy feat. But with some serious non-return valves, a half-way tank and two hefty pumps we did manage to get water to the house.

However there have been persistent difficulties and interruptions. The pipe keeps springing leaks; there are frequent air-locks; the mercury plummets and the water freezes; sometimes the pipe bursts. Problem after problem has seemed to whisper that water is to loom large among l'Avenc's early difficulties. In the spring of 2005, just when it appeared we had established a good and reliable supply up the pipe from Tavertet, the whole system seized up again.

The first pump (down at Tavertet, beside the village tank) had a struggle at the best of times, its job being to lift the water so far, but now it seemed to be pumping against an impossible pressure. Was there a blockage? Experts were called in and, laboriously, tested each section, section by section, of the long line. Finally they found the fault. Someone had poured liquid cement into the system, half-way along it, using one of the air-escape vents which punctuate it. The cement had solidified along a few feet of pipe, completely sealing it.

A bypass was put in place. A second tank, before the last climb, with a second pump for the second and final stage up to the house, was installed. It worked — it is working as I write — but 'How long, oh Lord, how long?' we cried.

Nevertheless, the road's resurfacing was our chance to bury a pipe in land that did not belong to Casals, and we were glad we had taken it. For years the local municipality had been promising to upgrade and surface the road, and now finally it was being done. Further, we had at the same time taken the opportunity to get the public right of way, and the road, slightly realigned so that it passed fifty yards in front of the house, rather than right under l'Avenc's windows. In an age when almost nobody passed this way the owners of l'Avenc might have regarded proximity to the track as an advantage, but we were looking towards a future time when an increasing number of tourists might want to take a back road with a stunning view – particularly once it was metalled.

It was to be surfaced in concrete: a narrow lane wide enough for one car, but with passing places – exactly what we had always hoped. Finally everything was graded and ready. There followed a fortnight of almost uninterrupted heavy rain: a complete downpour. A whole section of road a few hundred yards to the Rupit side of l'Avenc simply slipped over the cliff. In came the bulldozers to start all over again.

At one point within sight of Casals's farm, Rajols, the roadbuilders had been unable to complete the concrete edge of the road because the bank beside it falls away so sharply. The resulting indentation – a lethal nibble out of the side of the carriageway – is a hazard to any less than keen-eyed motorist. So the roadbuilders had improvised by painting a stone on the edge of this indentation in Dayglo pink.

One night someone scraped all the paint off the stone. The intention was presumably to imperil unwary visitors to l'Avenc. As an exercise in spite this must have been a lonely and laborious task. We spotted the minor piece of vandalism immediately, but did not bother to repaint the stone. What would have been the point?

What had we done to deserve this? Each of the four owners was about a quarter of a million pounds poorer than we would have been if we had never seen l'Avenc. Each of us had aged visibly in the six years since we had bought the property, and the strain of keeping the project on the road had played its part. None of us had ever seen the house as some kind of get-rich-quick scheme and none of us expected either monetary profit or the massed cheers of a grateful populace. But we were proud of what we were doing

and thought we had reason to be; each in our own way, we were
making a personal sacrifice so that the work could carry on. Costs
kept mounting. Difficulties kept multiplying. Red tape grew ever
more tangled. Deadlines kept being missed. All this was made easier
to bear when visitors from Tavertet or further afield – people we
did not know – stopped and wondered at what was being achieved,
and said how good it was. But, equally, every shaft of suspicion or
jealousy wounded us, staggering as we were, both financially and
in our spirits, under the burden of the project.

Spirits rose when in June 2005 the court sequestered Casals's
property of Rajols, in guarantee against the debt he owed us.
Spirits fell when it became clear this would take effect only if he
tried to sell it. They rose again in July when his lawyer requesed
a meeting – and fell when Casals turned up, shouted at us and
repeated his demands. They fell further when somebody blocked
our new pipe again. We repaired it.

Sometimes, at low moments, I would remember the time I had
first walked that way all those years ago, and found the house; and
the night the three of us had decided to go ahead and buy it. I
would think how different our lives would have been if none of
this had happened. Were we sure – were we absolutely sure – that
if we had the chance to walk that way again, we would take the
same turning?

Joaquim Casals's withdrawal of our water supply was for us a
real cost and an infernal nuisance, but if the difficulty with the
water had arisen from some natural cause – fractures in the pipe
or the drying-up of the spring – we would have faced the problem cheerfully. It was the anger and the hatred that made it almost
unbearable. We could not and cannot understand.

The demise of Bishop Galcerán was marked by the arrival of a
divine light from Montserrat. Sometimes, as I look towards
Montserrat from the big balcony at l'Avenc, a thought occurs . . .

And I banish it.

7. A Mission

The Water Wars baffled and infuriated us but they never held us back. In the seven years from 1998 to 2005 the house rose again – rose from the brink of ruin to becoming the near-finished home in the stunning place which l'Avenc is as I write.

The work had been far harder than we ever imagined, the sheer complexity of the project had often left me reeling, and the burden it placed on all three of us had at times seemed almost crushing. The cost has been huge and the setbacks many. Looking back on it now, it seems like such a mountain range of challenges, with each ridge, once climbed, yielding to a higher ridge in front, that if we had had any inkling of the journey ahead when we started then we might have turned back at the beginning.

Now, in retrospect, I even begin to forget the order in which we did things, or how our tangle of tasks interlocked, one with another; and why we did what we did when we did it – or failed to do the things which temporarily defeated us. If I am to tell you what we did, where am I to start? Perhaps the late-summer days I spent almost alone at the house at the end of the last century describe it best.

Before work started even on our first task, renewing the roof, I decided to spend a month at l'Avenc during the summer. This – 1998 – was the year we had signed the deeds of ownership, so by that August we had not long been owners.

I had become seized with the idea that what was needed before the workmen got started that autumn was a set of stone steps behind the house and outside it, giving easy access from one terraced level of ground to the next, twenty feet beneath. At the time it seemed such a big and important job and believing in it gave me one of the happiest summers of my life. I was not to know that my brother-in-law's more far-reaching plans for the project went beyond a set of rustic stone steps behind the house.

I slept out on the grass behind the house, at first under the stars, then in the house and, when the weather broke, in an old caravan my father lent me. Apart from overnight camping this was probably the first time anyone had stayed at l'Avenc since the last people to live there had left in the 1950s. I wrote a diary, which *The Times* published in the newspaper's Weekend Review. It reads now like the diary of someone slowly taking leave of his senses. This is what I wrote:

Monday Aug 10: *Invasion by cattle – Raid by mice – I begin my great project*
A cow wakes me, breathing heavily. She's trying to get in. I see her outline through holes and cracks in the wooden door to the downstairs hall where I sleep on the floor beside the stone mounting-block for departing horsemen.

Rise with the dawn. Shoo off cow. Boil a kettle of water from a cattle trough a kilometre away (there's said to be a pipe nearby but I can't find it). Spoon coffee into the mug. Pick up milk carton . . .

Shock of my life! Carton sealed but light as a feather. Close inspection shows tiny tooth marks pinpricked in bottom corner. Mice have drunk the milk. All of it – all my four cartons empty. Trail of tiny droppings – milk-gorged mice staggering home to sleep it off. The first food in l'Avenc for 40 years! Miracle recorded in mouse annals for succeeding generations: 'White Monday, 1998'.

Where are their nests? Holes in the walls, holes in the floors, holes in the roof . . . no way of keeping them out. I slept outside when friends were here but the thorns and thistles are bad and what if it rains? And wild boar. And mosquitoes. And flies. Think I'll sleep inside. With the mice. Ah well.

Today I build a stone staircase. There's no way up to the barn behind – a retaining wall ten feet high blocks access, except by a long diversion up a track. Wooden steps have collapsed. I shall build stairs up the side of the wall. Tons of granite slabs and rubble lie around so this will tidy the property too. My family say to check under rocks for vipers.

My first drystone staircase; nobody to consult; teach myself. I'll do it from first principles, plus string and pegs. Steep – 45 degrees. About 15 treads, I reckon, infilling with rubble. Rubble? I find a fossilized conch-shell, perfect, the size of my fist. Cattle invade – accustomed to shelter inside l'Avenc, but we've fenced them off. Cows furious, snorting, trying to get through. Repelled successfully.

Only two steps done by lunchtime. Arms ache with lifting. Neck burning. Cicadas screech. Getting hotter. Doze off in the shade, then work from five till dusk. Three steps complete. Put in long tie-stones, sledge-hammered into the wall.

I'm dirty and sweaty. Contemplate fetching bathing water from cattle trough. The obvious dawns. Bathe in trough – revenge on cows. Marvellous, stretched full out as sun sets, crickets sing. All around wild lavender, thyme and purple Viper's Bugloss; sloe-bushes loaded.

Return to survey my steps as owls hoot.

Tuesday Aug 11: *Two more steps – Moonlight dissolves walls*
Slept fitfully – shoulders aching. Awoke in the small hours. Silver light flooding through cracks in the rotting door, gaps between stones, holes in the roof and floors.

Moonlight turns the foreground into background. The moon is the foreground. Up with the sun. Finished two steps. So proud of this. Stick to the pegged string guide and it really works! Shall I have a plaque – 'these were steps constructed 1998 by MFP in his 50th year'?

Wednesday Aug 12: *My new home arrives*
Family bring lunch. Dad brings old caravan – got it up the track with the Land-Rover. Family depart. Install myself in chintzy plywood and plastic domesticity. Eat your hearts out, mice.

Thursday Aug 13: *Three more steps – Return of mice*
Losing interest in the world. Clinton, Monica somebody, who cares? 'He's just a womanizer, like a lot of men,' Mum said. Give up the news. Stone steps centre of my life. Two before lunch, another by sunset. Haul rocks up hill. 'I must work harder' (Boxer in *Animal Farm*).

Make packet soup. Knorr-Swiss. Spot tell-tale mouse-tooth marks in tinfoil. Gnaw-swiss! Laugh out loud at own joke. Drink soup from saucepan. Alone in the night, giggling in caravan. Finish rice wine left by friend from Japan, use eggcup as goblet. More giggling. How fast one could turn into oddball.

Friday Aug 14: *A boar, a sea of cloud*
Hear a boar squeal in the night. Awake before dawn and feel excited about steps. Stand in underpants, contemplate possible slabs. Whole valley filled with cloud as the sun rises – white sea at my feet. My staircase awaits.

Monday Aug 17: *My stone steps – strange voices*
I'm alone. All sense of time has gone and life's proportions shift. There's something in the news about the rouble – but the stone steps I'm build-ing are all that matter now. The work has been painfully slow – two, at the most three, steps a day – and backbreaking. I've moved (I reckon) five tons of stone and rubble. But I cannot lift or manoeuvre a flag wide and deep enough to form a single tread, so each step is a composite of liftable flags and wedges.

I work from first light till dusk, snoozing at noon but hardly both-ering to eat – getting thinner but feeling strong. I'm not lonely any more – I'm used to the silence. When family call by I find all the chat-ter noisy and end up unfocused, staring into space. I'm very happy. Before dawn, after the owls, I heard again something I thought I heard before: a low grumbling as of indistinguishable voices in a downstairs room or a strong current over heavy river-stones. It comes from no direction in particular. I cannot place it. There is nothing frightening about it: nothing frightening about anything in the air at l'Avenc.

Tuesday Aug 18: *A letter*
The family brought a letter, from Holland. A nice Dutch lady has read *The Times* and wishes to encourage me. She addressed the envelope to me at 'Casa l'Avenc'. But l'Avenc is a ruin unrecognized by the Spanish Post Office – not an address. And I – not being resident in Spain – am unknown to it.

She also omitted the province. All the Correos had to go on were the names of two small villages she mentioned (with question marks), some 30kms from each other. L'Avenc is in neither. Then she put the name of a town 40km away, and (in brackets) the route number of a local road – but l'Avenc is not on it and it is 100km long.

Mistaking the Spanish for 'road' she wrote, in effect, 'horse race'. We often praise the ingenuity of our British Post Office, but there are inspired postmen in Spain, too.

I can guess who this will be: Josep-Maria, a local farmer's son and keen sportsman. He temporarily lost his job as postman when the bureaucrats insisted only a qualified civil servant could do the job.

Catalan commonsense triumphed over Madrid red tape and Josep-Maria was reinstated. Thank goodness. He knows my mother, will have seen the envelope and put two and two together. This would be like sending a letter to someone not resident in Sussex, marked 'E Wittering? Petersfield? Chichester. Horse race A3. Britain.'

Thursday Aug 20: *To plaster, or not?*
An architectural historian points out small patches of primitive plaster clinging to the external stone. A grand house like this, he says, will have been plastered. Almost disappointing – the warm, rough stone was what first drew me to l'Avenc.

An authentic replastering with quicklime, though, would look anything but cold and hard. Should we? Such decisions are far off – the roof is falling in, for heaven's sake.

Friday Aug 21: *Steps near complete – Wild thyme in walls – Standards slip*
Only four or five stone steps to go. Now they go high enough for me to clamber up the rest of the wall to where my caravan is parked.

Superstitiously, I resolve at first to continue going the long way round, saving my inaugural ascent for the moment when the final tread is complete. But resolution slips. I tear wild thyme in tufts from the walls, where it's in the way – and remember the struggle to make it take in the garden at home in Derbyshire.

Later, alone, I start eating things from jars and packets, shortcutting utensils and crockery. I'm hardly Somerset Maugham's Englishman, dressing alone for dinner and reading *The Times* in date order, three months late.

I've only been here for a few weeks and already I'm wandering around in my underpants and drinking from saucepans. Beard growing. Grey! Oh no!

Sunday Aug 23: *I descend a well; a photographer pays a visit*
Belinda, my sister, is here. Today we explore the well. In front of l'Avenc stands a shoulder-high tower of old red brick. Peering in one sees that, below ground level, the shaft is lined in big, beautifully dressed, curved stone blocks. You can just see water below.

How odd – we're only a few hundred yards from the top of a 1,000ft rock cliff. We lower a 20ft ladder down the well – but still no floor. Attach a rope to the ladder and drop it further. The feet splash into water. I climb down the rope and descend the ladder.

There is darkness – with tiny, illuminated well-side faces peering down at me anxiously from above. This well is shaped like a mercury thermometer – long shaft and bulb below, where the well opens out into a little cave surrounded by rock. The water is about 2ft deep – cool, clear and clean, and seeping from the horizontal strata around me. There are tins and bricks and bottles to be cleared out with a bucket on a rope. Another day.

I climb back up, where Mercè Terricabras has come to take photographs. She has driven 20 miles, risking the dreadful track.

'You didn't say there was a well,' she clucks reprovingly. 'I need a special flash for wells.'

Monday Aug 24: *An incorrect expression – distant fireworks*
A hiker passes, observes my sweaty labours: '*No es matar moros!*' he says, meaning that it doesn't look the most fun in the world. Literally this means 'It isn't killing blacks.' Hardly sensitive, politically, but one has to remember the Moorish invasions, to which such idioms hark back.

After dark I hear a strange clap and rumble down on the plain. Distant fireworks! Tonight is the *Festa Major* of the town of Manlleu, where my mother has a school of English.

Tuesday Aug 25: *An important loss; a hallowed place; song of insects*
Can't find my only ballpoint. Frantic search for pencil, crayon, anything. These little inventions are so important to us diarists. Try scratching key

words on to notepad with carbon of burned-out matchstick-end, just to jog my memory.

In the evening I sit after dark in front of l'Avenc, listening to the night sounds. By noon or by night I always choose this place – plastic chair, the great façade of the house at my back, at my feet the cliffs and mountains, valleys and plain, the lights of Tona, near Vic, twinkling one way, those of Girona the other. I fancy people have always sat here. I listen to the crickets' song. Except it isn't. Listen properly – not blindly as though this were nature's equivalent of white-noise – and you realize there is not one insect's song, but the songs of half a dozen species: each quite different, some occasional, others continuous, some modulated, others a monotone, some percussive, some lyrical, entwined but unpick-able, woven together into a textured sound.

Wednesday Aug 26: *An open secret – A firefly*
Two more steps finished by dusk. Belinda says the people in Tavertet (the nearest village) seem pleased someone is rescuing l'Avenc. We had worried that people might object to foreigners – but apparently not: everyone who knows the house has been saddened by its ruin. My sister had not been mentioning my own interest from abroad – not to conceal, but to stay private. Fat chance.

Went to a roadside bar 20 kilometres away last week. 'Are you the brother of Mark?' asked the barman, whom I'd never seen in my life. 'You've got the same voice. So you must be the English journalist who's buying l'Avenc.'

I chuckle, alone after dark. Something catches my eye – pale green and glowing. I bend down to inspect: it is a firefly fallen by the wayside, flickering out. If they end the evening without a mate, that's it. Curtains. Glad I'm not a firefly.

Thursday Aug 27: *Labour complete – A storm*
The last step! Yesterday my staircase entered a cutting, passing into the retaining wall just below its rim. I can't believe I've actually kept to the string I strung between pegs to guide me, when I started. This looks, well, almost professional. But will anyone use my steps? Certainly I will. My father observes calmly that they're quite good. What an

understatement, Dad! My efforts have been Herculean. Just at the moment this feels like my big achievement of 1998. Tomorrow I leave l'Avenc, my holidays over. Don't want to go.

In the middle of the night a huge storm – thunder, lightning and bucketing rain – rocks my caravan. I stumble down with a torch into the old house. Water is pouring through the ragged ceiling, down the walls and through holes in the rotten floors. Poor old house. Nearly 700 years old [I did not then know that some was older than this], but now the elements are moving in for the kill. Every storm like this spreads the rot, weakens the timbers. This is no time to leave, with the autumn approaching and winter round the corner. It seems unkind to quit l'Avenc now – like a friend walking out.

I've just realized I'm talking aloud, alone, in an empty house, in a storm. Maybe it is time to leave.

But I came back often and as l'Avenc began to change, so did my life. A journey that had once been a rare event, to see my family at Christmas or Easter, became a regular escape from England. I have travelled it by plane, ferry and car and bus – but the best way is by train.

You can take the sleeper all the way from Paris via Girona to Barcelona, using the main line which runs right down to the Mediterranean coast and then follows it across the Spanish border.

I prefer a more exotic route, though. There's a sleeper from the Gare d'Austerlitz in Paris which turns right off the main line at Toulouse and heads up past Ax-les-Thermes into the French Pyrenees; you wake up with snowy peaks around you, to be deposited in time for morning coffee on the platform of a huge, half-abandoned, somewhat ghostly station at the frontier village of La Tour (in France they write 'Latour') de Carol. From here a little Spanish train headed for Barcelona takes you all the way down the other side of the Pyrenees, crossing the frontier at Puigcerda near Llivia and passing the ski-stations of La Molina. This is still my favourite way of going to l'Avenc, and of returning to England. Leaving London after work on Thursday, you can be in Barcelona for coffee the next morning; leaving Barcelona late Sunday afternoon, you can be at work in London by eleven on Monday.

The two nations' railway systems, RENFE and SNCF, seem to be trying to hide this possibility. Eurostar to Paris (Nord) is easy, but Gare d'Austerlitz looked for ages as if a bomb had hit it. From this dilapidated station, repair work and scaffolding everywhere, seemed to run all the lines that do not matter. On arrival you begin to fear you have been misinformed and that the 21.56 night-sleeper to Latour de Carol promised on your ticket is a fiction. The destination boards are blank.

Down one platform you spot an undistinguished-looking train, no ticket barriers, and a railway official camped on the platform with a makeshift desk and a sheaf of papers. Yes, the train exists and your couchette in a six-sleeper compartment (second class) is ready. It is perfectly comfortable if chance has not sent you a fat French chamber-mate who snores.

You awake briefly to some shunting before dawn in Toulouse, then drift back into sleep as your part of the train begins clickety-clacking up the branch line towards the Pyrenees.

At about seven you awake again, and peer behind the blinds. Snow-capped peaks, lit in the early sun, soar into the sky above. Streams rush by. The line is steep and the train, pulled by two huge electric locomotives, slows. After a stop at Puymorens to let off the Andorra-bound, and an interminable tunnel, the train pulls into its destination. Most French travellers have by now departed at intermediate stations.

Latour de Carol is a substantial station with rotting goods yards, few trains and a deserted customs-and-immigration cabin. With Franco's Spain officially neutral and France under German occupation, this must have seen some odd doings during the Second World War, and it still feels weird. Over the way you spot a brightly painted, graffiti-covered little local train, waiting on its immensely wide Spanish rails to start the three-and-a-half-hour journey to Barcelona; but it is hardly eight; time for coffee and a croissant. You can buy the RENFE ticket on the train.

As the sun climbs you descend, clattering down towards the

plains, the Mediterranean and Barcelona – and first Manlleu, the closest station to l'Avenc.

The single track weaves down a valley beside a road, criss-crossing the River Ter and plunging in and out of tunnels through the rock gorges that contain it. At stations, some abandoned, you pass the down-trains.

This is the loveliest part of the journey. The road above disappears as the track hugs a steep valley by a noisy stream. Outside, oak, beech and hazel crowd the track while the upper slopes are clad in pine and juniper. At one isolated stone village where the goats gather in the farmyard, the tiny railway station advertises sausages for sale. Shade fills the valley. Snowy hilltops shine in the sun.

The track enters a mountain, our tunnel performing a downward spiral to bring us out lower. Then a wall of warm, dry, crumbly rock towers straight up outside the carriage window, and straggling briers brush the roof. A great way to reach Catalunya.

There was plenty to come to Catalunya for. I have made much, maybe too much, of the struggle at l'Avenc – and told you nothing about the fun. Yet all the time along the way there have been moments, evenings, mornings, which outweighed every anxiety.

It is extraordinarily hard to describe these moments and even harder to explain them. Sometimes the big breakthrough or material leap forward brings only the satisfaction of one more tick in one more box on a mental spreadsheet; yet a September dusk creeping over the Montseny mountains – just five minutes of silent contemplation while the crickets sing – or a half-hour at dawn when for some reason you have awoken before the others and are alone at a window-ledge as the cool yellow of the morning sun strikes the pale brown of l'Avenc's walls; or the instant when you glance at the small carved head (of a monk) on the stone lintel above a door and catch him looking back at you . . . these fleeting moments can be weighed in the balance against the whole damn slog, and outweigh it.

In the summer of 1999 I turned fifty. I had planned to be in

Catalunya for the day, 7 August, but with no big celebration in mind, though a dozen or so friends from England were coming for a house-party around l'Avenc; some were to bring tents, others sleeping bags and camping mattresses for the dusty and dangerous floors inside the house; others had booked rooms at the Hostal El Jufré in Tavertet or were staying at l'Hostalot, my parents' house. My plan was for all of us to join with my family for an evening meal, either at l'Avenc or in Rupit.

In those days the cheapest flights were to Carcassonne in France, and quite a few, including me, came that way. Others had arranged transport independently. Most arrived on the same day, the eve of my birthday, and gathered for dinner in Rupit. The following evening we would spend at l'Avenc, if we could find a floor with no holes in it.

We made our way there. The air cooled as the sun set and by now a fairly large crowd had gathered around the big arched door. Belinda, Deborah and their children were helping to prepare a buffet. Tammy, Belinda's daughter, looking gorgeous, was serving Spanish *cava* – sparkling wine. As, for some reason, the door stayed shut, we all mingled together outside, chatting and sipping. A disturbingly elaborate sound-system seemed to have materialized and was being hooked up, its loudspeakers to either side of the house. People fell silent.

There was by now only a faint glow in the western sky, over Montserrat, and the stars were coming out. The sound of our temporary generator being started behind the house broke the silence, but the throb was quiet. Floodlights (which had been trained on the Renaissance façade of l'Avenc) faded up, and the stone glowed yellow. It was beautiful.

Then an orchestra struck up – or what sounded like an orchestra. The loudspeakers were playing the introductory chords of Delibes's 'Flower Duet' from *Lakmé*. But who would sing?

The old wooden shutters across the carved double-window on the first floor burst open. Out came two English sopranos. And sang. They were professionals. They were wonderful. My mother had gone up to them when she heard them singing one day in

Covent Garden market, and persuaded them to come to l'Avenc. Their duet was sublime. You can say *Lakmé* is corny if you like, but British Airways had not flogged the melody to death by 1999, and eyes filled with tears, including mine.

Light was beginning to creep over the eastern horizon from the Mediterranean before the last partygoers staggered back to their beds, with (in most cases) nothing stronger than *cava* coursing through their veins.

The whole night had been stupendous. But there had been that moment, just one, which had been transcendental. As the warm light flooded the front of the old house and every face turned up to the shutters opening at the window, and, 440 years after that decorated stone frame was put in place, a melody which had probably never been sung at l'Avenc before burst from the state room upstairs, I thought of the words of the Book of Revelations: 'And they sang a new song.' All that we had done at l'Avenc, and all that we were still to do, was worth this moment.

Moments like this recurred. In 2001 we decided to have a midsummer eve's party. In Catalunya the longest day, 21–22 June, virtually coincides with the Feast of St John (St Joan). As in other parts of southern Europe this is the occasion for the year's big bonfire night. What 5 November is to us English, the Feast of St Joan is to Catalans. So we would have a bonfire party at l'Avenc.

And what a party! Belinda and her husband like to do things big but this time they excelled themselves. There was a jazz band, a rock band, a Spanish crooning band and a sound system which would have brought down the walls of Jericho. Apparently the party could be heard at Vilanova de Sau (the New Town of Sau), whose lights can be seen twinkling miles away down in the valley below.

And what a bonfire! I have never seen so much scrap wood. We piled it high on the big apron of flat land in front of the house, and waited for the ceremonial torch-bearer to come and light it: it is a local ritual that he travels from village to village, homestead to homestead, with a lighted torch, Olympic-style, igniting each St Joan bonfire in turn (and quaffing another glass or two of *cava*).

Everyone was invited. By 'everyone' I mean just that. We stuck invitations on to posts and trees in Tavertet as well as outside the house, and people came from miles around, starting to arrive around nine, until the track was littered with cars for hundreds of yards in all directions. We made a token charge (not enough: we lost plenty of pesetas, but who cared?) for entry and to cover drinks, and had a proper bar, made from old planks, by the house.

By then we had the second-hand diesel generator (bought from the municipality of Tavertet) going, and its thud punctuated the night as temporary floodlights lit the façade of the old house, and all the lights we had strung along the walls inside illuminated the rooms and stairs – and holes in the floors. It was a wonder nobody fell through, for people wandered everywhere.

For most of the night (and many stayed until dawn) there were a couple of hundred people, yet the party passed without incident and without damage. I wish one could be as confident that one could hold a party in an ancient house in England, post invitations to the general public on lampposts, admit everyone without reservation, and escape without damage, injury or even a drunken brawl.

It was chilly but the stars were bright and the sky completely clear. Soon, though, nobody felt the cold. By ten people had begun to dance. Five hours later they were still dancing. It was unsafe to dance inside so we turned the dusty patch underneath the balcony into a makeshift dance area. Once people had started there was no stopping them – and even I, who never dance, was dragged into the mêlée.

Slowly, as the fire burned down to a sea of glowing embers, our two dogs crept back from the hillside, and a pale light flooded over the eastern sky above Girona and the coast, the party ended. It had been a magical night – and an occasion we were to repeat every June thereafter. It was our way of saying thank you to the whole surrounding area for the friendship and interest people had shown; and our way of showing that we did not want to be exclusive at l'Avenc, that we knew the house belonged not just to us four proprietors but to the whole Collsacabra.

8. A New Roof

Best, maybe, to begin not with what we gave l'Avenc, but with what l'Avenc gave us. Because for all my talk of dereliction and the brink of ruin, our starting-point – the house we bought as it was when we bought it – was a strong and solid building.

The foundations were good. They must have been. The most ancient part of the house had survived the earthquakes in 1427 which brought down a castle two miles away in Rupit, destroyed almost the whole of that village and the village of Tavertet, as well as virtually every other fine house in the Collsacabra, and reduced one of the closest big towns, Olot, to rubble.

In the Gothic half of l'Avenc what had sagged or subsided had long settled before the last century dawned. In the Renaissance half there was little sign of any subsidence since the rebuilding four and a half centuries ago. The walls were absolutely straight, without bowing or cracking anywhere. You could stand at the corner stone beneath the front façade, rest your head sideways against the wall's edge itself and, craning your vision up three floors to the eaves, detect not the smallest deviation in the ruler-straight line.

You could examine the great arch around the front door: hardly a pin could be inserted between those tremendous, smooth stones in their perfect arc. They say one should be grateful for small mercies, but the fact that this house was structurally intact was a small mercy only in the sense that it was easy to take for granted. We did not know when we started that no problems with subsidence would emerge. Had they done so then everything else we had to do could have been undermined. Our starting-point was a magnificent building, standing four-square on rock-solid foundations.

The roof, however, was about to collapse. The ridge beam was splitting, was held up (as I have described) with a prop made of an old worm-eaten poplar jammed into the rotting floor beneath.

Contrary to what those of us who are not structural engineers might guess, ridge beams of roofs do not take the bulk of the weight. This is distributed across the rafters which run down from the ridge to the eaves, like ribs from a spine. But the ridge beam, into which the top end of each rafter is fixed, keeps the overall structure straight, holding the balance (as it were) between the rafters to its left and the rafters to its right. If the ridge beam fractures, the rafters which it holds in place will drop, the boards laid horizontally across them will collapse, and the tiles resting on the boards will slip. The whole roof will cave in.

You could not, therefore, extract the ridge beam for repairs, or down would come the rafters. You could not lay aside the rafters, or down would come the boards. You could not move the boards, or down would come the tiles. So the first thing we had to do was obvious: we must remove the entire roof, and rebuild it. Under a renewed roof we could then get on with reconstructing the floors, doors, stairs and windows.

Joan Sarsanedas and his small team of labourers and craftsmen did this job, and it was completed long before our problems with the water supply began. As all the original timbers were of oak, we agreed that replacements must be in oak too. Sadly it is only from France that it is now easy to get oak timbers of any size in southern Europe. In Catalunya most of the ancient oak forests have been felled and replaced by pine. Sarsanedas was able to find the timber he needed, but this added greatly to the expense, not only for the purchase of new timber but also the working of such hard wood.

While we were about the job of renewing the roof over the sixteenth-century part of the house, we decided to raise it – the whole thing – by about two feet; and to replace not only that roof, but the roofs over the Gothic section of the house behind.

For all the cost and complication of the labours that would follow when the roof was done, and for all the comparative simplicity of this job, replacing that doomed roof was the biggest thing we did. No single phase of the restoration cost more. Nothing else we did 'saved' the house in a more clear-cut way. Nothing gave me greater pleasure, pride or relief.

These roofs were Joan Sarsanedas's masterpiece. 'One of the

most important undertakings of my life,' he told Belinda after it was all over, 'and of which I will be proud for ever . . . Belinda, I love l'Avenc as much as you, Quim and your brother do.' I believe he meant it. For Joan this roof was like a piece of fine furniture, hand-crafted not just for functionality but for authenticity and grace.

First, all the tiles had to be removed. They were extracted one by one and placed on wooden pallets which were wrapped in plastic and lowered to the ground by a crane. Some met their fate later at the hands (or hooves) of Casals's cows.

L'Avenc had been roofed in *teula arábica*, the Arabic tile introduced by the Moors a millennium ago which replaced the stone slabs that until then had been used for building in Catalunya (and can still be found). Once the tiles were off, the planks supporting them were removed, and then the old rib beams and ridge beam were taken down.

This last task was immensely difficult: requiring (in Sarsanedas's words) a combination of technique and *collons* (literally, balls). The whole building was then bound around the top by a ring of concrete and iron. This, and our wish for higher ceilings and therefore cooler rooms on the top floor, was the reason for the two-foot increase in the roof's height. We took the precaution of adding this invisible steel cake-ring around the top because, on close inspection, there had been some splaying of the top walls over the centuries. With the expert eye of a master builder who understood the juggling of quality with cost, Joan Sarsanedas commented that the sixteenth-century owners of l'Avenc had obviously run short of money as the project of renewing the house progressed, and he could see a notable lowering of standards and cutting of corners as one proceeded upwards from the foundations and approached the roof. This reinforced our guess that the reason why only half the house was ever renewed may have been the owners' financial difficulties.

The ridge beams were then refitted using a mixture of old and new wood; the rib beams were all new.

We decided at this point to make a slight but very noticeable change to the appearance of the house. L'Avenc had had minimal eaves: stubby, stunted things. This looked ungenerous and austere, and spilled rainwater down the exterior stone walls (the house, like most Catalan *masies,* had no guttering, and to introduce this would look quite out of character). I like eaves. The meanness of traditional English eaves is (to me) an unattractive feature of our rural stone farmhouses; and, while we would not have wanted l'Avenc to take on the appearance of a monstrous Swiss chalet, a little bit of overhang seemed to us to sit well with the overall spirit of the architecture.

One-inch planks were nailed down to the skeleton of ridge and ribs, spread with concrete, sheeted in lead, and sprayed with spongy orange heat-insulation.

Then the tiles were replaced, all at fifty feet up, using stairs as access and a crane, first manual, then electric, to lift and drop building materials. The great majority of our old tiles (those that had escaped the infernal cows) were reusable. Where replacements were needed we tried to use old tiles from places such as the animal sheds, so that the overall appearance was of finely graduated reds, pinky-oranges and whites.

We made heaps, too, of all the old oak roof timbers – blackened and incredibly hard with age – as we took them down. Sarsanedas would examine the timbers one by one as he did the tiles, deciding which we could reuse and which would need to be replaced. It might have been cheaper to burn the lot and replace them with custom-built new timber and tiles, but our aim was to restore l'Avenc, not build a replica house. Much of this wood had survived 450 years in good shape and about half of it was usable. Wherever possible we would put the old timber back where we found it; what found no place on the roof was used later in the cellar, kitchen and the holiday cottages, for beams, windowsills and mantelpieces.

Over much of this fairly tense period, scaffolding poles, timbers, tiles and builders' debris littered the land around the house; and as the shifting and lifting vehicles we brought in to move out the old and move in the new began to scour the dry ground to each side of and below the house, its fragile covering of grasses, thyme, blackthorn, box and juniper was clawed away in the burning sun of that summer of 1999. L'Avenc and its environs took on the appearance they were to keep for the next six years: that of a huge and ugly building site, a big, pale-grey gash across the hillside, visible from twenty miles away, over the other side of the Montseny mountains.

The shells of old buildings just above the house, and a big stone lean-to built beside the house as an auxiliary barn, were demolished and removed, and the old rubble was cleared away (to be replaced with new rubble).

It was sad to see. However temporarily, our hillside was being hideously disfigured by the work. In summer it was a pale dust-bowl, in winter a sea of grey and yellow clay in which people and vehicles slipped and slid, and which clung to your boots, a new clod with each step, until you could hardly lift your feet. And all this was carried into the house itself, which became impossible to keep clean, though we swept and swept, and mopped until mops broke. Six years of continuous battle against dirt lay ahead.

Thus began a time of dust and mud: dust hanging in the air, dust in our sleeping bags, dust in our boots, dust in our nostrils; mud smeared over everything. A longing grew in all of us, a longing for a distant day when we would have the final clean-up and then need to clean no more; when piles of rubble would all be carted away; and when my sister Deborah, Manel and their son, Adam – the nurserymen and gardeners – would replant the grass, box, thyme and juniper, and l'Avenc would be green again.

Somehow this new dawn always seemed about a year away. 'Next year,' we would hear ourselves saying, 'we can really tidy the site up, and begin planting.' But next year came, and we would be in the middle of an even bigger mess. We hoped the clean-up might begin as early as 2000; we hoped it might be in 2001. By 2003 we were sure it would be in 2004. But it would always be next year. And that was before, seized by his recurrent bouts of mad-mole-mania, Quim began the Great Dig of 2004 . . . but of that, more later.

Suffice it to say that there would be times when 'next year' began to ring hollow, and I would find it hard to believe the great day would ever come.

All this activity was exciting, though. Exciting, it seemed, not to us alone but to a great many local people. My very first impression all those years ago that l'Avenc was an almost unknown or forgotten place had quickly been corrected. People in the area had turned their eyes from l'Avenc, not because nobody cared, but because its dilapidation was so sad. The house seemed to have gone beyond the point where any owner was likely to find the resources to rescue it.

Now that the unlikely had happened there was a tremendous upsurge of local interest, most of it sympathetic, some of it rather anxious. At one point the whole ancient room below the kitchen, which had been filled with rubble (probably after the earthquakes) and then built upon, was hacked out. This left the arched kitchen and pillar above it suspended almost in the air, and on shaky ground. The aim of the excavation was to find out what lay beneath; but the municipal architect was watching. Almost throughout, Gil Orriols has quietly and sagely looked on, trusting that we know what we are doing. But this was almost more than he could bear. He was noticeably close to despair. Hands to his head he moaned, 'But there are no foundations! I am not responsible. I am not seeing this.' But the excavation went without mishap, and the cellars we have constructed in the stone rooms we found there are a good deal more secure than the rubble they replaced.

As the years went by, sometimes by our own researches and sometimes with professional help, we were to find out a great deal more about the history, especially the architectural history, of the house. But the full story remains hidden, and I believe always will. My sister took charge of these researches and probably now knows more than any other single individual, living or dead, has ever known about the story of l'Avenc.

The place, she thinks, probably first existed as some sort of *balma* (rock shelter) close to the *avenc* natural vertical shaft by the cliff's edge at the bottom of the meadows in front of the present house, where there is also a thin but fairly reliable trickle of water from the mud in the stream. *Balmes* were inhabited from the beginning of human settlement in the area, when safety was to be found in the hills ringing the plain. Some in Catalunya were still being inhabited up to the beginning of the Spanish Civil War. Several can be visited. The *balma* at l'Avenc would have been turned into a hut and shelter for animals, and finally walled in and made solid: an early smallholding or *domus*.

It begins to appear on medieval maps as such: *Domus de l'Avench*. The word *avenc*, incidentally, turns out to be of Indo-European origin (*abinko*) and can mean a subterranean cavity with vertical walls, or any well-like natural formation; it can be used of a column of water too, in the sense of a current.

L'Avenc is first mentioned on 4 August 1234, when a certain Pere of Avench swears that he does not have possession of some books the Bishop of Vic has been trying to get hold of. The house was by then, we infer, already a well-established homestead, the kind of place a bishop might come looking for his books.

From then on there are increasingly frequent references to the house and its inhabitants: wills, oaths, marriage documents, sales, dowries and the like. Our friend at Vic's episcopal archives, Rafel Ginebra, made for us as complete a collection as he could find: *referències documental relacionades amb l'Avenc, 2003*. The best known is the 1292 marriage between the Avench family and the Sacostas of noble lineage: when Bondia Sacosta married Guillem Avench, later to produce young Galcerán.

The house at the time would have been a traditional *domus*, perhaps (as I have said) with a watchtower where our stairwell now is, with the tiny Romanesque doorway still there – but now leading nowhere. The entrance to the old kitchen with its Templar cross probably dates from this time, as may the kitchen itself.

The cellar beneath would have been where the animals were kept. Some of the walls in this vicinity are particularly old. The Catalan autonomous government helped us finance a study in 1999 and 2000, and the method of wall-building was identified as *opus espignatum*, which could have been as early as the tenth, and no later than the thirteenth, century.

Our next point of reference is 1486 (nearly sixty years after the earthquakes which filled the cellar with rubble), for which we have the complete inventory I quoted earlier. The column which today reinforces the archway in the kitchen is mentioned then, and the archway is noted as being in bad condition.

We know little of the fortunes of the house until then, though we suppose it must have enjoyed its fat years as well as thin, for l'Avenc had become a substantial place and its owners substantial people.

The house's second age of prosperity evidently arrived in the sixteenth century, when the new wing was built – and must have departed before the whole design was executed: hence the half of the old house we still have. I call this the 'Renaissance' part of the house, and the older part the 'Gothic', but these terms are used for want of better ones, and because they are the descriptions given by Catalan and Spanish experts we have consulted.

They, however, use them rather differently from us. 'Gothic' in the northern European sense suggests a particular kind of ancient and soaring architecture, its lines emphasizing the vertical, its arches characteristic. But in the Westminster Abbey (or Hell's Angels) sense of 'Gothic' there is not much at l'Avenc which looks Gothic, except for one very fine window that turns out to have been brought from a house in San Julià de Vilatorta in 1883. 'Dark', 'higgledy-piggledy' and 'pokey' are the terms I would employ to sum up the feeling of most of the old part of l'Avenc.

As for 'Renaissance,' Iberians seem to use the term more to denote chronology than style. The new (1559) part of l'Avenc, though distinguished by height, light, confidence and a general air of intelligent and noble design, is in no sense Italianate, and the carved heads and columns, though lovely, have a strange primitivism about them. I've no reason to suppose that the 'Renaissance' wing of the house could not have been designed along pretty similar lines a century earlier, if only the family had had the money at the time.

Still, 'Gothic' and 'Renaissance' will have to serve, for the distinction between the two halves of the house is palpable. The sixteenth-century part (and possibly the seventeenth too, for we do not know when it was finished) is very planned, very rational, and it must have taken professional stonemasons and (we've been told) specialists and designers from Gascony to make the windows and doorways, which are typical of the other side of the Pyrenees, not of ours. In the dove-tailed door-surrounds each stone weighs up to 700 pounds: the largest of their kind in Catalunya.

The south-facing window with the exterior dated crest marks the marriage between the eldest daughter of the house and a man called Segimón Amat, from a famous and well-regarded dynasty in a town called Seva. It was the second marriage for both, and Segimón makes clear in his will that all his property will pass to the children of his first marriage. (The date, 1559, is incidentally the year Shakespeare's parents married.)

Additions to the house for animal shelter, less finely built, and the absence of either a chapel or a special balcony for drying maize, which those who could afford such things erected in these centuries, suggest a period of relative decline in the fortunes of l'Avenc's owners. The family name, Avenc, also disappears, and the house begins to attract owners who were not residents, but landlords from distant cities.

This was an epoch when money was more easily made in town than on the land, but l'Avenc was probably still a desirable agricultural holding. There was money in cereals, which were dried on the top floor of the house – where Julian and I have made our own apartment – whose walls still show the scratched, faded five-bar-gate style of tallying bundles.

Slowly, it seems, the estate went downhill. It begins to change hands more frequently – into the ownership of the Fontcubertas (another local family) and also the Bachs (the great house, Can Bach, is nearby). It then passed into the ownership of families from the town of Manlleu: Arnaus, Arqués, and finally, in the 1970s, Casals.

By then it had been totally abandoned and was falling into obvious decrepitude, though its dilapidation certainly began many years before. The last families to live at l'Avenc (not as owners but tenants) were the Juventeny and Arenyes families, and the son of the town mechanic in l'Esquirol, Josep, tells of his father, Domingo, living at the house as a boy and being forced to leave, along with his father and brothers and sisters, when his mother died of consumption. But others came and went, and though I say that the house was not properly inhabited beyond the middle of the last century, there are tales of two brothers who kipped regularly at l'Avenc – the house may have been their only shelter – who would go down to Rupit in the evening to drink, sometimes failing to make it up the hills home again afterwards.

The fall of the House of Avench was very slow. Right up until the last it gave work locally – threshing, digging and looking after the cattle. Visitor after visitor to the place has told us stories – remembered or, more often, recounted to them by the last generation – of coming to l'Avenc. Its location, half an hour's walk from the village, makes it the kind of trek every adult and child would remember.

And wish to make again. For the visitors never stopped coming. And as word got round that something was happening at last at the old place, they were beginning to arrive in increasing numbers – and always unannounced.

At one level this was an infernal nuisance. A sort of promenade was being established which started in Tavertet – especially on weekends and holidays – and turned back home at l'Avenc. This offered a gentle hour or two's walk (depending on your speed), with the bonus of something to see when you got there. Others came by car on Saturday or Sunday excursions with the family. All would stop at l'Avenc, where we would be slogging away at whatever was the task of the hour, and approach with a cheery wave, a *bon dia* and the implicit request to have a look round to see how we were getting on.

Such interest was kind, and we did not want to be rude, but – the place being no more than a building site and often dangerous (and our visitors being typically the elderly on an afternoon constitutional, or families with small children) – one could not just show them through the front door and leave them to nose around. We would sooner or later have had a granny through the hole in the top floor, or a toddler under a fallen oak beam. So one of us (and it was almost always Belinda or her husband as I was there less often and spoke no Catalan) would undertake to give our visitors a quick tour.

Not all our visitors were the soul of tact — tact being, in any case, not a particularly Catalan virtue. 'Would you like a photo against the back-drop of the house?' Belinda heard one elderly gentleman from Cantonigròs enquiring of his relatives and friends, after gesturing at what he considered to be the atrocities we were committing, oblivious of my sister's presence. 'Oh, not here,' a woman answered at the top of her voice, 'it's a ghastly mess.' Belinda was more exhausted than usual on that particular day. She says a lump formed in her throat which would not dislodge for the rest of the afternoon.

But most people were curious, understanding and kind. Too much so. With Catalans there is no such thing as a quick tour. This was the high-point of our visitors' Sunday expedition.

The centrepiece of a Catalan Sunday is lunch. This rarely starts before half-past one, and should not end before four at the earliest. I have successfully asked for lunch at four-thirty. It is always a family affair but seldom at home. Catalans do not dine much at each other's houses: they meet at a restaurant, and everybody pays their share.

There were good restaurants in both Rupit and Tavertet, and l'Avenc, half-way between them, became a favourite spot, after the cognacs and coffee, for a post-prandial stroll of a vaguely cultural nature.

In loud and excited voices, our visitors would ask all about the house, our plans for it and the history of our involvement. And as I've said, they (especially the elderly) would often have stories of their own to tell us: the house as they remembered it when young. I don't think any of us ever managed a tour in less than half an hour, and it was often longer. Meanwhile we would have had to drop everything until it was over. And though to each visitor his or her enquiries were fresh and new, we must have been asked the same questions hundreds of times. We joked that it might be better simply to hand visitors a printed sheet with the answers to commonly asked questions, of which the most common of all was 'And what are you going to do with it when it's finished?'

Our weary reply, which was the truth — that we hoped at least that the house might become a sort of cultural centre where people would stay and learn – was often met by a typically frank Catalan, 'Ah, I see – you mean haven't really decided yet.' Nobody was ever convinced, even as the work progressed.

It remains a mystery to me that the entire locality did not become gripped by the conviction that we must be Mormons with secret plans to build a missionary training college, or the cat's-paw for a wicked entrepreneur planning an animal-experimentation laboratory or a nerve-gas testing centre. No doubt some in Tavertet and beyond did speculate behind our backs that we were hiding our true purposes, and perhaps some still do, but in the face of our surprising vagueness about the reason for the whole project, our visitors were always very polite.

In fact, if you seek an explanation for the general attitude of encouragement and friendliness we encountered towards our work, it may well lie in Belinda's and her husband's patient willingness to keep taking people round, even showing them the rooms where at any one point they were living – rooms with clothes strewn all over the floor and dirty washing piled high in plastic bowls. 'They'll think we are all bohemian,' my sister would protest, as her husband invited total strangers into the mess. 'Well, we are,' was his good-humoured reply.

At least nobody in Tavertet can ever have gained the impression that we were trying to hide any part of what was going on at l'Avenc. And my sister's and her husband's enthusiasm for the house always did communicate itself to visitors. For their part, our guests were touchingly pleased to see the rescue of l'Avenc, and full of ideas about its past and future.

Viewed as a public relations exercise I think it was worth the time we took to be friendly and informative, but our friendliness was more than public relations: it was really heartwarming to feel that other people cared about, and liked, what we were doing. I used to feel impatient with these continual interruptions, and with what I thought was my sister's and her husband's excessive forbearance; but now I think they were right.

Perhaps partly as a means of escape, my brother-in-law decided to opt for ear-muffs and a glass cabin five feet up in the air: he bought l'Avenc's own earth-mover, a real monster, second-hand. After that it proved almost impossible to extract him from the driver's seat, and I sometimes suspected him of moving piles of earth and rock from one place to another, and then back, just for solitude and for fun. Where other fathers escape into the loft to play with their children's train-sets, Quim would lurch and roar around our twelve acres at l'Avenc, scooping up rocks and topsoil in his mega-bucket.

It was not long before a second-hand digger was not enough for this reincarnated mole. There had been a persistent problem with the brakes, and one afternoon the machine (with Quim in it) began of its own accord to trundle down the field towards the cliffs. Lesser men would have resolved to leave the digging to professionals. He bought himself a brand-new digger.

Day-by-day we were making a difference. How much of a difference had first been brought home when in the autumn of 1999 all of us had been confronted by a melancholy picture which had not been seen since the early 1500s: a roofless house. Momentarily, l'Avenc had lost all its air of solidity. There was something awfully bleak about the sight.

But now a new, sound roof was back, and remarkably fast. Beneath the tiles and above roofing boards, Quim had (as I described above) laid a complete layer of lead sheet. Part of his and his brother Francesc's family business was the recycling and rolling of lead, so they were well placed to provide what we needed at cost price; but even discounted lead is an expensive material. This, however, as he insisted, was l'Avenc's one chance in perhaps hundreds of years to give the roof a protective skin which would be as eternal as any human construction can be, and I'm glad we did it, though later we were to learn that unless you stand by a window, a lead roof wreaks havoc with mobile phone reception.

Joan Sarsanedas proposed that as we had had to dismantle two of the existing rickety old chimneys, and they had anyway been pretty woebegone affairs – in no way important architectural features – he should design new ones himself, in a style in keeping with the period of course, and unblock the almost hidden sixteenth-century chimney from the state room in the main house, unused for many years.

We agreed, thinking little of it. The result was one exceptionally stout kitchen chimney, very much in keeping with Sarsanedas's emphatic, no-nonsense, cigar-smoking character, and one totally different creation: a delightful, delicate little folly which seemed to me to betray an altogether capricious – even faery – side to the stolid and beefy personality I had before then associated with Sr Sarsanedas.

Here was a subterranean gaiety, almost Dalí-esque, which we had never suspected; here was Joan's Catalan *rauxa* (caprice) coming through, to match his *seny* (sense). For the next 500 years, long after he and we are forgotten, few will overlook those imaginative flourishes, dreamed up, perhaps, on a warm August afternoon. I had never realized that the human spirit can flower in the shape of a chimney.

Each of us who was part of this restoration can claim features of the new l'Avenc which were the special vision of just one of us. For all the big projects that Quim was to spearhead as part of the redevelopment, I think the most strikingly creative was his balcony.

Of the three of us, my brother-in-law is far and away the best spatial visualizer. A small businessman and son of a small businessman, with no formal training in art, architecture or structural engineering, he nevertheless seems able to build and hold in his imagination three-dimensional structures of quite a complex sort. He can somehow see where things will go, and where they will not, and how they will look.

All of us could see that there was something seriously wrong with the Gothic section of one aspect of l'Avenc – the downhill flank of the old part, standing above and alongside the Rupit–Tavertet track, and facing south. Though as you wound your way up the hill from Tavertet the splendid sixteenth-century façade of the new part – the famous 'front' – of the house with its arched door was what you saw, you then rounded a corner and passed beneath the whole length of the building. What confronted you, after the elegant geometry of the new front wing, was the bad stonework of the big, long, dismal, higgledy-piggledy wall, pitted with small windows, blocked-in windows and the remains of windows on various levels which I mentioned earlier. The blocked-in remains of an external door gave (were it still open) on to thin air about five yards up. I have already described the mess of what had once been a covered yard beneath.

Quim looked at this and saw a cleared yard, and out over it, standing on square stone pillars, a long, deep, high balcony going right up to the eaves. In the external wall it hung from he envisaged a big, heavy wooden door into the old kitchen. He explained his solution to Sarsanedas for both saw this as the least attractive flank of the house and agreed a plan was needed.

Their mutual understanding was immediate. The two men's thoughts and spatial comprehension have always gelled. While the rest of us nod intelligently and struggle to visualize what they mean, my brother-in-law and Joan quickly grasp a plan. And remember that it was Sarsanedas who had first seized the chance to buy l'Avenc. Even though he passed the parcel on, he had been at work on the house in his imagination since he had bought it in 1996.

Sarsanedas had visualized a sort of courtyard-cum-cloisters in the area covered by those unsightly outbuildings and broken walls. Santi Canosa, the first in a series of three architectural consultants we were to retain (they fell fast in combat, but we owe the plans for the roofs to Santi), guessed at what l'Avenc might originally have looked like, before the sixteenth-century restoration. He thought there would probably have been a tower. He proposed a new tower, as a solution not least to the problem of joining the Gothic and the Renaissance halves of the building, whose junction had always been an awkward affair, no less temporary in appearance for being more than 400 years old. Santi drew up a quick sketch, loosely based on other houses with towers in the area.

Quim stuck to his balcony concept, but wanted to incorporate the tower too. He has never been one to do things by halves. Joan Sarsanedas suggested inviting a well-known historian, Antoni Pladavall, to comment. Dr Pladavall said we should not invent history. Not only were we struggling with clay, stone and dust, it seemed, but we were caught between the opinions of architectural historians. There were times one muttered that all we ever wanted was a place to live. We abandoned the tower.

My brother-in-law remained keen on his balcony, which had never claimed to reproduce an original feature. He accepted Sarsanedas's proposal that we incorporate a new and crucial element to light the kitchen and stairway: a huge stone arch of a window, as wide as a man is long and twice as tall; a single pane glazed in eight thicknesses of reinforced glass. This would echo the great (supported) stone arch within the kitchen itself. Thus the long kitchen gained a full-length balcony, and the main stairwell next to the kitchen gained illumination from the arched window between.

So that is what we built. It was finished by 2001. The huge, double-glazed, plate-glass, arched pane had to wait until some of the construction work had settled down before we could summon up the nerve to install it. A terrified truck-driver succeeded in delivering the glass up the atrocious track from Tavertet without mishap; breaths were held as the earth-mover lifted the precious cargo . . . And – phew – nothing broke and everything fitted.

Today the balcony is one of l'Avenc's most obvious delights. It looks lovely from outside and beneath the house; and on summer mornings there is no more magical place to sit in the sun with coffee and croissants, and watch the clouds steaming up from the valley. On a hot summer night, with crickets calling and owls hooting, you can sip a huge glass of young, sweet Catalan red wine (served cold) and stare out towards the dark Montseny mountains – and wonder from how many other places in Europe it is possible to see so much forest without a single light.

But as the bulldozers roared, the cement-mixer clattered, the bills came in and clouds of dust blew across us in 2001, 2002 and 2003, it was probably only my brother-in-law who could hold in his imagination the final picture. 'Ah well,' I used to say to the others on one of my increasingly frequent trips from England, 'it will be done.'

'Easy enough for you to fly in, say that, and breeze off back to

Britain' was the obvious retort, but Belinda always managed
to suppress it. My sister was by now acting as the unpaid clerk of
works at l'Avenc, a job she managed to combine with teaching
English in our mother's school in Manlleu and working as her
husband's assistant and translator in their family business. She was
also bringing up three children.

Her husband, meanwhile, was spending every moment of his
spare time at l'Avenc – a great deal of it on his earth-mover. With
each succeeding month he seemed more absorbed in the project.
Of the three of us it was perhaps he who had been most hesitant
at the start; perhaps he had foreseen better than my sister and I the
enormous demand it was going to make not just on our finances
but on our time; but now he was throwing himself into the restoration with a vengeance. His brother, Francesc – a part-owner too –
gave us constant encouragement and stayed interested throughout,
but stood back from day-to-day involvement, seeing himself more
as an investor than a project-manager. I think Francesc felt that there
were enough generals already in this campaign.

He was right. But I would sometimes feel guilty at assuming a
good share of overall control of the project while being unable
to be on hand all the time as it proceeded – in the way my sister
and brother-in-law were.

Still, I was paying my share of the mounting costs, and working ever harder in England to keep up the payments. This was a
period when no occasion was too slight, no publication too minor,
no radio channel too obscure and no hour too early or too late
for me to contribute my three-ha'penceworth of punditry. Those
£30-plus-VAT payments for a quick ten minutes on any one of
a range of topics (and any one of a range of broadcasting outlets)
do add up, but it can become remorseless.

To make ends meet, Belinda and her husband were later to put
their little house, Casalons, not far away in the Collsacabra, on to
the books of a holiday-let agency. All of us kept up with the bills
but it was becoming a struggle.

And in the middle of it all, in the spring and summer of 2000,
career and curiosity took me away to the very ends of the earth

– to the frozen bogs and crags of the remote sub-Antarctic island of Kerguelen (Desolation Island) in the southern Indian Ocean – for a five-month stint on a French scientific base. Here, 5,000 miles from l'Avenc (and at least 2,000 miles from anywhere at all), I made a television documentary, started my autobiography and experienced some of the toughest and most frightening times of my life. This was the fulfilment of a boyhood dream not a mid-life crisis, but I have to admit it looked like a very passable imitation of one. I could keep in touch with developments at l'Avenc only by fax: no other means of written communication was available. I used to lie in my cabin, battered by the howling gale outside as the metal walls of my cabin were shot-blasted by sleet, and think of those warm summer evenings on the new veranda at l'Avenc.

On my return from the wastes of the Indian Ocean at the end of the first summer of the new millennium – a year on from that summer living alone at l'Avenc – my confidence grew that this was the end of the beginning. A corner had been turned. We had had carved on to an oak beam a crest with the initials of the owners' names – the A and P of Abey and Parris – intertwined beneath the year, 2000, and the stone now formed the lintel above the stone gate into the old part of the house, the kitchen and Quim's balcony.

These were days of rapid apparent progress. Looking back, it seems hard to believe it but we told ourselves that the hardest part was behind us. There were moments when we even dared hope we were approaching the half-way point. We were wrong. We had only just begun.

9. A Town Called Squirrel

From l'Avenc a path makes its way along the cliffs and then tumbles down the hillside through beech and oak into the village of Rupit.

Tightly clustered on a small platform of solid rock above a rushing stream (rushing, in fact, towards a 300-foot waterfall over the cliff's edge into the valley of the River Ter), Rupit's dark, narrow streets are overhung with close terraces of tall stone houses, almost all constructed in the same style and during the same epoch. In summer the village is always cool. In winter it is freezing.

There is nothing particular to see in Rupit – no monument, no cathedral or great house. What is left of the ancient castle, tumbled stones overgrown with wild thyme on an inaccessible rock above the village, is unvisited. What distinguishes the place is the whole, which is greater than the parts. This is an almost flawless example of a typical and unspoiled stone-built Catalan country village: a sort of paradigm.

There is a coherence and integrity not just in the village's architecture, but in the whole air of the place. It is tightly focused in both its fabric and its feel; there are no rich villas, no ostentatious flourishes and no hovels either; houses are modest, solid and homely, built of oak and stone. Everyone knows everyone today, just as they always have.

The little main street running above the stream that divides the village is only just wide enough for the few cars that try to make their way through. It is still paved with the tough, grey rock on which Rupit is built. At its heart this is still a farming village. The open balconies where corn was dried, the big oak doors for the hauling in and out of sacks of produce, and the hitching posts for horses and mules tell you all you need to know about what made Rupit tick.

Here in Rupit the mule and donkey substituted for the horse.

Only the *senyors* from Barcelona, or big landowners, often absentee, had horses and traps. Rupitencs (the vernacular word for an inhabitant of Rupit) had mules and *carros* (carts) and many just walked.

The reason Rupit is so pretty and 'typical' is that it was bypassed by those two destroyers, prosperity and the highway. A mile off the highway and along a dead-end road downhill towards the cliffs, Rupit was so poor and remote-feeling – and in winter, for those without proper heating, so cold – that it had been virtually abandoned by the 1950s, when the rest of Spain was beginning to look up. The local poet Miquel Banus remembers as a child seeing families leaving the village for ever, every Christmas, when rents were due.

Once a thriving agricultural settlement with a small textile and canvas factory of its own, it dipped fatefully below the level of self-sustainability and dwindled over less than two decades into a ghost village. Having all but died in the Middle Ages, and come back, it faced its second death (the fate of many beautiful rural villages across southern Europe) in the middle of the twentieth century.

Rupit was brought back from ruin by two strokes of good fortune. Though fast becoming just a shell, it was an enchanting shell. A trickle of *excursionistes* and wealthy people sought it out as a sweet rural backwater, bought houses for next-to-nothing, and began renovating and weekending – giving work to the few families left, and eventually attracting permanent residents back.

Then a heroic figure, Camil Pallàs, became municipal architect in the 1960s and 1970s. He had a vision for the village. Rigorously prohibiting any new building that did not conform to its character, he made innumerable enemies among local people who failed to recognize him and his vision as their rescuer.

Pallàs was Joan Sarsanedas's mentor. But only after his death has wider recognition come. There was a local 'homage' to him in 2004 to acknowledge the way he saved Rupit, and to atone for his unfair treatment during the transition from Francoism in the late seventies, when he was seen as an agent of the old order. Pallàs had later died with no public honour. I cannot say why (for there are surely greater injustices in the world) but I feel keenly for people who bear the slings and arrows of popular contempt and die before the day of which they must all their lives have dreamed – the day of recognition – arrives.

Right up to the 1970s Rupitencs could be distinguished on market day or on a provisioning trip to Vic or Manlleu, dressed as farmers had dressed for centuries: wearing spartan sandals and with a sack over their shoulder. Many could be seen walking to the bus stop to catch the ancient *barca* (boat), the local name for the blue bus that rocked and fumed like a steamship twice a day, up and down the C153 Vic–Rupit road . . . until the mid-eighties when, sadly, the bus finally expired. With the *barca* the sandal-shod, sack-carrying peasants also disappeared, never to be seen again.

The little village shops which during summer weekends give themselves over to hordes of Catalan visitors in search of rural trophies to carry back to the cities – cheese, sausages, fire-irons, honey and those confounded little red Wee-Willie-Winkie hats – are on a winter weekday morning still the centres of gossip and local chit-chat as wives and widows linger over the unhurried purchases of the morning. But the refurbished and expanded Hotel Estrella in the middle of the village, the new swimming pool and the big car-park on the road coming in tell a different story: of a local tourist industry that has been gently growing for about thirty years now – and if it grows much more is in danger of crowding the village out on the busiest weekends.

Very few foreign tourists seem to have discovered the village; its visitors are overwhelmingly Catalan, from cities like Barcelona and Girona and from the towns and villages of the surrounding countryside. Rupit is today sensibly conscious that its unspoiled appearance is what people come to see, and its councillors and mayors (of whom our master builder Joan Sarsanedas has been one) have been careful about building and rebuilding. The village has a strong collective sense of what is in keeping. So physically it remains intact; but sheer numbers, though important to the livelihoods of the villagers, sometimes threaten to overwhelm it.

It is best out of season. On a dank winter morning before the sun breaks through the freezing mist (as it fairly reliably does in the Collsacabra, shortly after eleven), with the smell of hot, sweet *coca* bread and coffee from the Forn de Rupit bakery which greets you at the entrance to the village, and the sound of Catalan women's voices in animated chat about nothing or influenza, the timeless regains its mastery over the touristical.

Rock defines the village. It is totally built of stone. Some of the houses are built straight into the rock. Paving is not necessary as the streets have been carved out of the natural existing rock. As you arrive, the little river (Riera de Rupit) greets you from its rock channel beneath the village, running towards the cliffs' edge a few hundred yards further on.

The houses above and around were mainly built in the seventeenth and eighteenth centuries, after the medieval collapse of the population, assisted by the two earthquakes and many plagues. The earthquakes brought down the castle above Rupit and some of the stone was used during this period of rebuilding which, because it was confined to a couple of centuries, helps give the place its sense of architectural unity.

We noted the dates carved into twenty stone lintels above Rupit doorways last time we were there. The oldest, beautifully decorated, is in the little square near Fonda Marsal: 1557. The newest, bravely and honestly carved above a door just as you enter the village, is 2003. But the great majority are between 1610 and 1693, and decorated typically with Christian crosses on a triangular mount, plus a couple of Templar crosses. Older window and door lintels have been reused, too, one with the date, 1677, upside down, incorporated by an illiterate eighteenth-century builder. He got the Christian cross the right way up.

The Carrer del Fossar, an uphill stone street and the most photographed point in Rupit, is scraped from the rock floor in a series of wide, shallow, regular steps: a small natural wonder. There are dovetailed doorways, wooden balconies, once-painted façades (exposed stonework is a fashion modern to Spain: in Catalunya all but the poor used to plaster stone with lime or paint, and l'Avenc was once externally plastered). The church is eighteenth century, and rather gloomy for my taste.

Rupit must have been all bustle and business in the seventeenth century when the office of notary public, which stayed in the same family for 500 years, was the grandest job of all. The family, Soler, owned one of the few houses which is majestically richer than any other in a village notable for its egalitarian style. At the end of the village the Solers' coat of arms, the sun, is still visible on the door.

Rupit's dead-end-ness makes it. The buttock-clenchingly narrow main street stops at a cliff. The village grew around the castle and goes nowhere. Even today, with its summertime coach-parties and busy restaurants, you have the feeling that Rupit is hiding.

Climb the interminable stairs (up which I once piggy-backed my mother to win a bet) to the restaurant at the head of the village, l'Hort d'en Roca, and you will find the end wall of the cave-like dining room (by the crackling fire) is a huge boulder. The furniture is antique and the paintings unusually interesting: the restaurant is kept by Nuria Sellabona, the wife of an artist of real distinction, Bernat Sarsanedas, famous in Barcelona and the brother of our Joan Sarsanedas.

Nuria's two daughters, Ester and Silvia, and her son, Joan, wait at table. It is all about family, in Rupit. Call in at the busy Cal Estrella, which (a rare thing in the Collsacabra) attracts guests internationally: Estrella, who runs it, is the daughter of Estrella, who founded it seventy-five years ago. Her daughter-in-law Susana has made the Internet work for the business. Will Susana's daughter carry the business on? Her name? Estrella.

Walk down the main street, then left up the hill, up the carved, stepped carriageway of the Carrer del Fossar. Or cross the gorge which separates the two sides of the village, where you will need to take the swaying cable-strung suspension bridge whose main cables are secured into the rock at either side. Everything is secured into rock. There are even houses which are part-underground.

L'Avenc belongs to the village of Tavertet but Rupit is our local showcase. It is where we go for bread, for groceries . . . and for lunch. After a late-morning walk along the cliffs you end up virtu-ally falling out of the undergrowth overhanging the edge of the village. But where to eat? Rupit now has a good half-dozen restaurants, cafés and bars, all full on Sunday lunchtimes but almost empty for the rest of the week. Although in summer they depend on tourists they all keep their local flavour. Cooking in Rupit is a family business – and a serious one.

At l'Hort d'en Roca the duck (*ànec*) is delicious, cooked as mountain food should be in large portions from simple ingredients. Pears, pine nuts, garlic, tomatoes, olive oil and meat – especially pork but rabbit, wild boar and duck too – are the staples of every menu. Although Rupit is not so far from the sea, this is the cuisine of the uplands not the coast. There is fresh trout from mountain streams and the leathery salt-cod ubiquitous in southern Europe from Portugal to Provence, but the delicate seafood dishes of the Costa Brava are never seen here.

Instead Rupit prides itself on *botifarra amb mongetes*, the long, pure-pork Catalan sausage grilled with white beans fried in olive oil and pork fat. This is the food that carries with it the soul of the Collsacabra, honest, affordable and simple, washed down with cold red wine and the salty fizz of Vichy Catalan water.

There is none of the elegance of dining in rural France, even though the border is not so far away. Rural Catalan style tends to be more homely than chic. Fluorescent strip-lighting lingers on in restaurants and so do televisions, though nowadays every house in Rupit has its own and there is no need to go to the village bar to watch Barça – Barcelona FC – play not just for team pride but for their nation's too.

Most of the time we eat at Fonda Marsal, the closest Rupit has to a village pub but now an expanding restaurant too. The proprietor, Jaume (James), was my mother's English student (he has to be cajoled into displaying his learning, however) and in the years since he took over from his father, Jaume too (who took over from his grandfather), he has been building the business up into quite a place. There's a huge dining room out over the river, and a balcony planned. You can sip Fonda Marsal's staggeringly large gin and tonics. In winter the big room is often closed and we sit in the old bar and dining room which has served Fonda Marsal for seventy-five years. On the wall is a wonderful portrait of the grandparents who founded the business, now yellowed with the years, the pair painted by the imperfect yet perceptive hand of a village artist in the formal costume of 1920s Spain. I do not know whether Rural-Iberian-Edwardian is a style known to art historians, but it should be.

All the pork dishes are excellent – mercifully, because once you have removed anything connected with pigs from a Catalan menu you have ripped the heart out of it, as my poor vegetarian mother and sisters frequently complain – and the *escalivada* (grilled or roasted oiled strips of aubergine, tomato and peppers) is always good. The resolution to eat less meat, however, which I usually keep in England, breaks down in Catalunya.

The wine is even better. Jaume is proud of his cellars, for in wine he is a real specialist. There, cut into the rock under the house, he keeps his great oak barrels and the sulphur sticks he uses to fumigate a barrel before refilling. I suspect I am a disappointment to him, however, because his house wine – a sweetish, young Catalan red always served cold, in endlessly refilled bottles, that is included with the bread in the cover charge – is usually good enough for me.

Jaume once directed me to his wholesaler of wine, oil and vinegar in nearby Roda de Ter and I bought seventy-five litres (at one euro per litre) and a beautiful new fifty-litre oak barrel, and took them back to Derbyshire in my pickup truck. Now Quim has bought barrels for our old cellar at l'Avenc (the rooms we hollowed out from the rubble left by the earthquakes of 1427) and is learning the techniques of fumigation which Jaume has taught me, and which involve a great deal of coughing and spluttering as acrid white sulphur-dioxide vapour comes pouring out of the barrel into which you have lowered your blue-burning wick of sulphur.

There is another restaurant in Rupit where the *botifarra* and beans always seem to taste especially good, and it is the place my family call the Upstairs Room, for the fairly obvious reason that the street door gives straight on to a staircase, and the dining room is at the top.

There's little remarkable about the place – just a big room with a low, beamed ceiling up some stone stairs in a seventeenth-century stone-block house on a narrow rock-paved street in rural Catalunya where the food is cooked on an old cast-iron stove . . . but I love it. Years ago three women – Mariona, her mother, Carme, and sister-in-law Laura – decided to carry on the business, which had been going for 125 years, after Laura's husband died young. '*S'ha de tirar endavant*,' the Catalans say when hardship strikes: 'One must pull the cart forwards.' Tony Blair might consider the phrase as a useful variation on 'move on'.

Rupit is one of only three settlements of any size along the thirty-mile stretch of road that forms the backbone of the Collsacabra. The C153 rural route starts down on the plain of Vic and ends down on the plain of Bas in the volcanic region of La Garrotxa not far from the sea. Between them lie the hills of the Collsacabra and through these hills the road climbs a couple of thousand feet gently, then plunges fast back down again through beech and oak forests to the plain.

About seven miles before you reach Rupit you will pass the edge of a small town not much bigger than a village, called Cantonigròs. The least picturesque of the three settlements, Cantoni (as everyone calls it) works the hardest to deserve its visitors – and does so once a year with an extraordinary music festival which draws choirs from all over the world. Choirs and traditional dancers perform in an atmosphere close to that of an eisteddfod. Cantoni has done as much for the Collsacabra in the twenty years since it started its festival as a score of state-funded tourist offices.

Not far from Cantoni is a small turn-off from which an unpaved road leads to a place very dear to Catalan hearts in the Collsacabra: the church (or *santuari*) of Sant Julià de Cabrera. But the Sant Julià is usually dropped, and it is commonly known, as is the mountain on which it is perched, simply as Cabrera. It is a sublime spot: not so much by virtue of its sweet stone church, though it is a Romanesque gem, as by virtue of its position. Right at the end of a high ridge with a narrow flat top, Cabrera looks out over the whole Collsacabra, with the snow-topped wall of the Pyrenees clearly visible along the horizon behind it. At its feet the ridge tumbles and crumbles down into the valley, and steps have been constructed so sightseers and pilgrims – even the elderly, if they are determined – can climb to the top. And they do, especially on Sundays and feast days, when special services are sometimes held in the church. El Santuari de Cabrera reminds me very much of the rock-hewn Coptic churches in the mountains of Ethiopia, to visit which the faithful have to make a strenuous morning's climb. Many of them were constructed around the same time as Cabrera.

The church is one of a whole string of hermitages, chapels and monasteries located in the most remote and breathtaking positions in the Collsacabra. Such outposts are thought to have been once the sites of primitive castles or *torres de guaita* – watchtowers to guard against the Moors in the eighth and ninth centuries. Two other equally isolated mountaintop sanctuaries, Bellmunt and Sant Miquel, are visible from the Santuari de Cabrera. And you can see out to the very end of the three-mile-long, flat-topped arm of cliff – like a giant geological aircraft-carrier – which stretches out towards Girona, dominating the coastal plains. It is called El Far – every plane on its way in from England to the Costa Brava flies right over it – and there is a big sanctuary church (and an even bigger restaurant) there. The priest runs both.

El Far, Cabrera, Bellmunt, Sant Miquel, beautiful Sant Joan de Fàbregues near Rupit . . . and have I mentioned La Salut – also with breathtaking views and restaurant attached: even the most sceptical atheist could spend a happy week walking from one pious pinnacle to the next.

But piety is not what distinguishes the little town of Santa Maria de Corcó, down the road towards the plain of Vic. This is a rebellious place not a contemplative one. For a start it defies its own name, St Mary of the Flat Hills. No one who lives there calls it Santa Maria, let alone Santa Maria de Corcó. Most call it Squirrel. Or, rather, most call it l'Esquirol, which is Catalan for squirrel.

It is also an insult. Which came first, the name or the insult, is a mystery. Some say it is the original name of a community that sprang up (without a church before the mid-1800s) so named because the hostals and restaurants were all near a farmhouse beside the royal road, *camí reial*, called l'Esquirol because it had one in a cage.

Across the Iberian peninsula a 'squirrel' has become the slang term for what in Britain we rather less charmingly call a 'black-leg' or 'scab' – a strike-breaker. At the beginning of the last century, during a general strike of textile labourers in the area, mill-workers from Santa Maria carried on working. Whether the sobriquet was named after them, or vice versa, the name came to be used with affection. To sum up: a caged squirrel may – or may not – have given its name to both a town and a tendency.

Now the locals rejoice in it. The town has taken its insulting nickname to its heart, though not all of an older and more religious generation would agree. 'L'Esquirol' has the edge for another reason, however: it is an unashamedly and cheekily Catalan word, so the break with the old name can also be taken as part of the renascent Catalunya (*Catalunya renaixentista*). Road signs which omit the colloquial alternative get 'Santa Maria de Corcó' aerosol-sprayed out and replaced.

By day the town looks pleasant but undistinguished. To those who live there (like my youngest brother, Mark, his Catalan wife, Isabel, and their son, David, and little daughter, Iris) it is a friendly community, quite tightly knit, with everything – shops, school, bank, pharmacy, surgery, good restaurant and relaxed little café-bars – you could need; but visitors would notice no more than narrow streets and steep lanes crowded with unpretentious stone houses, and a wide but unremarkable view across the dusty plain.

The church, which (as is usual) dominates the town from raised ground, is imposing, with a big angular tower. Though of traditional design, much of it is recent. Like many churches in Catalunya, Santa Maria's was burned out during the Civil War.

But once a year in the middle of August, the soul of the devil seems to take over this gentle place for one night at the end of the week of l'Esquirol's annual fiesta. With friends and family a couple of years ago, I went to see how.

We had parked in the main square but something seemed strange: ours was the only car there although there were no notices

forbidding parking during the fiesta. We were about to walk over
to the bar when a bystander politely suggested we move our car
from what we now realized was an empty square. We did, thinking little of it. But as we drank beers in the cool of the evening
outside the bar near the church, which has a talking parrot (the
bar not the church), I had no idea what was about to hit us.

Somebody had said there would be fireworks, and at ten there
was an almighty bang. 'That's the warning rocket,' said Deborah.
Suddenly all the town's lights went out. I noticed people – what
looked like half the town – crowding towards the open space
beneath the church. Why were all the younger people wearing
wide-brimmed straw hats? Why had the children swathed their
faces in scarves? Why were those youths wearing devil's horns?

Then it started. These were not fireworks. This was a deluge of
fire. This was a rain of terror. A man in a straw hat holding above
his head what looked like a devilish candelabrum – a great spiky
reindeer's antler of a thing made of iron, festooned with dozens
of tiny finger-length packages, cylindrical in shape – ran into the
middle of the crowd.

There was a flash. All the fingers on the candelabrum exploded
into light. With a deafening, fizzing whirr, they began twirling like
Catherine-wheels, showering sparks. For the minute the eruption
lasted this diabolical machine became a spitting, flaming, crackling explosion of light.

I say 'showering sparks' but that hardly captures it. It was more
like being under a minor volcano. Thousands of tiny points of fire
came cascading down on to the heads of the crowd, who began
to dance. Someone was beating a drum in a slow, ominous rhythm
which I can only describe as satanic. The crowd leaped higher as
the fire rained down.

Another candelabrum was run into the crowd. Cheering and
stamping, the whole assembly moved off in a cloud of sulphurous
smoke, a warlike procession dancing down the street. Amazed, we
followed.

Gunpowder candelabra, at the top of each a small Christian
cross, seemed to be arriving from nowhere, but soon we realized

that the same structures were being continually rearmed with fresh gunpowder fingers pulled from a hundred stuffed pockets. The downward slope of the lane beneath our feet ran with sparks like a river of brimstone. Young men and children made daredevil rushes to get right beneath the fountain – dancing round the mouth, as it were, of the volcano itself, which in a geyser of fire cascaded in sparks in a wide circle all around.

This was the paradox: you were of course safest from the danger if you never came anywhere near. But if you must come near, if you were curious, then you were safest joining forces with the devils who were its source. Those who flirted at evil's edge stood the greater chance of being burned.

There was no light save from the sparks. In lulls between the firing up of new stacks of gunpowder sticks there would be darkness and hush. Then the bang and crackle and the blinding orange flame would light up the street again, illuminating the faces of scores who watched from their balconies, or from within. The drum would beat and the dancers would move on.

In bursts of fire and deafening flashes of light, the cavalcade proceeded to the bottom of the street. Almost unnoticed, the corner of a wooden balcony of a house on the corner caught alight. A couple slipped from the crowd and appeared upstairs to extinguish the flames before they could spread. In the square below a whole blinding salvo of new explosions awaited – and then, drums thumping, we made our way back uphill, up another narrow street.

How many barrels of gunpowder were consumed in the twenty minutes of mayhem it took us to make the journey to and from the front of the church, I cannot estimate. For hours after I could hardly hear.

Was it over now? From within the belfry of the church tower, a hundred feet above us, came a huge explosion. All at once, rockets started firing from inside the tower, shooting off in all directions like a wild salvo of mortars. A Niagara of orange sparks cascaded over the edges of the belfry. The belfry itself was billowing crimson smoke as rockets shot out. The whole church had become a sort of arsenal of fire. I could not help but reflect that this church had been torched and partly destroyed during the Spanish Civil War. Was there any conscious or unconscious reference to that in these fearsome celebrations?

This had not been just merriment, a celebration of light and colour; there was something dark behind the exuberance, something meant to frighten. The church tower spitting flame and red smoke, the crosses dancing on the top of the fizzing, crackling candelabra, the mobbing of the devils by children . . . To me they seemed to be saying that in the end God and Satan work together, terrorize together, and are to be respected and feared together. The undertone was dualist, Manichaean.

On a map of north-eastern Spain, see if you can find l'Esquirol: one small dot among many. Looking at it, you wouldn't expect much. I hadn't. But after that night of 17 August 2001, those images will invade my dreams for ever.

10. A Cave

It was by coincidence that we had found ourselves beside one of Spain's and Catalunya's great national walking paths, but the discovery triggered in my mind an idea which in time was to become one of the most straightforward parts of our plans, and the most easily realized: converting the ruined cowsheds attached to l'Avenc into a line of stone cottages for walkers and tourists.

Right past l'Avenc's front door ran a road which was as old as any in Spain. Excavating around the house we scraped clear the big flagstones which once paved it. Beneath the cellar, when we had cleared from it the rubble of the fifteenth-century earthquakes, we found traces of what an architectural historian told us was probably a Roman track. It was hardly surprising that there would have been a road running along the top of these immense cliff-systems for as long as there had been human beings there, but this one was important: it was the continuation of a commercial and trade route up from the valleys and plains into the mountains.

Iberia, where distances are large and towns and villages often sparse, is criss-crossed by the ghostly traces of what was once an immense network of packhorse routes, whose habit is to take the most direct line between settlements – any path, however steep, up which a horse or mule can pick its way – where modern highways will take the long way round. Some of these old routes have found a new incarnation in the form of walkers' trails, called (in the world of hiking and rambling) *Grandes Rutas*.

The *Grandes Rutas* of Spain cover the whole country, and within Catalunya the *Senders de Gran Recorregut* (as the GR routes are called there) form a great web from the Pyrenees down to the inland plains and the coast. L'Avenc is on the GR2.

The path climbs up through a gap in the cliffs by Tavertet. It has come from the other side of the Montseny mountains to the south, wound its way over the mountains, down into the valley of the River Ter, and then, after scrambling up over the cliff-systems' edge and into Tavertet, it turns right and heads for Rupit, running along the clifftops and beneath l'Avenc. After that it winds down another cliff-system on to the plain of Olot, and heads for the Mediterranean end of the Pyrenees.

It is a popular route – but so are most of the GR paths. Catalans love outdoor walks and nature-trails, and town and city people are especially keen. They take their pastoral pleasures rather gravely, buy the right walking gear, get the necessary information and are proud to behave as responsible hikers. To Catalans, *excursions* (the word is the same in Catalan but has a more derring-do ring) are more than a pleasant day out in the country: they are felt to be a sort of homage to the natural heritage of Catalunya. For some Catalans walking in the hills feels like almost a patriotic act, and might be accompanied by outdoor readings from books of Catalan folk poetry. To them the countryside is not just a physical but a cultural experience.

I suspect that during the Franco years when Catalan language and culture were being suppressed, the apparatus of state bore down more heavily in the towns than in the villages, and more heavily in the villages than in the fields. Perversely, the outdoors offered a kind of privacy where Catalans could be themselves. An idea exists – though I have never quite heard it voiced – that the 'spirit' of Catalunya is to be found in the woods and mountains.

Maybe they are not so different from us in this. Catalans share with the English not just St George (Sant Jordi is their patron too) and football but the paradox of being a predominantly urban people who, asked to paint a picture of their nationhood, would fill it with symbols of rural life: simple, bucolic and pastoral, and strikingly small-scale.

We English might choose foxhunting (still), thatched cottages and willow-lined streams; a Catalan might choose the narrow streets of stone-built villages such as Rupit, country-cured ham, the snow-topped Pyrenees and the *sardana*, the communal country dance of

Catalunya. Every Catalan has his or her native town or village, every Catalan 'comes from' somewhere, and where you come from is an important part of you. Getting out into the country means getting back into what you are, and Catalans do it by the coachload.

Every Saturday and Sunday the rural restaurants (of which there are tens of thousands, some of them up unlikely tracks and in the remotest places) are packed. From about two in the afternoon, when lunch starts, until about five, when those with packed schedules may have to peel off early, huge family groups, from wrinkled grannies (*iaies*) to the smallest children (*nens*), tuck in, all talking ten-to-the-dozen in loud voices as they consume an insane amount of pork and staggering quantities of beans. Pigs' cheeks (*galtes de porc*) are specially prized. It must be a nightmare to be a rural restaurateur in Catalunya, with all your business packed into about three meals; and many country restaurants do not even bother to open outside the weekend.

Eating is not the only pursuit, though. Sightseeing is as beloved of the Catalans as it is of us British. Those too old or too young for trekking peer from the coach windows, or pile into the little shops of villages like Rupit to buy souvenirs of honey and Ratafia, the treacly bitter herb liqueur made in the village, which I have tasted but never been able to enjoy drinking. The able-bodied go hiking.

In the Collsacabra the fences are usually pretty rudimentary, and higher up in the Pyrenees there are no fences or boundaries at all. But Catalans are rule-conscious people and (unlike some of their militant rambling English counterparts) would feel uncomfortable to be off the beaten track. So the set walking routes are hugely popular, ancient tracks and bridleways with a history of their own, and a range of maps and guides directs walkers down them, advising on flora, fauna and history, and the places to stay along the way.

The routes, almost all off-road, are well marked with small red and white bands painted on to rocks and trees and kept up by members of the enthusiastic Federació de Entitats Excursionistes de Catalunya. A modest hundred miles in length, our GR2 is one of the country's shorter routes, but only a few of the long-distance ramblers who pass l'Avenc would be walking the whole thing.

If I had a fortnight to spend on an ambitious GR itinerary, I would combine two routes: the GR11 and the GR2. The route takes us right through the hinterland of l'Avenc and into the stupendous mountain range which frames Spanish Catalunya, the Pyrenees. Let's follow it for a while.

The GR2 begins at an altitude of only about 1,500 feet in the village of Aiguafreda (which means 'cold water') on the extreme western tip of the Montseny mountains. With a population of some 2,000 inhabitants, this was originally a tourist centre for middle-class Barcelonins and has many second residences. Not least because the Barcelona to France train has stopped here for over a hundred years, Aiguafreda and its neighbouring staging posts were among the first villages in the nineteenth and early twentieth centuries for Catalan excursionists to flock to from Barcelona at weekends, when the idea of getting back to rural basics – walking in the mountains and drinking the spring water – first caught on.

Here you are at the foot of the western slopes of the mountains – just over the top (as it were) of the skyline you can see from l'Avenc, and down the other side. The Montseny mountains are a natural park of more than a hundred square miles and include three substantial peaks just under 6,000 feet.

Though tourists flying over the Pyrenees and into Barcelona from northern Europe might think these mountains an extension of the Pyrenees, they are really a quite separate massif, not so high, milder in climate (they overlook the sea) and a completely different ecological zone. The Montseny massif was declared a natural reserve of the biosphere by UNESCO in the 1970s, on account especially of the varied mix of plant life which its wide range of micro-climates at varying altitudes produces.

As our walk climbs from Aiguafreda towards and then along a side ridge of the Montseny, the hiker will only occasionally get glimpses out over the coastal plain behind, because the whole range is quite densely forested in oak, beech, evergreen oak and conifers. The spirit of the Pyrenees is open: pale rock, snowfields,

Alpine pastures; the spirit of the Montseny mountains is dark green and closed. Almost the whole range appears to be virgin land: there is not much sign of agriculture, past or present, apart from corn and vegetable patches near the hill villages, herds of goats and grazing cattle with their clanging, almost mournful cow-bells; and the area is very thinly populated.

Nor are the Montseny as wet as the Pyrenees, where you are seldom far from a rushing stream or snowy mountainside. Deeply indented by a few small rivers hidden in their gorges, these peaks and high hills are otherwise quite dry. But the wildlife, which is abundant – wild boar, hares, badgers, red squirrels, pine-martens and marmots, as well as many birds of prey – know where to drink.

I always think of the Montseny mountains as a kind of secret. Not literally, of course – the rich from Barcelona have for centuries kept little villas up above the cloud-line there. But for an impressive mountain range beneath which Spain's busiest motorway (from France) passes, which is visible from the whole Costa Brava (millions of clubbers and sun-seekers every year must look inland fleetingly and notice it) and which is situated almost in Barcelona's backyard, this beautiful range is surprisingly little known or visited. Indeed there are not many roads.

Walking there a couple of years ago, we parked beside the only road which goes over the top and took the path running to the highest point, up the ridge called Matagalls. You start in steep beech forest. The smooth, grey, twisted roots, closed canopy above and bare leafy ground beneath give the feeling of an enchanted wood. You climb hard through beech until you are almost at the top. Then you suddenly emerge on to the long strip of bare ground which follows the ridge. From here you can see l'Avenc across the great valley of the River Ter to the north; and behind it the whole Collsacabra, the foothills of the Pyrenees, and among the Pyrenean peaks on the horizon, the enormous massif of Mont Canigou, which is visible from across a huge area of coastal south-eastern France.

We stopped at the beacon on the top for a while, then carried on towards the other end of the ridge of Matagalls. Our path petered out. Soon we were back among the trees, stumbling down a precipitous slope and close to being lost. We saw through the undergrowth what looked like a little chapel on the edge of a cliff – and it was: an extraordinary place, built into the side of the rock, sheltering a shrine, and apparently abandoned. We stumbled on – and came upon a sort of alley. It led to a half-ruined monastery with a stone spire, where some kind of restoration seemed to have been underway, but there was nobody there. I saw from a rough sign that the place was called Sant Segimón. It was another half-hour before we reached a proper road. This was a day which in recollection feels – felt to all of us – like a kind of dream. That is the quality of the Montseny mountains.

The GR2 (from which we have just made that temporary detour) does not go right over the top of the Montseny: for this you could take any one of many smaller hiking paths. A company called Editorial Alpina publishes good detailed maps and guides. Divert along one of these side paths if you want to get into the heart of the Montseny. I would.

The GR2, meanwhile, sidles up the western slopes, passes a reddish stone village called El Brull on its way over, then, after crossing the ridge, descends through pine, brambles and evergreen oak to the lower slopes. You could stay here awhile in the pleasant little town of Sant Julià de Vilatorta.

Then the path climbs again, up to the top of a ridge where the most amazing castle, Sant Llorenç del Munt, sits on top of the world. This ridge takes you above Vilanova de Sau. The old town was transported here when the bottom of this valley was inundated in the last century to create two enormous lakes, the upper about seven miles long, the lower closer to ten, both snaking round the corners cut by the old gorge of the River Ter.

High above here sits l'Avenc: you can just see it on top of the red gritstone cliffs, distinguished until recently from the surrounding woods by the huge piles of rubble and earth created by our building work but now, thankfully, blending back in as the greenery returns. At night from the house we can see the occasional flash of a car's headlights as someone returns home to Vilanova or a late visitor searches out the remote Parador de Vic-Sau, a traditional hotel on the water's edge deep in pinewoods at the end of a dirt road.

On foot, though, you take the path crossing the big concrete dam holding back the upper of the two lakes, the Pantà de Sau. From June to September it is hot and humid, almost tropical, down here, utterly different from the mountain air on the cliffs above.

Standing on the wall of the dam, you can look along the lake behind it to where the stone spire and bell-tower of the eleventh-century Sant Romà de Sau pokes its sad head above the surface. It can be explored when the waters are low. Drying mud and broken stones mark where the congregation once sat; the roof is long gone. Outside, the streets of the old lost village can be traced by the piles of white rubble, a few walls still reaching up above head height. It is a melancholy place. Once this must have been a familiar landmark for the family who lived in l'Avenc, a community they could see from above and reach by scrambling down the cliff path. Now it has been lost beneath the warm, green water.

So look downriver instead to the next lake, even more remote, the Pantà de Susqueda. A track, barely drivable, follows its shore all the way through to the end of the mountains. You can walk this in five or six hours until, after the last gorge and a third small reservoir, the track becomes a road, emerging on to the coastal plain, only ten miles or so from Girona airport and the Costa Brava. A few years ago I walked up from the plain, following this track.

You enter a closed world – literally so, for in medieval times this river valley was settled and farmed, but after the Middle Ages became depopulated and in the last century was finally drowned. But the emptying of this valley began before it was sacrificed to provide power and water for the air-conditioners and golf courses of the coastal resorts.

Was it a loss of confidence in the region after the earthquakes which destroyed the town of Anglés, not far from where this road up the valley begins? Was it a plague? There are so many fine Romanesque and Gothic churches ruined or still standing, and after the seventeenth century building seems to have picked up again; but in between a sort of hole. It makes the partial rebuilding of l'Avenc in 1559 most unusual.

Down here by the Pantà de Susqueda everything has reverted to nature. Trees clothe the steep hillsides and crowd the shores, and in summer the valley is alive with butterflies. The only trace you will see of its human history is the occasional glimpse of stonework, throttled by roots and trees; or an unexplained copse of flowering cherry trees, apples, walnuts, figs or sweet chestnuts, once tended but now gone wild.

Walking past one of these in 2004, we stopped to rest in the heat of the day – and spotted the top of the steep hump of the slender medieval bridge of Queròs just awash, for the lake was very low. Across the other side you could see the ruins of the village and its church. I swam out to the bridge and stood there, the waters of the Ter now lapping at my toes where once they would have flowed thirty feet below me in the drowned gorge.

It was sad. We are very used in our era to bewailing the spread of humanity, the retreat of nature and the advance of all the works of man. But here in the valley of the Ter I felt just as I had in the forests of the little island of São Tomé, off equatorial West Africa, where the jungle is coming down from the mountain and strangling the elegant wooden verandahs and slim columns of abandoned Portuguese colonial coffee and cocoa plantations. I felt sorry.

Men and women had a place down here by the Ter. They made their gardens, their habitations and their fields here. It was not the kingdom of rats, ants, foxes and snakes alone. They cut back the throttling ivy and cruel brambles; they kept the nettles down.

I regret their departure. The earth is ours also. Those who deify Nature with a capital N should reflect on the paradox that just as surely as it is in the nature of a cat to hunt or a bird to fly, so it is in the nature of man to keep 'nature' at bay. Even as I stood on the bridge at Queròs I could touch with my toes the loosening mortar between the stones, and it made me sad. I have offered you in an earlier chapter my hymn to l'Avenc's ruin. Let us have hymns to restoration too.

But again we have digressed from the GR2, which, as it crosses the dam wall, switches from the southern half of this landscape – all those hills, valleys and mountains to the south of the River Ter – to the northern half. South of the Ter is called Les Guilleries, dominated by the ridges and peaks of the Montseny. This is steep but flowing land. North of the Ter is the Collsacabra, characterized by cliff-systems, platforms of meadows and sharp, small flat-topped mountains. This is more abrupt, broken, geometric. This is where l'Avenc is built. Further north again, the Pyrenees begin. That is where our path is heading.

First it must climb the cliffs to Tavertet. Pause before that ascent at the friendly La Riba hotel, which overlooks the lake, drink a beer or a lemonade in the shade on the lawn, and then set out on a little concrete road which the path soon leaves, heading for the foot of the cliffs. Look up at those huge flanks of grey and red rock – layered like a Liquorice Allsorts – and you may see 1,000 feet above you, perched on the edge, Tavertet's 1,000-year-old church.

Cyclists must take the long way round, sticking to the concrete road which eventually winds its way up past the isolated eleventh-century church of Sant Joan de Fàbregues, past a needle of rock stuck out like a flagstaff posted over the whole valley – a favourite winter's afternoon walk from l'Avenc – and into Rupit. But the walking route goes by Tavertet – and so do a few of the local sure-footed horses, their striking looks and flighty nature betraying their Arab bloodlines. On horseback or on foot, you follow a path which marches up to the cliff's bottom, at first incredulous at the map's claim that the GR2 climbs it. But it does. The path finds a way to zigzag up a sort of gully, and you emerge breathless on the shelf where Tavertet sits.

Tavertet is our village, a relaxed, loose-knit little place. On a rock spur at the end of a lonely, beautiful (and lethal) road, snaking for eight miles around the cliffs, the village is on the way to nowhere. From Tavertet you can see Vic spread out across the plain 2,000 feet below; the eagles that hover along the cliff could fly there in ten minutes, but coach tours cannot easily take in Tavertet on a Catalan wood-and-mountains day out, so the place sits peacefully in the sun, among its grey rocks and dry forests of evergreen oak, juniper, thyme and rosemary. Visitors come to stay, not just for lunch.

Remote as it is at the end of a dead-end tarmac road, Tavertet feels anything but godforsaken. Perched near the edge, the small church of Sant Cristòfol has a timeless sense of calm and grace; its Romanesque central nave, dating from the eleventh century, and its Gothic additions, are in good repair. The lovely miniature, round, domed apse at one end has been restored to its original state, and at the other a restrained eighteenth-century bell-tower has been added. The church keeps a notable fifteenth-century alabaster carving of the Virgin Mary. Sant Cristòfol is right in the midst of the village, by its little square.

To either side of Tavertet's rock-paved streets are stone houses above whose doors dates from the last three centuries are carved; around this nucleus spread streets of houses new and old, all built in stone, many of them second homes where families come on holiday. The village has a super outdoor swimming pool – big and modern – open to all, with the best view from any pool I've ever swum in.

Tavertet makes no bones about being a resort as well as a village. At an altitude of about 3,000 feet its splendid position has been noted for centuries. There are restaurants: the classy Can Baumes for instance, which offers more ambitious dishes than most rural restaurants and a menu bound in goatskin. The proprietor, Joan Reixach, works in a bank during the week and in the restaurant at the weekend. His wife's family have lived in Tavertet for the past 800 years. This sums up Catalunya: work, family and heritage.

Just by Can Baumes, a restaurant called Fabas Contades has now reopened, and is run by two chefs who serve tasty portions of a size which it is possible to imagine actually finishing.

Or try the cheerful and busy restaurant and bar Can Miquel, with tables for a cold drink or coffee under the trees outside and, within, a country store, El Rebost de l'Isabel, attached – which the resourceful proprietor has stocked with good local cheeses: goat's, cow's and sheep's, and a nice balance of practical groceries and rural delicacies. That the shop has recently started to include in its wares vegetarian hamburgers and soya milk tells you something about how Catalunya is changing.

On the walls by the open fire in the restaurant there is a mounted wild boar's head surrounded by the tufts of the tails of every beast the owner shot by what an engraved plaque says was his eightieth year. If a would-be restaurateur doesn't have a boar's head at least (and preferably some other small stuffed mammal too), he might as well not bother opening a restaurant or bar in the Collsacabra. Dead animals are as obligatory on the walls of the Catalan country restaurant as are copper kettles and polished horse-brasses in the English rural pub.

I do not care for shooting, but the wild boar is not an endangered species in the Collsacabra. Though you only rarely see them, the enormous creatures are everywhere, devastating to trees and bushes when a mood of rootling comes upon them. Some say this explosion of the boar population arises from the accidental mating of wild pigs with domesticated ones, the latter having been bred to produce litters of up to twelve, while in the wild the litters are rarely more than four.

Some years ago the proprietor Miquel's wife died wholly unexpectedly in an awful attack of asthma. She had been a mainstay of the family business. In shock, Miquel and his daughters virtually closed down for ages, but at last decided to give it a go without her. They have gone from strength to strength, and Can Miquel is one of our favourites. In Catalan *can* means 'place of' or *chez*; Cantonigròs, the name of a nearby town, means 'Big Tony's Place'.

The tiny museum in Tavertet is more endearing than comprehensive. The display is eclectic and rather sweet. There is a £1 coin on show next to an ancient reversible spanner, antique farming equipment and a photographic souvenir of a local cave, the Cova del Forat or Serrat del Vent (it is known as both). There is no mention of the Spanish Civil War. Every Catalan village has its memories of that terrible time, and the memories divide people.

There are places to stay in Tavertet, too. Best known among them is the Hostal El Jufré in the street named after our own bishop, Galcerán Sacosta. It is an airy, open and comfortable place to stay. Some of the rooms look straight out over the valley: a wonderful view. Can Noguer, another bed-and-breakfast, occupies what once was the town hall. There is a pleasant, shady yard in front, outside the bar – a place where we often sip beers, coffees or (my teetotal mother's favourite) Bitter Kas, a petrol-pink concoction of tonic with Cinzano-ish herbs. Can Noguer is a fine _masia_ standing at the end of one of the three streets that run parallel with the cliff's edge.

That 800-foot cliff would be a horror to any English mother of small children. Toni Molina, the mayor and a builder who helped with the construction of the cottages at l'Avenc, was born ten feet from the brink. His Tavertet-born mother, Maria, had met his Andalusian father, Antonio, when (in hopes of finding female company one weekend) he climbed the cliff path from the reservoir below, where he was a labourer. We asked Toni whether as a cliff's-edger born and bred, he could remember any accidents befalling unwary children in Tavertet. 'No,' he said, 'we just knew where the cliffs were.'

Tavertet is very quiet on a weekday and pretty quiet even at the weekend. There seem to be almost more restaurants than people during the week, and more excitement among the dogs than the human inhabitants: Toni's dog Lluna, a frisky white husky, greets every visitor like a long-lost friend, while Miquel's street-wise dog Tom is famous locally for being able to outrun speeding cars. On being accused once of letting his dog roam the streets too freely, Toni said, 'Mayors often donate something of value to their village, I'm giving Tavertet my dog.'

Stand in the stone yard in front of the Hostal El Jufré and you find yourself in the very place I started, thirty years ago, on that first hike to l'Avenc. Walk, as I did, eastward along the clifftop track out of the village (abominably rough; it is the GR2), past the house of Raimon Panikkar, a respected and now-ancient Indian-Catalan philosopher whose personal quest is to unify world religions, and who holds a monthly session based on theology and mysticism. Then pass the village's big round water tank. And within a hundred yards Tavertet is behind you.

You are heading for l'Avenc. You will reach the house as I first did, though perhaps by the time you read this they will have paved the track. The GR2 follows it all the way, though after some open scrub and box-bushes close to the cliff's edge, another track veers off to the right among the groves of oak trees you walk beneath. You can take either – they meet up again on the other side of l'Avenc. The lower track hugs the cliff's edge, passing close to the circular concrete cap which guards and closes off the top of the *avenc* – the natural vertical shaft of unknown depth after which we think our house was named.

I want to go down there. It seems likely to me that there is a honeycomb of caves behind these cliffs and beneath l'Avenc. We have evidence for this. In the wooded valleys behind the house there are two more of these shafts, both crudely fenced to protect cattle. In neither case is it possible to say how far down they go as they quickly narrow and bend. And in a rock face not far from l'Avenc on the Tavertet side whose location Toni Molina and I have agreed we should not publish, is the entrance to something far more interesting: the Cova del Forat del Vent, pictured in the museum. This is said to be the longest gritstone cave in the world, and one of its entrances is right next to l'Avenc.

Small, lithe, young and athletic, Toni Molina is one of the valiant four who gave evidence for us in our efforts to recover our water supply. He is a 'can-do' mayor: and when his village, too, ran short of water he decided to do something about it himself.

The answer lies in the cave which runs more than two miles through a rock arm of the hills above and behind Tavertet. The Forat del Vent presents an incredible challenge. It also contains water, which is how Toni first found himself learning the way in. Over months, he crawled back and forth dragging in the pipe that now supplies Tavertet, and our house, with water.

Both limestone and lava typically produce extensive cave-systems, but gritstones and sandstones – the Catalan word for this category of rock is *gres* – do not. This rare and fragile network of caves, properly penetrated only in the 1970s and still by no means wholly explored, needs to be protected from the pressure of too many inquisitive potholers. The reason is simple: the cave is dangerous, fragile, sometimes inundated, and the bed of many underground streams. Blind galleries lead off, some many hours long. The Federació Catalana d'Espeleologia controls access to a cave system which needs protection, not only because deep within it is the source of Tavertet's main water supply but also because visitor numbers would quickly overwhelm it.

The location of the entrance at the other end – the Tavertet end – is obvious. It is right beside a rough track which leads direct from the village to the town of Cantonigros. Only a few feet in diameter, the small natural tunnel in the rock face is securely barred by a massive concrete block, which can be winched up and down. From this gate emerges a pipe carrying water to Tavertet. At the other end of the cave – two and a half miles through it, or five if you walk the long way round by the GR2 – and hidden in the woods near l'Avenc, the cave's mouths, covered in leaves and rocks, are known to only a few. *Forat* means 'hole' and *vent* means 'wind', and I had always been curious to know what could be windy about so protected a system of hidden caverns. I was to find out.

Ever since getting to know Tavertet I have wanted to visit that cave. I have never been caving, anywhere. Just after my fiftieth birthday and only a few weeks after returning from Desolation Island in the year 2000, I got the chance. Toni Molina, who was thirty-one at the time, took me. He was already taking a group of Catalan cavers, and agreed to include my nephew Adam, my friend Julian, another friend, Nick, from England, and me. Five Go Caving.

This was Toni's fifth venture into the Forat del Vent and by now he knew what he was doing. He was thoughtful enough not to tell us until later that on an earlier expedition he had spent seventeen hours going down (or up) a gallery which had turned out to be a dead end. Still, he knew now which turn not to take, and in any case he was an experienced caver.

I am afraid we weren't. Our failure to supply our own water-proof over-clothes, carbide head-torches or knee-high boots, Toni may not have found surprising, but our arriving in shorts and T-shirts cannot have inspired confidence.

Still, he took this in his stride and supplied what was missing. That we had no idea how to abseil, that my closest approach to this sport was observing on television protesting lesbians abseiling at the Palace of Westminster, I never mentioned. I always reckon that there is no better way to acquire a skill than urgently and under force of circumstance.

But we were under a misapprehension about the Forat del Vent. I was not surprised when entering beneath the concrete block to have to crawl, but I thought that might be the end of crawling for the day. When people say 'cave' I think of Plato: of vaulted caverns, cathedral-like in their grandeur, of high rock walls and flickering firelight. The Forat del Vent was different.

Bright, hot daylight gave way to a dark, steamy cool.

'At first you will crawl,' said Toni. A little disappointed, I still thought he meant on hands and knees. My heart sank as, one after the other, the group in front of me flattened themselves on to their stomachs and slithered into six inches of cold, running water, beginning to wriggle and caterpillar along a passage about eighteen inches high. This continued for about a quarter of an hour. For though our — my — idea of a cave is of some brooding, lofty, orpheic underworld, Forat del Vent was different. Really it was just a two-mile crack beneath the mountains.

At times the passage would open into a gallery, and there were small halls and chambers the size of a parish church, like London Underground stations. But between these ran a jagged tube whose dimensions often barely exceeded the girth of a slight, narrow-shouldered man. Jordan would not have made it.

And this tube was an artery carrying water and air, both running against us. Yet it was very beautiful. Crawling along on your stomach in a damp cave can be curiously uplifting. As minutes gave way to hours and we wormed, splashed, clambered and stumbled our way forward, we passed galleries where the brown gritstone walls and ceilings had been penetrated by calcium-bearing water. Stalactites and stalagmites, and huge coral-like formations in pink and white hugged the sides or hung from above like organic furniture. This was Walt Disney meets Gaudí meets Gothic, in the dark, 1,000 feet under our mountain. It was magic.

And always – and this was so strange – there was a wind: a cold, clammy, sometimes vaporous breeze, blowing with gentle insistence along the tubes. That wind is the remarkable feature which has given the cave its name. It arises not only because the cave is open to the atmosphere at both ends, but also because the l'Avenc end is much higher than the Tavertet end, the flowing water cools the air within the tunnel, and the colder air sinks and flows down towards the lower end. The temperature near the Tavertet entrance was pretty constant – and remains so, said Toni, through winter and summer – at about 60°F.

Soon, soaked, our boots full of water, we began to shiver. Eventually we reached a round hall perhaps half the height and breadth of the Central Lobby of the House of Commons. We were on its clay floor. Toni pointed to a rope hanging from a ledge about forty feet above us. 'We go up,' he said.

'How?' each of us wondered. From his rucksack emerged harnesses, clips and a strange ratchet device which my father (a power engineer) told me was called a 'come-along' clamp in the pylon-fixing business.

I wasn't at all sure I wanted to come along. Nor was Julian. Nick looked terrified. But making a fair show of hiding his dismay that we were all completely unfamiliar with this device, Toni demonstrated. It is easy, actually, once you get the hang. Soon I was hauled, relieved, on to the ledge above. One by one the others followed. All of us made it.

The next five hours were the most spectacular – and exhausting.

It was unreal. What made the galleries through which we plunged (at times almost swam) so weirdly dreamlike were the long, jagged, calcium cornices which, like horizontal blades, lined the corridor walls at different levels. Imagine a picture rail running along the wall at neck height, but sticking six inches out and sharp as a razor. These had perhaps been created as accumulated tide marks in a bathtub might be: by different levels of calcium-rich water in different seasons. Even now, in August, quite a torrent was running through, still followed by that clammy wind. When we turned off our torches the effect was nightmarish. Pitch black, water rushing past your shins, a damp breeze in your face and a radar-sense of rock, inches from each ear.

I did not like it at all. I was not afraid but felt out of my element. There must be something in serious cavers which responds positively to these underground sensations: but not in me. I cannot have been a mole in any previous life.

Just over a mile into the mountain and after some four hours, we turned back. Most of us were beginning to tire, torchlight was weakening and all were cold. Secretly, each had asked himself how the descent down the rope up which we had come would be accomplished. Maybe Toni had explained, but I do not recognize the Catalan for 'abseil'.

We reached the ledge. Below there was only a black void. Toni's mate climbed into the harness, to which he attached a rope running through a complicated eye. Then he threw himself from the ledge and, suspended on the rope, swung violently across the void, hitting the rock wall on the other side, and bouncing off. In mid-air, he began to pass the rope, the tail-end of which he held behind his back, through the eye, dropping as he did so, until he reached the floor far below. He had obviously done this before.

I never had. Toni hitched me up. He seemed confident on my behalf. I thought, 'Well, you've got to trust somebody,' so I threw myself off the ledge.

Bang. I hit the opposite wall and swung back. Wallop. I hit the next wall. But I was secure, if airborne. Once I realized that, fear left me. Feeding the rope through the eye and dropping like a spider, in little swoops, I touched down. This was fantastic.

An hour later we blinked into the late afternoon August sunshine. The concrete slab was winched back down over the mouth of our secret cave. Hands still shaking, we drove away, cold and hungry, for we had not eaten all day. At supper, outdoors, on a verandah in a village restaurant near by, I joined my aunt, Christine, who had just arrived from Britain. 'What news of the Liberal Democrat leadership election?' I asked. 'Oh,' she said, 'I can't remember the names, but I think that gingery one is winning.' He did win. Odd that I should be writing this now, in the year the gingery one has faced his second general election.

Emerging from the Forat del Vent, the real world of British politics re-enveloped me, and the shadows fled. Or was that cave the real world, and is the gingery one just a shadow on the wall? Plato would know.

. . . But I have taken you far from the GR2, few of whose hikers will know, as they pass round a corner over the stream and see l'Avenc up a gentle hill ahead, that the astonishing other-world of the Forat del Vent lies so close to their path. One day I shall crawl right through, starting from the secret mouth to the cave at l'Avenc.

11. An Unanswered Question

Through all these diversions, work at l'Avenc was plodding relentlessly on.

If plod suggests weariness, that is often what we felt. Months would pass and it would seem no discernible progress had been made. Morale would drop. Then there would be a small leap forward and we would tell ourselves it was all worthwhile, all going fine. And then another barrier or another reverse and our spirits would fall again. But inch by inch we were getting there and perhaps you do not want to hear about each inch, but further milestones were passed as the old millennium turned and a new one began.

Somehow, the biggest jobs were the least dispiriting. The new roof, the new balcony and the holiday cottages (whose story I tell a little later): obvious successes to notch up, for they were jobs with a beginning, a middle and an end, and when they were complete you could stand back and take a snapshot for the album and think: that's it; done; finished.

Likewise with the entire exterior of the house (both the Renaissance and the Gothic parts). Here was a job even I could understand. Every external wall had to be repointed. Over the centuries, mortar had crumbled away, stone had fallen out and there were holes all over the place. Making all this good had been a mammoth task but a relatively simple one; the result, still the old walls, still the old stone, but secure, sealed and tight, was a pleasure to contemplate.

If only for the purposes of keeping up morale, I would recommend anyone undertaking a seemingly endless task like this to set themselves a handful of projects that have real shape, that are doable and once completed make an obvious difference, so that – like God at the end of the sixth day after Creation – you can put down your tools, inspect the work, and (echoing the Almighty) say quietly to yourself: 'Behold, it is very good.'

Not that anything we achieved was done in six days or anything like it. Often enough, only divine intervention looked capable of getting us through. But on we ploughed.

We had begun work on the most painstaking and most expensive stage of all, where for months — even years — the results hardly showed: the internal reconstruction of the 'noble' sixteenth-century part of l'Avenc. Agonizingly slowly the house was coming together within.

In a way, and colossal though the project of removing, raising and replacing the roof had looked at the time, the new roof had been the easy bit. Well, not easy, but simple. Not only because the work was physically straightforward but also because it didn't interlock with other tasks, the planning of this operation was uncomplicated. The same had been true of the holiday cottages: starting almost from scratch had made it easier. The balcony, too, was, for all its size and ambition, a bolt-on feature: we put it there, and it was done.

I remember sauntering around our newly roofed l'Avenc as the cement-mixer whirred and the walls of the holiday cottages rose from the ground in line by line of neat stonework, growing almost before our eyes, and thinking, 'New roof. Walls made good. Cottages growing like Topsy. Hey! We're well over half-way there. Just a matter of fitting it out inside, now, and landscaping the surround.'

Perhaps it is lucky that neither the scale nor the expense of what we still had to do had properly dawned on us — let alone the time it would take to do it. Otherwise we might have despaired. We had by then, at the start of the twenty-first century, already spent about half a million pounds on l'Avenc, of which the purchase price was less than a third. None of us had wanted to run up big debts or take on new mortgages, so the four of us were doing it out of our savings and our joint earnings, aiming to keep more or less abreast of each other in our total financial contributions.

This meant that from time to time we simply ran out of money, and would have to delay. Sympathy for any of us would be misplaced; we were lucky to have relatively high-earning jobs. All

I can say, though, is that in the face of the major restoration of an historic building, no high-earning job is high-earning enough.

The four of us discussed taking out a big loan. It made obvious sense. We could then proceed as the demands of the project dictated. Building slowly is inefficient, and maybe (we thought) with a major push we could get the whole thing done in one huge and expensive heave.

But somehow we lacked the stomach for surfing the lending market. At heart we were petits bourgeois, we Parrises and Abeys. True, my earnings were now in the upper rather than the middle bracket; true, my brother-in-law was part of a family business of substantial worth, and they knew how to manage finances. But Quim's father had made his way up from nothing by hard work, setting savings aside, reinvesting, and building a business slowly from its own turnover and profits. My father had started as a night-school-taught apprentice electrical engineer, and though the factories and businesses he had finally come to manage had operated as big business does – on borrowing – we had never as a family had any kind of debt beyond mortgages for our family houses.

At fifty I had reached a stage in my life when I had no borrowings at all – not even a mortgage – and it felt good. I did not want to return to the housing debts of my younger days. This was of course irrational, but in all sentient creation unreason runs deep where questions of storing, hoarding, eking out and buffering oneself against risk are concerned. Even as I write this I have just broken an expensively capped front tooth by biting a near-empty tube of shaving cream in order to extract the last scrap. Thus in pursuit of one pennyworth of soap has been incurred an expense of about £300. It's stupid. And I know I will do it again.

With hindsight, however, our policy of doing a bit at a time, standing back, taking stock of progress so far, moving on in our minds to plan the immediate next step, then slowing down or pausing until we could afford it, was inefficient. Work teams got disbanded; skilled tradesmen couldn't be assembled in the same place at the same time; once we had resolved what the plumber should do the electrician had started another job elsewhere; and when we finally decided where to reuse a heap of old tiles the cows had stamped on them and broken every second one. As a piece of folk wisdom, 'one step at a time' sounds sage advice, but in this case the wisdom was doubtful.

Of course we never stated it to each other like that. Perhaps we were not allowing ourselves fully to acknowledge that we were turning our eyes from the middle and longer term, and shying away from the hurdle of confronting the whole project as a concept, and making big decisions about how to finance it and how to staff it. One reason for this reluctance to confront the overall picture was that we probably had differing ideas about what that picture should be. For at the heart of everything we were doing lay an unanswered question: what was l'Avenc for? How did we see its future, decades hence? Slow progress at least gave us time to think, and we avoided some big mistakes which, in a rush, we might have blundered into.

My brother-in-law did think long-term – he thought very big indeed – but much of his thinking was around the periphery of l'Avenc itself, the ancient house, the core of the project. Quim had plans for the site overall. He had in mind a modest-sized leisure and residential complex. A little further round the hillside, behind the house and rather out of sight (where when we bought the property had stood a ruined and useless stone shell, now demolished), he envisaged a terrace of self-contained apartments or small houses. He had occasionally mentioned the idea of constructing a swimming pool and discreet parking arrangements, and perhaps a garage of some kind. But it is only now, as construction draws to a close, that I realize how big his ambitions really were.

And we had not even sorted out planning permission properly. The British sometimes have the idea that Spain is a kind of Wild West where you can throw up any building you like, wherever you like. In the past this has been true of parts of the country – along some of the coast, for instance – particularly during the last years of the Franco regime. But public administration in Catalunya is mature and advanced, there exists a complex framework for

the protection of valued landscapes and historic villages and buildings, and though some builders in some locations do seem to
get away with more than others, we were in the same position as
most people who live in Catalunya. We would need a lot of
permissions from a lot of authorities. The process was slow and
maddeningly bureaucratic.

We all decided that there was no harm in making the applications while deferring the decision whether we should really go
ahead on the bigger stuff until much later. We did so, and spent
a fair sum on architects' drawings and site-plans. Looking back
now I am glad we held our nerve and persisted with our ambition. But at the time it caused more problems than it solved.

First, it made the planning applications needed for the
smaller-scale work in hand – on l'Avenc and the new holiday
cottages – part of a much more ambitious and problematical application. Not speaking Catalan, and not spending enough time on
the project when I was in Spain, it was never quite clear to me
whether our grand plans were slowing the determining of the
immediate application. I always hoped that it might be possible
to agree the l'Avenc sections of the application while deferring a
decision on the broader plan. That never happened.

Thinking on such a big scale did also muddy the water when
decisions had to be made on things like plumbing and electrical
power. Were we at stage one of a bigger, staggered project, or was
our work on the old house and the animal sheds freestanding: a
restoration project to which something extra could always be
bolted on in the years ahead?

For as building work progressed, we had to develop our ideas
of what it was all for. Each of us had our own enthusiasms. When
my sister had told casual visitors that she saw l'Avenc's future as
a kind of cultural centre she meant it, even if her hearers remained
a bit woolly about the concept.

As she saw it, l'Avenc's location, in a breathtakingly beautiful
position on a mountainside with sublime views in all directions,
isolated, unspoiled and serene, pointed to one clear purpose. It was
an outstanding ancient building which breathed history and whose

external and internal architecture communicated a kind of cultural stature. And it was big. There were three great rooms capable of seating an audience of a hundred or more; there were rooms which could be used as dormitories.

The dream was for l'Avenc to become a sort of Aldeburgh of Catalunya, centred not only on music and the arts, but on philosophy and learning, and the exploration of beliefs and ideas. She could envisage festivals and seminars taking place there, as well as debates and performances.

None of us rejected this vision of a future, but to me it was not the first purpose of the house. L'Avenc's status would have to grow with time, and we could start small, try hiring the house out for functions of different sorts, and see what demand there was. How far the family would manage events ourselves, or how far we would let others do so, was also unclear. A gradual start to using the house in this way would allow us to experiment.

Nor need the idea of a cultural centre conflict with our living there. There was space on the top floor for two generous apartments to either side of the top-floor state room, one for my sister and her family, and one for Julian and me. There was space on the first floor for an apartment for Francesc's family. And there would always be the holiday cottages for friends and relatives.

For me, simply staying there was enough of an ambition. I have no wish to emigrate from England, and Derbyshire will always be my home, but holidays, weekends and winter breaks seemed from the start to be a glorious prospect. I may have daydreamed about making l'Avenc the venue for political summits – if you can have Bretton Woods or the Camp David Accord, why not the Treaty of l'Avenc? – but I knew that this was only a fantasy.

Yet from the day we bought l'Avenc I had another aim, too. I made it my personal plan that we should turn its little row of three tumbledown stone sheds into simple holiday cottages. I was anxious for l'Avenc to become again what the old house must have been for so many centuries: hospitable, a place of shelter. A single, isolated habitation among wide and empty lands is a refuge or it is nothing. At the rough end of the range I wanted us to provide a patch of grass where hikers could pitch an overnight tent, a standpipe for water and a shelter for storms. At the more comfortable end, we were creating a handful of dwellings where visitors could come for a week or more.

This was almost my only certainty about the future. I have never been sure what purpose we would find for the most imposing parts of the house, the reception rooms, the grand entrance hall, the high-ceilinged parlour with its carved fireplace. But it had seemed a sensible, achievable first step to make small dwellings out of the line of ruined agricultural buildings, detached from the main house, that came with the property. Unlike the main house, these structures were of no architectural importance or sensitivity, and we had a free hand.

All of us were agreed on this. After all, we would have to do something with these buildings: we could not leave them in the ruined state in which we found them.

We also needed somewhere which would be habitable soon at l'Avenc. The restoration of the main building was beginning to stretch forward indefinitely as work took longer and costs mounted; Quim kept thinking of new and more ambitious plans, all of them good, but none of them quick or cheap. And whenever one of us tried to clear a little corner of one of the big rooms and make a clean and comfortable nest where for a few days we could sleep and keep a suitcase of clothes and a washbag, the dust would settle from above and the builders and their machinery would invade from every side.

Besides, I was becoming impatient to establish an income, however small, from the project. I just wanted to see something, anything, in the credit column of the balance sheet. After a couple of years of the huge outlays which went into demolishing, reroofing and building the balcony, and the lengthening prospect of years of plumbing, plastering and electricity, not to speak of rebuilding the floors and staircases (oh – and don't forget we haven't yet got any windows or doors), I thought it would be modestly helpful to our battered bank accounts but (more importantly) good for our morale, if we could prove to ourselves that there were customers for our project out there in the wider world, that at least something at l'Avenc could make rather than take money.

As ever, it fell to Belinda and her husband, to Joan Sarsanedas and Toni Molina, to turn ideas into buildings. We didn't need to poke around the old stone sheds for long before it became clear that the roofs were rotten and would have to be replaced; that the floors had long collapsed and would have to be built again; and that the walls were unsound and would have to be reconstructed. In short, what was needed was a complete rebuild, from the foundations up. And we didn't need to poke around much longer for it to emerge that there were in fact no foundations – or none to speak of.

These had just been animal sheds. There were three in a line, snaking uphill from the main house, beside the track. Just below and separated from them by a narrow passageway to the back of the property, there was also a fourth stone building, a kind of hovel, half-heartedly attached to the Gothic section of the house. All faced south-east, straight into the morning sun, and looked right out across the valley to the Montseny mountains. So the potential was there, but when it came to realizing it we had a fairly blank sheet of paper to draw on.

We were unhappy with the way the Gothic half of l'Avenc fizzled out into broken walls and blocked windows, so – just as the balcony had tidied and graced the side of the house – we would make a clean end at the top, beyond the old kitchen, with a big, heavy kitchen door, a stone-paved yard and a properly roofed wood shelter. This would cut and clear away the tumbledown link between the main house and the small, half-attached hovel, which we would rebuild. We would recreate it as a whole and freestanding cottage with a living room, fireplace and open-plan kitchen downstairs, and (there was just space for this) two small bedrooms and a bathroom upstairs.

This, we thought, might one day be an extra holiday cottage; and for the time being it could be the first properly habitable and self-contained dwelling at l'Avenc, which all of us could use. I started to call it the janitor's cottage because that looked to me like a possible future use for it.

Next, above that cottage, came the narrow passageway which we would leave in place. To the other side, above, were the three animal sheds which we would demolish, using the stone to build a terrace of three small cottages side-by-side and adjoining each other. They would be aligned facing the track as the animal sheds had been and occupy more or less the same space, but they would be about half as high again. This would allow for two storeys to each cottage. Each would have its own front door, and they would all be different, with characters of their own.

The whole terrace would be roofed in the same red, Mediterranean pan-tiling which roofed the main house, but so that the profile was not too high this would be quite a low roof, and upstairs rooms would have sloping ceilings, especially low at the front. Each would have its own fireplace and small chimney.

The first cottage (closest to the main house) allowed for two small bedrooms and a bathroom, and a living room and en-suite kitchen downstairs – much like the janitor's cottage. Its front door would open into the passageway at the side but most of its windows would face forward. The view would be splendid.

The second (in the middle of the terrace) was rather smaller. We decided this cottage would not have a full top storey, but instead one huge room, with a sort of mezzanine platform along the back where the roof was high enough – like a big minstrel's gallery with a wooden balustrade. That would be the bedroom. The living area would be the whole ground floor, with the kitchen and bathroom tucked beneath the balustrade and chairs, sofas and table at the front.

The third, farthest from the main house and at the top end of the terrace, would have a complete first floor with two small bedrooms. On the ground floor everything (except the bathroom) would be open-plan.

The work on the holiday cottages started in earnest in 2000, after we had put the new roof on the main house. Little else that we have done at l'Avenc has proceeded quite so smoothly or according to plan. Unlike with the renovation of the main house, we were not wrestling here with an ancient monster with a character all its own; we could impose our own ideas and plans, and we did.

It was finished faster than we expected, and the results were more charming and characterful than we expected.

In all our minds – even in mine, the originator of the holiday-cottage idea – this part of the project had been very much a sideline. 'Oh, we'll tack on a little terrace of houses; then one day we can let them out to visitors' had been the thinking. 'And we'll make them solid, good-quality, but basic, nothing remarkable.'

We did not plan to cut corners, of course: it's one of the facts about l'Avenc's rescue of which I'm proudest that nowhere (even when seriously strapped for cash) were we ever willing to cut corners. But the cottage plan had started as a bread-and-butter element in the bigger picture.

Yet as each cottage took shape it took on a life and personality of its own. The designs were really quite quirky, and much the better for that. The janitor's cottage felt like a miniature family house, compact and comfortable. The bottom dwelling of the terrace of three, with its front door at the side, was cosy and quaint, full of turnings, nooks and crannies. The cottage at the top end was simpler, lighter and airier. And in mid-terrace the open-plan cottage with the mezzanine gallery had an avant-garde feeling, like an artist's studio.

The janitor's cottage was completed well ahead of the others because all of us, especially my sister and her husband, needed somewhere away from the dust and clay to lay our heads when we stayed overnight at l'Avenc. In the event its completion co-incided with their decision to put their own home, Casalons, on to the books of a rental agency. They needed the money. This was a period when the work at l'Avenc was gobbling up euros even faster than usual, and at least in the summer moving out and letting their house to visitors would bring in some extra income.

Casalons is unusual: it has a big swimming pool. Quim had been let loose with his digger, and turned a steep hillside in front of the house into a sort of sky-pool on a hanging apron of lawn, with absurdly steep terracing all the way down the hill beneath it. With views of the Pyrenees behind, views of the swimming pool and oak-woods in front, Casalons looked as though it should be easy to let.

So it proved. The auguries for our holiday cottages were good. This would surely be part of l'Avenc's future, and something which, because it was uncomplicated and we could all agree easily on it, we pursued unhesitatingly from the start. Casual observers and local residents probably have the impression we see the project in a straightforward way as a commercial venture and an upmarket leisure complex. But we do not and never did.

At most, tourism and hospitality will be part of the house's future, but if there's one thing that's clear to all of us it is that this will not be the whole of it. But what that future will be, heaven – and I suspect l'Avenc itself – knows.

12. A Different Spain

What would our visitors, when we could persuade them to come, explore?

Every year tourists crowd the beaches down by the coast – beaches you can see from the little hill above l'Avenc, and from which the whole sweep of the Pyrenees and the tops of the Montseny mountains are visible. I dare say that with a sufficiently powerful telescope on a sufficiently clear day we could actually see these hordes from l'Avenc, all huddled, shrieking together along the seafront like penguins in Antarctica, facing the ocean with their backs to a majestic and unexplored continent behind them.

They have wheels, these holidaymakers. Many have driven from their home countries, or hired cars at the airport. A little further down the coast hundreds of thousands of weekenders fly into Barcelona, right over the Garrotxa (pronounced *garotcha*), the Guilleries and the Collsacabra. They must see this dramatic land-scape from the windows of their aeroplanes.

Yet almost none of these visitors ever visit us. If they did, they would share my feeling, I think, that we are all in on a bit of a secret. I did once see a Japanese tourist in Rupit (she looked rather lost) but the rest of the world has stayed away. From the day my family arrived in Catalunya more than thirty years ago we have wondered why this part of Europe was so little known beyond the coast. We have been waiting, and still wait, for the day its fame would spread.

That could be a mercy: we might be overwhelmed. But I do regret the timidity of so many foreign tourists. I would like them to know and enjoy rural Catalunya and all the places my family know and have explored there. The real Catalunya, our Catalunya, is so close and they are missing it.

Maybe families who have set their hearts on a buckets-and-spades holiday by the sea, or 18–30s who want nothing more than to drink and dance into the small hours in the bars of Blanes or Tossa del Mar, have no interest in motoring inland. Maybe an extended weekend break in Barcelona does not lend itself to hopping on to one of the hourly trains from the Plaça Catalunya up into the Pyrenees, though it is only a couple of hours.

Or maybe people do not know about these places, and never think to find out. But there are rainy days on the Costa Brava. There are heatwaves on the coast when a picnic from the boot of your car by a mountain stream not ninety minutes from the beach, would be a good way to cool off. Or you could drive to Molló, or Setcases, ask one of the bars there to make up some ham or cheese rolls, buy a bottle of country wine and a local map, stuff it all in your rucksack, and start walking.

You do not need strong boots, or much more than a good sunhat and a water bottle. And there is so much to enjoy. From Rupit the path that passes l'Avenc swings north and heads for the very end of those mountains, just before they dwindle into the Mediterranean in an unreal landscape: the dry, pale, bleak, knobbly coastal hills near Cadaqués and Port Lligat where Salvador Dalí lived and worked.

But first the traveller has to drop: about 2,000 feet into the plains around the large town of Olot. Napoleon's army came up from the French Languedoc this way, en route to sacking the monastery at Montserrat. There is a variety of paths and packhorse routes down the steep mountainside. One passes my parents' house, l'Hostalot, crossing the stream below it over a small medieval stone bridge near which my mother once found a small button by the path, with an N engraved on to it. It is likely to have come from the tunic of one of Napoleon's troopers.

If you take that route you will pass a rather grand, dark and austere rural Catalan mansion called El Grau.

El Grau has a history. In earlier centuries this house was a judicial headquarters, and the room where convicted criminals used to be hanged is still there. Earlier yet, the place was a hostelry for travellers coming up from the coastal plains and from France, for the royal road (*camí reial*) passes it: a wonderful packhorse route diving down towards the plain of Olot. The house looks out across the plain.

Though the path is now almost overgrown and forgotten, it is possible to see through the nettles and tree roots the beautifully laid stone steps which made the steepest and wettest stretches passable. The house enjoys a full view of the path and the mountainside; and vice versa: a facility of which full advantage was taken in the Middle Ages by enterprising staff at Grau who had made a private arrangement with a company of bandits using a cave half-way down the mountainside.

It is said by some that Joan Serrallonga (whose house in the Montseny mountains you can see from l'Avenc) was the leader of these brigands. But Serrallonga (though no philanthropist) has something of the status of Robin Hood in Catalan tales from history, and it is hard to separate fact from myth. Tales of banditry and derring-do are attributed to Serrallonga rather as quotable quotes are attributed to Dorothy Parker or Winston Churchill.

Whoever these bandits were, they had a key accomplice: a planted collaborator. Their plant worked at the hostelry at Grau. By hanging towels – as if to dry – out of a window, he alerted the bandits to the departure of richly laden guests travelling down the path; thus the bandits were ready to leap from their cave when their prey passed.

More like a long, narrow, very deep gulley in the rock than a true cave, the den could easily hide a small posse of men and a couple of horses. My brothers, sisters and I located it many years ago, but having located it, we always seem to lose it again when next we are looking. It truly is – and was – an elusive place, almost magical in its disappearance. You can walk right past without seeing the hide.

It is fun to skulk there, invisible from the nearby path, look up the mountain through the dripping trees (these north-facing slopes are almost always cold and damp) and see the old stone walls of the house and its little windows. How many bandits crouched where we crouch, how many unsuspecting travellers and their mules, newly refreshed at Grau, passed this way to be mugged?

But fate caught up with the highwaymen. They were finally rounded up – and one was hanged at Grau. What happened to their accomplice in the hostelry is not recorded.

The path is probably safer today than it has been in ten centuries but I would not go that way. My family have found a sublime detour. To the north, as the path tumbles over the cliffs, is a tiny peak – a small promontory out from the cliffs – and on it, often with a red-and-yellow Catalan banner flying, is the hermitage (*ermita*) of Sant Miquel.

The resident hermit has long departed but we can be sure he will have enjoyed the view. The location is rather like that of a seaside pier, but out over the plains far below, rather than the ocean. To the east you can see as far as the coast, to the south you look along the cliffs and mountainside, and to the north the Pyrenees frame the view. In the foreground, however, is a most beautiful small mountain: an isolated ridge called Puigsacalm, which means 'calm peak' in Catalan.

It is hard to describe what is so very striking about Puigsacalm, but it is a landmark with which everyone in the plain below is familiar. You can walk to its highest point: from Sant Miquel there is a path, well marked, leading along the eastern slopes of the hillside, damp with little springs and rivulets and thick with ferns and box bushes through which the path sometimes makes a kind of tunnel. Half-way along, the path climbs to the top and switches sides, clinging to the western slope: an exceptionally fine beech forest whose floor is a carpet of daffodils in April. You then have to climb round the back of Puigsacalm to ascend to the top, but the climb to the beacon is worth it: from here there are magnificent views of the Pyrenees, which suddenly seem to have come much closer.

Far below is a small town called Les Preses, really an outskirt of the regional capital, Olot: a big, solid, bourgeois and rather prosperous town, with fine avenues lined by massive London plane trees and grand and gloomy Spanish-Edwardian houses built for doctors and lawyers, an old-fashioned theatre, and the kind of central park in which well-dressed women of a certain age walk their toy dogs past cast-iron drinking-fountains beneath high trees.

Olot was flattened by earthquakes in the fifteenth century but has long resumed its quiet predominance over a strangely private inland plain. The town is hardly more than an hour's drive from the Costa Brava but I have never encountered a single foreign tourist there. Olot is long-established, secure, self-respecting, economically important, rather cultured, quietly rich . . . and almost unknown. It could be a fictional town, the essence of a provincial town, like George Eliot's Middlemarch.

You are in another Catalunya now, down on the Olot plain. Here the world looks towards Girona and the coast. The roads are long, flat, fast and straight: put your foot down and you could be in the south of France within the hour. Trucks and vans roar by; industrial estates hug the highway; the land is rich and fertile; the sun is warmer and the growing-season longer. Fields of maize rustle in the breeze; there are orchards of fruit-trees, roadside nurseries, roadside bars − even a roadside brothel.

All at once the Collsacabra seems to have receded far away, up in the high hills behind that great green wall of an escarpment you have come down. The climate now is almost Mediterranean, and more humid − it rarely freezes hard or snows − and you will even see the occasional brave clump of red or purple bougainvillea climbing a wall. Palm trees too survive. Gardens are lush.

Behind Olot, there is a quite remarkable micro-region. The Garrotxa is, like the Auvergne in France, something you don't quite expect to find in Europe: a region of volcanoes. True, they are long-dormant if not extinct, but no amount of brambles, evergreen oak and beech can conceal the classic shape of a volcano. Within not many miles there are scores − about forty in all − of modest-sized conical hills; and a handful of them are proper craters, with scooped-out bowls in the middle, the ash long buried beneath a carpet of verdant undergrowth.

This odd place is hardly a secret: the zone is a protected area, and walkways and information centres have been created for visitors, yet it has somehow never made much mark on our common European knowledge of our own continent. Were the Garrotxa a region of England it would be as famous as the Cheddar Gorge or the Norfolk Broads. If there were extinct volcanoes with perfect cones in Ireland, they would be the stuff of folk songs and legend. In France the volcanoes of the Auvergne are widely known. But the Catalan Garrotxa has remained in the *Mastermind* category of 'specialist subject: vulcanology'.

The Garrotxa was never 'discovered' – locals have always known about it and landscape artists have often painted there – but it was a Scottish-born traveller, scientist and liberal patron called William Maclure (1763–1840) who brought the volcanoes to the attention of science, after travelling to Olot in 1803. Maclure became known as the father of American geology, and wrote a detailed account of his investigations.

This was followed up by one of the nineteenth century's most eminent geologists, Sir Charles Lyell (1797–1875), a friend of Charles Darwin and a modernist whose avowed aim was to 'free science from Moses' but who struggled morally with the concept of human evolution. Lyell was an original thinker and a clear and stylish writer whose great contribution to geology was his insistence that (to put it crudely) geology is still going on and the formation of the earth is a continuous process; it follows that we should study the 'modern causes' of ancient events rather than think of the formation of the earth in terms of one-off cataclysmic shocks in a long-gone epoch beyond our reach.

In the middle of the nineteenth century Lyell travelled to the Auvergne, to Etna and to Olot, and there is an account of his Garrotxan sojourn in the third volume of his famous *Elements of Geology*.

Volcanoes of Olot, in Catalonia: I shall first direct the reader's attention to a district of extinct volcanoes in the north of Spain, which is little known, and which I visited in the summer of 1830.

The whole extent of country occupied by volcanic products in Catalonia is not more than about fifteen geographical miles from north to south, and six from east to west.

It is evident that the physical geography of the country has under-
gone no material change since the commencement of the era of the
volcanic eruptions . . . [and] if the lavas could be remelted and poured
out again from their respective craters they would descend the same
valleys in which they are now seen and reoccupy the spaces they at
present fill.

Lyell found that 'most of the Catalonian volcanoes are as entire
as those on Etna, or in the neighbourhood of Naples'. He
concluded that the rich plain on which Olot stands was 'produced
by the flowing-down of many lava streams from the hills into the
bottom of a valley, probably once of considerable depth'.

The largest crater of the whole district occurs farther to the east of Olot
and is called Santa Margarita. It is 455 feet deep and about a mile in
circumference . . . It is richly covered with wood, wherein game of various kinds abound.

They still do: deer and wild boar, though the wolves have been
hunted to extinction. Today there are stables nearby, the hills are
as richly forested as they were in 1830, and you can go riding in
the woods. Rare pine-martens and genets are to be found, and
the Garrotxa is said to be home to many snakes, including adders.
For this I cannot vouch but I have noticed a profusion of lizards,
happy in the volcanic rubble beneath the greenery.

The last eruption is thought to have taken place about 17,000
years ago, and nobody is expecting another soon. Nor was Lyell.
Talking about the last great shock in the fifteenth century (which
shook l'Avenc too), when 'the whole of Olot, with the exception
of a single house, was cast down by an earthquake,' he suggests
that the cause was not volcanic, but resulted from the settlement
of vast caverns beneath the surface of this part of Catalunya. He
reports the sinking of several houses into the ground, and the
practice of rebuilding on top of the rubble – just as appears to
have happened in what is now our wine-cellar at l'Avenc. Lyell
was plainly much struck by the Garrotxa.

So am I. I love volcanoes. I make a bee-line for them wherever I am in the world. I've peered into craters or inspected lava
flows in Bolivia, the Atacama, Ethiopia, Tenerife, Congo, Hawaii
. . . the list is exotic. But the Garrotxa is quite different from all
of these. It is as though some almighty hand had taken a typically
bare and grey system of cones and craters, and clothed their naked-
ness in thick green fur. The Garrotxa is the right shape but the
wrong colour and texture: a sort of joke, like a patch of tarmac
upholstered in green baize. There's something slightly weird about
this bizarre corner of Catalunya.

Away from the highway, your path takes you through wild
country, past the volcanoes and into the empty hills which line
the passage from the maize-fields of Olot down to the coastal
plain. To your left you will bypass a very strange town indeed:
Castellfollit de la Roca. The town, whose population is only about
1,000, is extraordinary and not just because it contains what must
surely be the world's only museum of sausages, an odd place that
must seem unsurprising to carnivore Catalans but is bizarre to
everyone else.

Drive down the main street and you will see nothing unusual:
a rather shabby place, you may think; undistinguished. You may
notice that in the middle of Castellfollit the main road takes a
very sharp bend to the left, but roads sometimes do: you are
unlikely to guess – in this case – why; there are houses to either
side of the road, as you would expect.

Soon you are out of the town, and notice that the road bends
right, doubles back on itself and descends a small escarpment rather
steeply. Then you cross a river, and the road follows it downstream
on the opposite bank.

Look across the river and up. There on the skyline is Castellfollit
de la Roca. But it is on the edge of a cliff. The whole town is
strung out along the top edge of a huge, bare wall of solid volcanic
rock. People's back windows give straight into space. So would
their back doors, if they had any. The front doors on your right-
hand side, which you have just driven past, are the only way in.
All they have at the back is a giddying view over the cliff. It is

as if a fissure had opened up across the middle of town, half the
town had sunk into it, and the other half had been left teetering
on the brink. That is why the highway makes its sudden bend to
the left after entering Castellfollit. The road would otherwise
plunge straight over the edge.

The inquisitive Sir Charles Lyell found and recorded this minor
wonder. His notes are drier and less breathless than mine:

A lava stream flowing from a range of hills to the east of Olot descends
a considerable slope until it reaches the valley of the river Fluvia. Here
for the first time it comes in contact with running water, which has
removed a portion, and laid open its internal structure in a precipice
about 130 feet in height, at the edge of which stands the town of
Castell Follit.

Castellfollit de la Roca has remained what it was then: famous
within its region, unknown beyond it. The same is true of Besalú,
which the GR2 goes right through. The medieval quarter of this
town is very fine, and the medieval bridge, lovingly restored, one
of the highest and most impressive examples of these steep and
slender arched stone constructions which abound in Catalunya: I
have seen none better. There is an ancient church with alabaster
windows, staked around with the dark needles of cypresses. There
are some exceptionally pleasant restaurants. Climb the bridge and
you will see that you have reached the edge of the wide, flat,
fertile coastal plain which lies behind the crowded beaches of the
Costa Brava.

Mercifully, that is not where the path is going. From Besalú,
however, the GR1 does run all the way to Empúries, close to the
classical ruins on the coast at Empuriabrava. It will be an unusual
sort of walk, across a cultivated and populated coastal plain, and
one day I shall try it.

But in winter. Parts of the Costa Brava are beautiful, especially
the little bays further south, the six-mile sand beach at Pals where
my family have a flat, and the curiously blank hills around
Cadaqués, but the best time to visit is off-season, between late

August and late May. For let us make no bones about it. Catalunya made a disgraceful mistake towards the end of the last century in letting mass tourism trash her once-delicate coastline. The motive was profit and the results were brutal. Those pine-clad, rocky inlets and tiny fishing ports were a fragile patrimony and many of them have gone, passed beyond repair and remembered only by elderly Catalans and travellers who visited before the 1970s.

There are just a handful which have retained their ancient shape, and they tend to be year-round resorts where the better hotels and restaurants stay open all winter, and where the rich have kept development out: for, hidden away from its soulless and now rather dated package-holiday zones, the Costa Brava has always had its complement of mature villas and discerning visitors, though in the high summer you'll struggle to reach them. Large parts of the coast are simply swamped. The heat is sweltering and the traffic jams lead (should you reach your destination) only to parking congestion, and (should you manage to park) beach congestion, followed (if you can even get through the door) by restaurant congestion, followed by indigestion.

We often recommend friends to seize on a sunny winter weekend (the weather is stable), fly to Girona, and stay in one of the nicer places. S'Agaró is elegant and well kept, with some extraordinary colonial houses on the seaside path. Sant Feliu de Guíxols, Llafranc, Tamariu, Sa Tuna or Sa Riera have not lost their charm, and, a few miles inland (where the shore used to be), medieval, walled villages such as Pals and Peratallada are untouched by mass tourism.

The Roman and Greek ruins at Empuriabrava appeal even to non-ruin-bashing types like me. So does the food. The rugged dishes of the mountains around l'Avenc give way to delicate flavours: anchovies fresh off the boat in the harbour, lemons, squid, basil. It is no surprise that this coast contains what is said to be Europe's best, and certainly most creative restaurant, El Bullí. There is an energy and innovation here lacking in the hills not far inland.

But I like the hills. So for all the attractions and noise of the coast I would go north again, through the wild and beautiful lower foothills of the Pyrenees, heading for La Jonquera, by the frontier with France.

I have yet to explore these hills. They are remarkably empty and fairly dry, for the most part little-grazed, clad in Mediterranean evergreen oak, juniper and thyme, and crossed by few paths or tracks. There are almost no proper roads at all, and no paved ones. Here there will be deer, boar, wild goats and squirrels. The path, which along this section is a bridle-path too, crosses a series of ridges, each a little higher than the last; and it will be a warm day's walk to the Pantà de Boadella, a big lake with two long arms, behind a man-made barrage. From the ridges there will be clear views of the whole wall of the Pyrenees as it descends towards the sea.

Look out for Canigou, in France, over to the west and higher up the range: at some 9,000 feet it is not the highest peak in this part of the Pyrenees but it is indisputably the most majestic. Belinda and her husband have climbed Canigou in fog, completing the whole ascent and descent without ever being able to see where they were.

Her friend Maite has bought a small, abandoned 1920s hydro-electric power-station, a few miles from a small town called Darnius. The place used to supply the town of Figueres with power, and was finally shut down in 1960. It is situated in a most unexpected place: by an unpaved road through the woods where the lake begins. Maite and her husband, Miquel, have turned this into a pretty classy hotel with an excellent restaurant.

In April 2004 we all drove there – my family, that is, and friends – to celebrate my father's eighty-first birthday. The lunch lasted until night had fallen. With the river running by, the situation was tranquil, and the building itself is a folly, with a tower and turrets. The enormous pipe coming down from the mountains which used to carry water to the turbines runs almost into the dining room; and Maite has even retained the power-station's somewhat brutal name – La Central. She has built a swimming pool, spa and sauna for guests, of whom the more energetic arrive on foot along the GR2 on organized walking holidays; and some even on horseback, coming through the woods where Maite and Belinda go riding. They say (I am no horseman) that this is the ideal way to get through the relentless terrain and see the countryside fast.

One day I'll follow the path all the way up to La Jonquera – the next stop. There will be a big decision to make when the path reaches its end, near the ridge of the Pyrenees, in a gap in the mountains over which the coastal motorway from Barcelona to Perpignan and Marseilles passes.

Do I turn right and go east where the mountains slip down into the Mediterranean, meeting it near Cadaqués – or do I turn left and head west along the ridge as, en route for the Atlantic, the Pyrenean range climbs to its highest peak in Catalunya, the 10,500-foot Pica d'Estats (an easy ascent) and then (in Aragón) its very highest peak, Aneto (11,165 feet)?

Either way, east or west, I shall be on the GR11, one of Europe's great walking routes. This follows the ridge, sometimes right along the top, with French Catalunya to one side and Spanish Catalunya to the other (and you can see out almost, you feel, to infinity), and sometimes beneath it on the Spanish side.

The GR11 goes right to the edge of Catalunya and beyond. There are youth hostels along the way (I have stayed in a couple: simple, friendly, and with good homely hot food) and so no need for a tent – but no problem about camping for those who wish to. This is huge, open, unfenced country, with springs and streams wherever you look. The rule is that a one-night stop, from sunset to sunrise, is allowed almost anywhere.

How best to describe the Pyrenees? I love these mountains but struggle for words which capture their bare, crumbly and rocky magic.

If the Alps did not exist, the Pyrenees would be the best range in Europe, and every child's idea of what a mountain range should be. But the Alps are so spectacularly . . . well, *Alpine*: so steep, so high, so classic in their fairytale majesty, that the big, rugged 300-mile wall of the Pyrenees mountains has tended to be overlooked.

Yet they dominate. And separate. They dominate the histories, the wars, the peace treaties, the frontier-making and the cultures of the peoples who live around them. They have separated nation from nation. They have held back the Moors to the south, and to the north thwarted the French and discouraged the Nazis. From what is now France in the Middle Ages they have ushered Cathar refugees over their hidden passes in the night. It was not called France then; it was Catalunya – or Catalunya del Nord, as it is still known among the nostalgic, rather as Taiwanese conservatives call Beijing 'the bandits in temporary control of the mainland'.

These mountains have given ancient shape to the economics of the regions they separate. Their peaks and passes have defined the arteries of transport into the Iberian peninsula. In the hills and valleys and mountain fastnesses Franco could not reach, they have saved Catalan culture; and they have doomed the ambitions for modern statehood of Catalans and Basques straddling both sides of the range, condemning both peoples to homelands cut in two.

These are not high hills, they are real, grown-up mountains, more like the Rockies than the Pennines; but though they have their towering peaks and vertiginous faces of bald rock, they do not soar as the Alps do. Most peaks have a shoulder you can climb; most slopes, though they are relentless, are the kind you can cling to; and everywhere there are passes through to the other side or ways up to the tops of the ridges and down again, if you are prepared to scramble over crumbling granite. It has become almost a cliché among European historians to call the Pyrenees 'a wall' to the movement of peoples and armies, but we are not talking Hindu Kush here: the Pyrenees are the kind of wall you can clamber over. You cannot surge in a mob over the Pyrenees but you can scramble through in small groups with all your worldly goods in your knapsack.

When my family first settled in Catalunya and we would go walking in these mountains, it was not uncommon to see Franco's Guardia Civil in pairs and trios, combing the mountainsides for escaping 'enemies of the state'. Sometimes they came home with a catch, handcuffed and dejected. But mostly they didn't. Over a million passed this way during the ebbs and flows of Republican fortunes during the Spanish Civil War. If you know your way through – as in my patch of the Pyrenees I now do – then you can make it across to France in the dead of night.

Ask me for my overriding impression of the high Pyrenees and I would talk about exposure: a feeling of being a small dot on a bare hillside. Wide, open mountain flanks carpeted in short grass and small bright flowers, blue, mauve and yellow; gentian and juniper bushes; very few trees; patches of grey shale or exposed rock; pale, wet scree slopes; deer and wild goats breaking cover and leaping away; the strange, bird-like shriek of marmots among the rocks in the gorges below; the sound of cow-bells clanking far beneath you from the sharpening valleys which slope down from the summits; in summer merciless sunshine and a clear blue sky; in winter the same clear sky but pale, with all the peaks snow-clad and glistening white; a pair of chamois goats clattering away over the stones, and hawks and golden eagles hovering. Brown granite crumbling like fudge; the ecstatic song of the lark; pink azaleas native in June and the smell of a hillside of broom in flower – the smell of chocolate.

Abrupt blasts of wind hissing across the rocks, the whoosh of a vulture's wings, ants and lightning: more than anything, though, I would report a feeling of freedom to roam. The Alps can be claustrophobic. You can be trapped by the topography. The Pyrenees are different. There is always a way through. I cling to the illusion that if I took a big flask of water and filled all my pockets with Mars bars, nuts and raisins, then, carrying only a lightweight blanket I could walk from the Mediterranean to the Atlantic, keeping Spain to my left and France to my right, with only the sun and stars to guide me.

Much further west there is an epic national park called Aïguestortes (twisted waters) where one climbs on to a high shelf of land near the French border (to walk down into France would be a wonderful two-day hike), and here during one of the spectacular electric storms which roll around these mountaintops I have watched lightning strike a rock face and remove a whole slab in a burst of smoke and dust and falling rubble.

But my favourite walk is classically simple, and follows a long stretch of the GR11. It goes up to the top of the ridge, along it and down, and takes all day.

To start, we had to get to a place called Nuria. Nuria has a rather basic ski-station, a church and place of pilgrimage, a grey stone barracks of a hotel, and the top terminus of a most unlikely electrical funicular railway built in the 1930s and still served by some of the original wooden carriages manufactured in Switzerland by the Brown-Boveri company.

The line begins at Ribes de Freser, a pleasant riverside stop on the main road from Barcelona, goes over the Pyrenees by way of Ripoll and Puigcerda, Bourg Madame, Ax-les-Thermes, then down to Toulouse in France. The mountain-route international railway I described, running from Barcelona to Toulouse, goes this way too, stopping at Ribes de Freser before disappearing into the side of a mountain, to corkscrew up and out. This way it makes it up to the well-known ski-station of La Molina, before heading into France and through a monumental tunnel.

But if you get off at Ribes you can catch the little funicular to Nuria. It takes about an hour and the journey is stunning, running beside the tremendous rock flanks of the mountain, with cascades of mountain streams foaming into the gorge below. Nuria sits at more than 6,000 feet, in a wide bowl formed by arms of the high Pyrenees, along whose tops there is snow for most of the year. In winter Nuria too is deep in snow.

We wasted no time there, but set out along the banks of a river rushing down from the ridge. After a few clumps of stunted pine, we were on open mountainside, little blue trumpets of flowers almost iridescent at our feet. We reached the head of the valley and climbed the scree – there is a path – up to the ridge.

We were on the border. You could see France, almost, it seemed, to Toulouse. You could see Catalunya almost to Barcelona. You could see the coast. It was windy up there – we were just below 10,000 feet – and you could feel the altitude when you tried to run. We ate some chocolate and marvelled at the view.

Then we set out along the ridge. It was like walking on the ridge of a snaking roof. Below on the Spanish side there were pastures, quite dry, and ant-like cows whose bells we could just hear. It looked as though you could run all the way down to Barcelona. On the French side the landscape was darker, more wooded, with lakes and tarns. And all you had to do was keep to the ridge and walk east, towards the rising sun.

On the ridge, which undulated and wound its way between rotting, needly turrets of rock with names such as Pic del Gegant (Peak of the Giant), there was no water and the landscape up there looked more Martian than Earthly, scraped by snow with hardly any vegetation, and weird patches of red-coloured, grey and yellow shale – sometimes a whole mountainside. From here I was later to walk all the way down into France. There is a wonderful path to the little town of Mont Louis, passing a primitive but welcoming French youth hostel and then picking its way through a theatrical gorge which it crosses and recrosses on narrow iron bridges, and finally reaching what the French call the 'Little Yellow Railway' which runs from the coast up the French side of the mountains to Bourg Madame. I've come up that way too, and you can do it easily in two days.

This time we were not diverting to France. After a while the path swoops down a wide mountain flank past a stream and pastures, then over another ridge and plunges into a secret valley, thick with pine at the bottom, past screeching marmots, and into the village of Setcases. *Setcases* means 'seven houses' but this pleasant mountain resort village has grown. We ate *entrepans de pernil* (baguettes of country ham), drank a few beers, crossed the river, and carried on west.

You climb and climb, at first through pinewoods, but then out into the clear again, following the red and yellow paint markers for your path. After a couple of hours we were back in open pasture – occupied, to our surprise, by fat carthorse-style horses, left there to graze free in summer. Then the path wound itself on to a long, descending arm of a hill, and we staggered weary but content into the old stone village of Molló.

Turn left on a main road which passes below this town and you climb back over the top, past the frontier, and down into the

French town of Prats de Molló (*prat* means field in Catalan, and is a common surname with none of the English connotation). But turn left and you can hitch-hike, as we did, down into the old-established mountain town of Camprodòn with its famous, high, medieval stone bridge, its dark, narrow streets, its chocolate shops and its hotels.

Not so far to the west, quite close to Andorra, is the Pic d'Estats – and a more dramatic mountain (though not so high) called Pedraforca (Forked Rock) which does literally consist of a 2,000-foot-high rock, about a mile in circumference at its base, split vertically into two, like a couple of peach halves. Pedraforca can be seen for fifty miles: it is visible from the rock promontory above l'Avenc, about five minutes' scramble up from the house.

Andorra you can take or leave. By rights Catalans should love the tiny state because it is the only country in the world where Catalan is the national language; but to me, and to many Catalans, the place breathes greed. Andorra, which is a tax-haven, can best be described as an extent of wild, high and mostly uninhabited and trackless mountain, cut by one big valley filled with duty-free shops and the brass plates of businesses nominally registered in Andorra. This is Andorra la Vella, the capital and only town. At a glance you might characterize the principality as a monstrous supermarket stuck on to the edge of some ski-slopes.

A brochure I consulted recently advised that the main activity in Andorra, apart from skiing, was duty-free shopping. 'Perhaps the most interesting thing in the town,' it said, was the thermal baths. And that is true. They are extraordinary. The interior of the Caldea Spa is laid out *à la* Hanging Gardens of Babylon, with indoor–outdoor pools, fountains and waterfalls, saunas, hot-tubs, Turkish baths, hydrotherapy, sunbeds, massage room and even a grapefruit bath. It is all rather wonderful, but this and the duty-free shopping somehow jar not only with the beautiful Pyrenean backdrop, but with my boyhood idea of Andorra as a remote and tiny mountain country, and a stamp-collector's dream.

Still, let us not be harsh – though Catalans, embarrassed that the closest thing there is to a Catalan state looks like this, are

sometimes harsh. There are some wonderful small-scale
Romanesque churches and ecclesiastical treasures; and there is at
least one pretty little road up a side-valley and a range of fine
views so long as you stand with your back to Andorra la Vella.
Besides, the Catalan town of La Seu d'Urgell is only three miles
away, whose cathedral, with its thirteenth-century cloisters, is a
small wonder of the Catalan Pyrenees. Here our old friend Galcerán
Sacosta, working as a teenage trainee, will first have been spotted
as a potential bishop. Andorra was part of Urgell's diocese.

Sadly this is all far from the modern ethos of Andorra. Some
Spanish shysters actually register their cars in Andorra (there's always
something dodgy about that big 'AND' on the back of a BMW)
and the country's tax-haven status is an infernal nuisance to the
French and the Spanish governments (both make sporadic attempts
at subjecting departing motorists to customs checks, causing sudden,
unpredictable and horrendous queues) and no doubt both would
love to be rid of it; but Andorra's enduring if limited 600-year-old
independence can be ascribed to centuries of a kind of nervy
stand-off between its two big neighbours, each watching the alignment of their Pyrenean frontier with a wary eye, each alert for any
attempt at readjustment by the other side. Were Andorra to lose its
statehood, it would have to go one way or the other, so both have
preferred to accept the status quo. The quirkily enduring nature of
Andorra's statehood is nicely indicated by the titular 'co-princes'
which until recently history had bequeathed the principality as its
rulers: the Bishop of La Seu d'Urgell and the President of France.

About twelve miles further along the Pyrenees towards the
Mediterranean – and witness to this neurotic history – is what
must be one of the quirkiest border arrangements in history. Llívia
(pronounce it as if the second 'l' were a 'y': *lyeeve*-ya) is a minus-
cule Spanish enclave just a few miles into French territory, near
the border town of Puigcerda (pronounced *pooj-ser-dah*). It covers
less than six square miles and consists almost entirely of a town
of about 1,000 souls.

In Roman times Llívia mattered. In the Middle Ages there was
a castle – now in ruins. The community, though never much larger

than a big village or small town, was given city rights by the king.
They little knew how this was to shape Llívia's whole future.

In 1659 the Spanish–French border was realigned by the Treaty
of the Pyrenees. The lawyers got to work, and in 1660 a new and
consequent treaty established the exact frontier through this part
of the Pyrenees, called the Cerdagne ('hog country'). The treaty
established that half of the Cerdagne (in which Llívia was situated) was to go to France, including 'the 33 villages' in that sector.

Then the lawyers went into overdrive. Spain refused to hand over
Llívia, arguing that it was not a village but a city, and so could not
have been within the purview of the treaty. France was forced to
accept this, and markers (there are now forty-five) were put down,
indicating the shores of this Spanish islet in the French ocean. They
remain objects of hatred to some. Spain (probably mindful of the
impertinence of Llívia's existence) has forever distrusted French
intentions there. It all boiled up some years ago in a series of bizarre
disputes with a Clochemerle quality all their own.

Are you sitting comfortably? It's not too complicated as long
as you remember that the Spanish point of view is basically that
Llívia's apparent failure to touch Spanish territory at any point is
just an unfortunate mapmakers' oversight, best remedied by imagining a kind of metaphysical cord connecting the enclave up to
Spain, and passing invisibly through French space; while the French
point of view is basically that Llívia is a ludicrous untidiness, a
hangover from history, which *la France* mentally swept away long
ago, but cannot, for tiresome diplomatic reasons, actually remove
from the map.

A minor road (the D68) connects Llívia to the Spanish 'mainland'. This represents the metaphysical cord. The D68 is at one
point crossed by the larger French N20. Drivers on the N20
heading for Spain pass within sight of Llívia, over on a little hill
to the left. But in the last century it used to be forbidden for
foreigners on the N20 to execute a left turn on to the D68. Instead
– should you wish to visit Llívia – you had to enter Spain first,
go through passport control, then take the D68 all the way back
to Llívia, crossing the N20 rather than turning off it. This selective

Galcerán's original seal is kept at Vic Cathedral

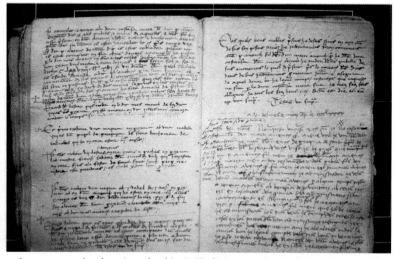

Inventory stored at the episcopal archive in Vic listing every item in l'Avenc in 1486 and mentioning its ruinous state due probably to the earthquakes of 1427

In the 1930s, everything, including a kitchen sink, was once in the state room

Posing for *The Times*

I was the first down the well

Deborah and I pushed
our way into the rotting
interior

The cracked ridge
beam: the roof was
propped from the
floor below

Belinda in the old bread oven

An internal arch was supported by a stone pillar after the 1427 earthquake

This Gothic door was built for a smaller race of men

Holiday cottages, before and after

An emergency
water tank arrives

Quim and his
helpers stand
proud (*right*), but
Christina (*above*) lets
the strain show

The sad room we stumbled upon thirty years ago, now restored, and cheered by Andrew Hubble's chandelier.

The Catalan Donkey is distinctively marked and twice the size of other donkeys. It is coming back from near-extinction

As minutes gave way to hours, we wormed, splashed, clambered and stumbled our way onward through the cave . . .

The house changed with the seasons; but its majesty and tranquillity remain the same

prohibition on a traffic manoeuvre must be the only case in legal history of a nationality-dependent clause in a highway code.

In the 1970s, arguing (which was true) that 'their' road, the N20, carried more and faster traffic than the Spanish-controlled D68, the French traffic authorities gave right-of-way to the N20, installing Stop signs on the D68 (which, being in France, was after all a French road). Thus was Llívia's umbilical connection to the Spanish motherland cut by a requirement to give way – and to French drivers!

The Spanish were outraged. They considered the Stop signs a breach of their right to a direct and unfettered link between Llívia and Spain. The French replied that to give a minor road precedence over a major one represented a traffic hazard. The D68 was not a *cordon sanitaire*, they argued, and along it the French writ should run.

There was a stand-off. In the night, Spanish irregulars would execute commando-style raids into France, uprooting and removing the road signs. Patriotic Frenchmen responded by lightning strikes on the forty-five markers delineating the enclave. The French local press dubbed it '*La Guerre des Stops*'. To misquote Maréchal Bosquet's remark on the Charge of the Light Brigade, '*C'était la guerre, mais ce n'était pas magnifique.*'

A truce was agreed. A viaduct was built with Spanish public funds, on French territory, taking the D68 over the N20.

Then in 2001 a similar dispute boiled over, this one involving a less important crossing, with the D30, which arguably also 'interrupted' the D68. This time cooler heads prevailed and a compromise was reached – an arrangement which didn't absolutely require any Spaniard to stop on the journey to Llívia, though he or she would have to slow down. A roundabout.

Lest you suppose that in a new millennium anyone on either side of this dispute is growing up, I must now report another row. In the original haggle about Llívia's status, the Spanish had agreed to cut the town loose, as it were, with no territorial cordon, in exchange for ownership of a large area of French property around a nearby lake, which stockaded Llívians were to be able to use for grazing and forestry. In 1831, however, after a series of court battles, they lost the land to the east of the lake. But they kept the land to the west.

Then, not many years ago, in an act of monstrous audacity, the French built a hotel on it, l'Hotel Bones Hores (good, or perhaps happy, hours, in Catalan). The name might be Catalan but this was a French-owned hotel. There followed a huge battle in civil litigation. The upshot is that the hotel is to revert to Llívian property (but on French territory — are you still following me?) in 2030.

We should all be there to celebrate.

13. A Chandelier

We have been lucky in the tradesmen who have helped us turn our plans for l'Avenc into reality. It is true that work was almost always slower than we hoped or planned. Spain's fondness for an enormous holiday throughout August did not make things easier, especially because during winter months the claypit into which the rain turned the whole site seriously hampered progress every year. That did not leave a lot of time for building.

August has often been maddening: you simply cannot find anyone to do anything. But almost all the labourers and craftsmen we have employed on the project, or who have worked there under Joan Sarsanedas's direction, have been honest and conscientious, and we have found carpenters and stonemasons whose skills are rare these days. Some have shown a touch of genius.

Books about the experiences of English people building or renovating abroad tend to be sprinkled with hilarious accounts of the eccentricity, duplicity, unreliability or sheer incompetence of local tradesmen, and if that had been our experience it would have been amusing to record it. But we grew to like the people who worked for us at l'Avenc, and to value their work.

As a work-site this was a terrific place to be in. Catalans are no less conscious than their visitors of the beauty of their surroundings – perhaps rather more so than some of the world's labourers – and the stonemasons, joiners, plumbers and wallers who have toiled in sun, rain, snow, mud and dust at l'Avenc always seemed to appreciate its spectacular situation. More than that, they often shared our pride in the project itself. There has been a sense of rescue about it; and the place we have been rescuing has struck everyone working there as worth our efforts. All are touched by a sense of privilege to be there.

At first none of the workmen on the site was directly employed by us. Joan Sarsanedas brought his own men; and skilled workers such as the carpenter Josep Pujol, who made all our windows to Joan's design (a challenging job because we wanted the frames to be virtually invisible from the outside), and Pep Solà, our intrepid plumber, were self-employed. Pep would arrive as on a storm, plumb like a tornado for a couple of action-packed hours, and sweep away again.

As the work proceeded and we became more confident ourselves as site-managers, it made sense to retain a couple of workers whom we knew and trusted and who enjoyed working at l'Avenc, as our full-time building staff. Deborah's co-worker Desi loved helping housekeep there. Jordi Ballana, born in a local farmhouse, looked like Hagrid from a Harry Potter story and was ace at driving Quim's digger: considered, deft, the opposite of rash. Jordi was a quiet man with a dry sense of humour, a peaceful presence at l'Avenc. He never missed a day.

One of Quim's family business employees who helped us regularly with the building, Ramon, was a different sort. Resourceful and determined, he could be relied upon to arrive at the crack of dawn – he loves the sunrise – and push any job through to its finish. He was stone-deaf as a child, and became the first person in Catalunya to use a computerized hearing-aid, inserted into his head like a bionic man. He was charmingly intent on learning English. To watch Ramon at work lifting and carrying, fixing and shelving, you would not think that in 1982 he won second prize in the Paris tango championships.

The chap who did all our stone walling and facing – a dogged, solitary job – was the youngest of our workforce, Abel. Once, when we had a vast sofa to lift up to the top floor, Abel took one end and three men, including me, took the other. Lifting rocks does that for you.

Sometimes, workmen past or present have asked if during their holidays or rest days they could bring their families or friends to show them the great project in which they were involved. It is touching when this happens. A feeling has grown that l'Avenc is more than a private house which we are doing up for our private pleasure, but the property too of everyone in the locality – part of the heritage of the Collsacabra.

This sense of a shared ambition was not a marketing exercise devised by us to neutralize possible envy or hostility in the surrounding area. It has not originated with us at all. It has been communicated to us through the interest and pride that those who visit on business or as sightseers seem to feel. At first we thought it rather a presumption. At first we were sometimes irritated by the way people who had no connection with l'Avenc and were not paying for its restoration would talk in a familiar tone as though the place were somehow common property ('our' patrimony as local people). But quickly we began to feel pleased and complimented by the familiarity.

As a *Times* and *Spectator* columnist I encountered something similar. Right at the start, just after we had bought the house and short of a subject for my fortnightly *Spectator* column, I described the winter's night we spent there which I thought might be of passing interest to readers – but that was all.

I was surprised at the response. Dozens wrote to me to ask more about l'Avenc. A little later my editors at *The Times* asked if I would write something on the project for the paper's Weekend supplement. A family friend and professional photographer, Mercè Terricabras, drove up from Olot and took some pictures and I gave these to the paper too. Again the response from readers was enthusiastic.

Thereafter I would write the occasional column or diary about l'Avenc – rarely more than about one every year – and find readers tremendously inquisitive and encouraging. There I was, a writer who liked to consider himself a serious commentator on politics and world affairs, delivering weighty columns every week on war, peace and the future of the world – and whenever I went out to supper people would ask, not 'What are Tony Blair's chances at the next election, do you think?' or 'How confident are you of your fascinating analysis of Shi'ite intentions in the new Iraq?', but 'How's l'Avenc doing? Have you got your water supply back yet?'

It happened once that more than a year had passed without my taking up the story again. Readers began writing to ask if all was

well – or had we given up at l'Avenc? They were concerned that
they had heard nothing. They wanted to encourage me. I did feel
encouraged. They felt somehow part of the project, having followed
it in the paper, and some asked if I could write a monthly column
about it. Instead I decided to write a book one day.

But before I could begin, I always knew the job ahead was
colossal. Rescuing and reinstating the interior would prove a long
campaign on all fronts. The problem was that we could not start
from scratch, which would have been so much cheaper and simpler;
nor did we want to. In bits and pieces, what we wanted to keep
was already there, and these precious bits and pieces we had to
cherish and restore, while renewing, chopping away, shoring up
and slotting in, all around the ancient core.

And this – curiously – was an intellectual challenge as well as
a physical and financial one. Before putting in a new floor you
needed to decide where the electrical conduits and the plumbing were to go and how to take account of them; and before
deciding on the plumbing and electricity you needed to think
where the lights, switches and loos were needed; and before you
decided on that you needed an overall plan for the layout of parti-
tions, doors and walls; and how could you plan the layout when
we still awaited planning permission for the new septic tank and
soakaway system?

The tank, a thirty-foot resin-built, livid yellow-enamelled
monster (we called it the Yellow Submarine), had already arrived
and was sitting in the yard outside, shimmering balefully like some
great beached cross between a whale and a mutant banana while
we puzzled: assuming that permission finally came through, should
we have dual-plumbing so we could use run-off rainwater and
recirculated waste-water for a non-potable supply – and how could
we decide on that until we knew how short of water the property might be, depending on whether we ever got our water back
from Casals, which was up to the court, whose decision we had
but from whom we still awaited judicial execution?

And how could we finalize the liquid-gas water-heating and possibly central-heating system until we knew how much electricity we

would be able to generate? The gas tanks had already arrived and awaited burial, sitting by the well like two twenty-foot black torpedoes and (with the Iraq war looming) in imminent danger of being bombed by the Americans as suspected weapons of mass destruction.

And if we were indeed to have a water-circulated central-heating system and dual-plumbing system, hadn't we just finished and nailed down the new floor without having put the necessary pipes in? And who's that knocking at the door? The man who was going to dig the trench up the hill to bury the cable from the wind-turbine, for which permission hasn't yet been granted, to the domestic electrical system whose design still awaits our concluding plans for the gas, whose tanks were rusting in the yard.

Perhaps men and women whose business it is to plan great construction projects – professional people who know about flow-charts and critical-path diagrams and just-in-time deliveries and the planning of cash-flow – will read this book and snort. Welcome, they will laugh, to the world of construction. Does Mr Parris suppose that it is any different for anyone else who must plan a project in which different things have to be ready at different times, some waiting upon others before they can be started? Building a house, they will say, is an inherently complex business; building or rebuilding any house is. The Parrises and the Abeys had builders: so what is this fellow huffing and puffing about?

I am not complaining, only trying to convey how dispiriting sheer complexity and the tangle of missed deadlines can be, especially to amateurs who have bitten off almost more than they can chew.

Many of the challenges we faced and the problems which tormented us were – it's true – of a kind which anyone who tries to rescue a large and ancient building will face. But one or two were avoidable and with hindsight should have been handled differently. An English friend, Andrew Hubble, had fallen in love with l'Avenc from the start and had become increasingly engaged in planning and installing the power circuitry. He would wail good-humouredly that specifications kept changing. This was a problem which we had to acknowledge had dogged us at many turns: the avoiding or delaying of key decisions meant that work was sometimes done which later had to be undone.

A stonemason would be chiselling away in one corner while a plumber soldered copper fittings in another, both blithely unaware that the consequence was a PVC waste-pipe heading ultimately for a piece of stone which hadn't been in the plans when the plumber started. An electrician would be laboriously chasing conduitry through cement rendering and plaster which, had the builder and the plasterer spoken to the electrician before he plastered, could have waited. At one point the power cables from the solar panels up on the hill had just been buried and connected when a new piece of bulldozing commenced behind the house, ripping through the cables.

Andrew, a bright-eyed, soft-spoken, super-civil and super-conscientious chap, but meticulous to a degree which could make working in the chaos that was sometimes l'Avenc a nightmare, longed for a set of clear and final plans. With his partner, Steven Preston, he had invested a modest sum in the project: a drop in the ocean but a heartening vote of confidence; and as Ryanair flights from Stansted and East Midlands to Girona grew steadily cheaper, Andrew, who was self-employed, found himself volunteering more and more often to fly over for weeks at a time. He got on well with the Catalan tradesmen and labourers working on the site and steadily assumed the role of electrical power consultant. He is a careful – sometimes too careful I, one of nature's bodgers, would occasionally complain – but indefatigable worker and his only vice is electrical goods showrooms, where he will stare at light-fittings for hours on end, like a rabbit at a snake, until gently led to a place of safety.

Andrew was involved from the start in designing and developing the 'green' system of power generation I wanted for l'Avenc. He remains probably the only man who wholly understands all its elements and how they fit together. This may explain his haunted look.

Early in this book I described my horror of pylons, poles and overhead wires; and my ambition that l'Avenc should stand, as it did when I found it and as it always had: alone and untangled on the mountainside, wired to nowhere. None of us wanted to see a line of the over-engineered steel or concrete poles they use in Spain, strung out along the clifftops.

It was from this that our plans for a self-sufficient power supply grew. In time the technical challenge of achieving this for what was becoming a hamlet of dwellings began to interest and animate us as a project in its own right, so that we sometimes almost forgot that it had never been our intention to sponsor a significant experiment in autonomy of supply, along environmentally friendly lines, for a complex of buildings. We just wanted electricity.

Our original idea had simply been to manage without poles. As we waded deeper and deeper into the technical complications (and the expense) of pioneering a very substantial green energy system – and in the end waded so deep that it would have been a shame and a waste to draw back – we swung between enthusiasm and frustration (and even, sometimes, despair). We had entered the field quite early in its development in Europe; our experience, our successes, failures and costs would be among the early experiences of an industry which would one day be available more widely and cheaply.

It is lucky we saw it that way. Maybe we were just making the best of a tricky situation. Because in retrospect the easier and cheaper way of achieving the aim with which I started would have been to dig a big, long, deep trench for the couple of miles to Tavertet, and pay to be connected up in the village to the Red Eléctrica de España, the national grid. In the end we had to dig a trench anyway – for the emergency water pipe.

I think my brother-in-law would have preferred this. My evangelism for autonomous power never really inhabited him, but he became as engaged as anyone else – being on-site and directing operations he had to be – in the technical challenge. He developed ideas of his own to take mine forward, with one of the most exciting of which, 'co-generation', we are still wrestling as I write.

Madcap or not, by 2005 we were getting there. I sense your eyes glazing over. To the layman a description of electrical circuitry may have the power to send a person to sleep. But believe me, to us at l'Avenc that kind of thing has had us sitting bolt upright in bed, sleepless into the small hours, wondering how it could all be juggled. We have eaten and drunk, lived and breathed the discourse of wiring these last seven years

More than anyone else Andrew Hubble, assisted by Pep and Albert, has pulled together our planning and kept a supervisory eye on the work whenever he visited. He was forever trying to ban the more power-hungry of Quim's toys, fighting a vigorous but at times losing battle on many fronts, against hair-dryers, dish-washers, tungsten light-bulbs and electric ovens.

Behind it all lay the simple idea that we generate, store and distribute our own power. We aimed to rely on the sun and the wind. So in place on the hill surrounded by box bushes is an array of photovoltaic cells, a great, silver slab of circuitry that is now our main source of power and which we have done our best to protect from the curious noses and hooves of local cattle. My brother Mark's ponies carried up hundreds of buckets of wet cement to fix the panels in place, and the cable is safely buried in a 3-foot-deep trench up a 45-degree slope hacked into the soil by Peter, a West African refugee. It keeps the lights on. But our ambitions for l'Avenc require more power than the sun can ever provide. So our hopes lie in a 10-kilowatt wind turbine and charger. As I write this it is still in kit form at the bottom of the hill, awaiting planning permission. But how could we build it without getting the machinery up to the top of the hill, which would need a large helicopter, which might or might not be available after Catalunya's summer firefighting helicopter fleet was stood down in autumn? The turbine's diameter is about twenty-five feet, and the supporting steel pillar is about fifty feet. On top of the hill this will look smaller than it sounds, but it will be conspicuous. I admit it – for all my adversion to poles and pylons, we will end up erecting one. But only one.

Until we do, most of our power has come from a large diesel generator. This red monster is second-hand, bought from the village of Tavertet, whose power supply it used to support. Its reassuring thump and its less-than-reassuring fuel consumption have been our constant companions at l'Avenc for four years now.

From these different sources power is sent into the basement of the house, where it is stored in a lead-acid battery system.

That description does not do justice to the majesty (or horror, depending on your perspective) of the battery room: a chamber about the size of a generous bedroom, almost filled with what to the casual observer looks like enough car batteries, neatly stacked, to kick-start the entire field of the Monte Carlo car rally. This is our reservoir of power, sufficient to keep the lights on in the winter and at night when the photovoltaic cells, which provide a continuous supply during daylight hours, stop.

My brother-in-law, as ever, is not content with this small-scale system. He will soon buy what is known as a co-generator, a gas engine, in other words, which drives an alternator to produce electrical power, but instead of dissipating heat into the atmosphere provides hot water for the domestic supply.

In theory, a co-generator is a cleaner and leaner means of generating power than an old-fashioned diesel engine, and should be able to replace it. But 'in theory' is the operative phrase. The development of this technology for medium-sized applications like l'Avenc is still at a relatively early stage. Were we a small town or hospital, or (at the other end of the scale) a single dwelling in the Outer Hebrides, we would have found products better suited to our needs.

Electricity means light; light is beautiful, but it also transforms. By the end of 2004 the first stage of our power system was in place and so were the switches and spotlights and cables we needed but which ensured that l'Avenc would never again be seen in its pure, untouched medieval aspect.

In installing the trappings of the modern world, however, I wanted our work to be in keeping with the spirit of the place. The scale and the proportions of the state room at l'Avenc called out for a chandelier. Yet a remote and fortified rural mansion in the mountains, whose great days had been in the Dark and Middle Ages and whose final flowering had been in the sixteenth century, wanted nothing to do with 'elegance' or the refined and delicate good taste of later centuries. This was no château or stately home: not a house where the minuet would have echoed down the corridors, or porcelain graced the shelves or velvet the curtains. The spirit of the house was solid: stone and wood, not silk and crystal.

Rural Derbyshire in England where I live shares with rural Catalunya a sort of fortitude of artistic spirit. In the small town of Tideswell Andrew knew a designer in ironwork who worked in quite muscular designs, befitting a tradition of the plough and barrel, of labour and harvest, of beam and ironwork, such as was l'Avenc's.

We asked him to take one of the small chandeliers he made, and magnify it into a grand chandelier: bold and heavy in black iron. The result was huge. It was as tall as a man, as wide as an armchair and as heavy as a motorbike. The next challenge was to get it from Tideswell to Catalunya. But I have a Vauxhall pickup truck, and our Tideswell chandelier fitted easily into the back.

Too easily, really. It seemed a waste not to take something else. On a cruise down the Thames in 2003 from Tower Hill to Clacton-on-Sea, on the world's last ocean-going paddle-steamer, the *Waverley*, I had in a moment of madness purchased the ship's diesel generator and dynamo. The weather and the ship's bar were to blame. It had rained in sheets from the moment of embarkation until our arrival at Southend Pier, and so heavy was the rain that it had been impossible even to discern the banks of the Thames to either side.

My friends and I had resorted to the bar. After several whiskies I took a turn around the ship. It was possible to inspect her engines. Here I saw that, after a refit, her original dynamo, post-First-World-War, and the 1940s Perkins diesel generator which had been the last to drive it, were for sale for a few hundred pounds. I love old machines.

I don't know what possessed me, but I bought both, landing myself with a drive to Glasgow to collect them later from the ship's Clydeside workshop. They were extremely heavy – not far short of a ton between them. But, chocked up with logs and strapped down to stop them rolling around, and crowned with the magnificent Tideswell chandelier, they set out for France and then the Spanish border, with Julian and me at the Vauxhall's wheel. We looked like travelling scrap-metal merchants. Miraculously we were not stopped by the police or customs at the border.

Perhaps the whole expedition sounds crazy to you. It seemed crazy to us. I wished I'd never bought the generator and dynamo in the first place. The arrival of Quim in his digger, bucket waving in the air like some huge stick-insect's feelers, to unload the iron-ware from the back of my truck, completed the farce. But the digger did the trick; the chandelier fitted (just) through the window; and the generator and dynamo were unloaded without damage. I shall not forget the moment we finally hoisted the chandelier into position in the state room, and stood back nervously to see how it looked.

The light makes that room, and for hundreds of years, I hope, will be its centrepiece. And best of all (from Andrew's point of view) it carries low-wattage light-bulbs, twelve of them. It is, as I said to him, a festival of energy efficiency.

As for the generator and dynamo, we knew a man in Cantonigròs who restores old engines. We are to install the two machines in a special room down among the batteries and generators, for use in emergencies, and as a sort of exhibit in the history of electricity generation. For both generator and dynamo, it had been a long journey from the world's last ocean-going paddle-steamer to a fortified medieval mansion in Catalunya.

14. A Dog's Life

Once, not so long ago, donkeys and mules would have been tethered outside l'Avenc's arched front door, for transport to Tavertet, Rupit, Olot and Vic. Useful for ploughing, they would have worked the fields too.

Mated with the mares of horses, the *Guarà Català* donkeys produced the biggest, strongest and most useful mule in the world, which Catalans call the *matxo* (pronounced as in the Machu of Machu Picchu). Native to Catalunya, and an animal for which the country used to be more famous than today, the *guarà* is a beautiful creature, strong, noble and hard-working, which for many centuries was the backbone of rural transport right across the region.

These donkeys are most strikingly distinguished from your common-or-garden *burro* or seaside donkey by their size. They are as big as a small horse, and half as powerful again as a regular donkey. In l'Avenc's heyday as a growing house in the Middle Ages, these would have been the most common pack-animals in the carriage of goods and people to and from the valley beneath and down on to the plains of Vic and Olot. They would have passed along the track below the house in a regular traffic. They would have carried from the *alzina* forests down in the Guilleries the huge cargo of charcoal which was one of the region's principal exports – bound for as far afield as Toledo and later Madrid, where throughout Spanish history the shortage of a local supply of fuel had dogged development.

It was only towards the middle of the last century, when the internal-combustion engine began (later in Spain than elsewhere on the continent) to make great inroads into transport and agriculture, and tractors, lorries and automobiles were gradually taking the place of animals, that this creature fell from prominence and use.

In the 1950s, as thousands became redundant in Catalunya, some

50,000 *guaràs* were exported by sea to the Indian subcontinent, for use in post-colonial India's new army.

Some remain in Catalunya; near Tavertet there are enthusiastic and expert breeders and growing interest in the breed. I hope to see them at l'Avenc again – though with our luck they will probably destroy all the young trees.

They will not be the only animals to make the house their own. Tom and Jerry, our two dogs, were brothers, part of a litter from Belinda's Alsatian bitch called Lluna and a roving Catalan sheepdog who belonged to Joan Sarsanedas. So in their origins – by the owner's bitch, out of the master builder's dog – Tom and Jerry were l'Avenc's from the start. If a monument should ever be raised to the small band of dependables who made the whole thing possible, Tom and Jerry's names should be right up there with the other heroes. Tom was dark with a tan bib, and Jerry was light tan all over.

At first they were sent to be friends and guardians to my father and mother. My parents loved both brothers, and the dogs loved them: faithful companions, calm, steady and clever. But sadly there was an exception to their placidity: the very sight and smell of sheep seemed to stir in them some inbuilt breed-memory inherited from their Catalan sheepdog father. Sheep fascinated them. Without proper training, though, the instinct misfired and they started chasing rather than herding. My parents could not control this, and when finally a neighbour's sheep perished it was decided with sorrow that Tom and Jerry must be put down.

Then came a lucky escape. Quim's family enterprise had acquired a business in Girona surrounded by a large, fenced outdoor compound. Guard dogs were needed, especially for the hours of darkness. Tom and Jerry's death sentence was commuted to life imprisonment, and they departed dolefully in the Toyota for their new and circumscribed life down on the plain.

But they took to it. They barked well at night, and by day made friends with the watchmen and all the staff. Tom and Jerry became popular dogs, and their behaviour was impeccable. Maybe they sensed they were on probation.

Then came parole. As the store of plant and equipment at l'Avenc began to grow, we needed to think harder about security. Later, Belinda and her husband started staying often in the janitor's cottage, but at first we were leaving the whole place – effectively unlockable – unguarded at night. Rather to my surprise, nothing was ever stolen, until one night a little portable generator, bought by my mother as a present for l'Avenc, disappeared. Our thoughts turned to the possibility of getting a guard dog. Well, what about Tom and Jerry?

Thus was a life sentence in Girona commuted to early release for good behaviour. At l'Avenc, which was unfenced, they could roam free. They were warned that if there was another sheep-chasing incident it would be curtains for both of them, but sheep are not kept in those pastures and the cows were more than a match for any dog. Indeed we would have been happier if the pair had adopted a more aggressive attitude to those fierce beasts, who seemed more wildebeeste than cow, and wanted the house for shade and as a place to trample over builders' supplies and pee in bucketloads over the sand and cement.

Tom and Jerry's copybook was never blotted again. There was (it is true) an unexplained incident in which one of our much-loved cats, living in the janitor's cottage, was found lifeless and slightly chewed, but our two dogs' pleading and innocent gaze convinced us that they had had nothing to do with it. From 1999 onwards, l'Avenc was never deserted. Tom and Jerry had moved in.

They loved it there, and we loved them being there. At night they stayed within the main house, barking from the balcony; and by day they were allowed out. Every afternoon their owners would arrive to feed them their daily ration of dogmeat and biscuits; and (when there) the duty fell sometimes to me.

I grew ever fonder of the pair. Though inseparable, they had sharply different personalities. Tom (the dark one) was always the leader; Jerry followed. Tom was more confident, Jerry more careful. They ranged freely all over the hills and pastures around l'Avenc, but always returned home to the house in the evenings. Neither was happy when separated from the other, and neither ever ventured out alone.

The pair did a kind of dance together, which they perfected over the years. This would begin with mock-snarling and wrinkling of the upper lip, after which, beautifully synchronized, they would rear up on their hind legs and box each other with their front paws, like hares. Finally, standing on their hind legs, they would lock front legs and close their jaws alternately over each other's throat, growling deeply, but never actually biting or drawing blood.

It was staged. It was amicable. But for those unfamiliar with the routine it was terrifying to behold. Tom and Jerry liked to begin their fight-dance when a car full of strangers arrived, or hikers passed in front of the house; they never played like this when they were alone with us. It was as if this was a kind of display, calculated to impress upon any visitor their terrible fearsomeness and wrath: a sort of animated 'Beware of the Dog' tableau. Some visitors were too scared even to get out of their cars and would watch, frightened faces pressed to their windows, as Tom and Jerry performed.

And how I wish you could have heard them sing.

It has to be true about wolves and full moons because as the moon waxed, Tom and Jerry's nightly howling sessions grew in volume and passion. This happened most often if you let them out after dark, though sometimes, locked in, if the moon was visible from the balcony, they would sing from there. They would stand close to each other, facing the moon. Tom would begin to howl. Jerry would join in. For a while both would howl in a kind of point and counterpoint with each other. Then, while one continued howling, the other would launch into a descant: a high-pitched *yip-yip* belted out rhythmically on one note, while the deeper-pitched howling rose and fell beneath it.

'Listen to the children of the night, what music they make,' cried Bela Lugosi playing Count Dracula in the 1931 movie. Listening to Tom and Jerry you knew just what the Count meant. It was night. The moon was full. It was their time.

Tom and Jerry were by now the oldest permanent residents at

l'Avenc by a long chalk, and I noticed that on our walks (Julian and I would wander the hills with them, seldom seeing them from one valley to the next as they zigzagged the countryside, sniffing everything in sight) they did not tear around quite as fast or as far as they had used to do; and that Tom's black muzzle was now peppered with rather distinguished little flecks of grey.

Then in 2004 he died. It had for years been his habit to run at the wheels of cars, barking madly – but nimbly steering just clear of falling under them. Perhaps his nimbleness was beginning to fade, or perhaps he just slipped, but Tom went under the wheels of a car driven by one of our friends from Tavertet, a splendid person whose pleasure and kindness it was to drive over whenever we had large numbers at the house, and bake delicious pizzas in the large and ancient wood-fired bread oven in the kitchen.

It was not her fault, and we all felt sorry for her. If our dog had not run under her wheels then sooner or later he would have run under somebody else's. Which particular set of wheels destiny invites us to run under – those of us whose habit is to bark at other people's wheels – is immaterial.

Poor Belinda was miserable for days. But Tom had been ten years old, and, given the rollercoaster ride on which fate had carried him, he had lived a happy and lucky life.

When it comes to animals though, some of my family would go much further. Indeed they have. When my mother decided to close her school of English in Manlleu, she used part of the proceeds of the sale to commission a local sculptor, Salvi Aulet, to carve for l'Avenc a statue of the patron saint of animals.

Neither she nor he had a very clear idea at the outset what, once he laid down his chisels, the result would look like. It was beautiful. He carved in a golden-coloured wood a figure, about half-size, of the saint with small animals around his feet. It was at once clear where it should go: in the big hall on the ground floor, into which the arched doors open and where there was once (and still is, in the ancient farmhouse, Corcó, in Manlleu, where my brother-in-law Manel's parents, Isabel and Josep, live) a stone dismounting-block for horsemen.

The wall you face as you enter, by the stone stairway up into the house, has an empty alcove. It was just the right height – high above our heads, for this is a lofty hall – and wide enough too: as though made for the carving. We placed my mother's gift there and admired the result. I hope St Francis will stand in his place at l'Avenc for ever.

His influence has already been felt. While l'Avenc was progressing, my sister Deborah and her husband, Manel, were overtaken by a kind of mid-life conversion to the animal-rights movement. Of all the things to take on in Spain, opposing bullfighting must be one of the most quixotic. But they decided, bravely, to do it – and have met with success.

It began with their reputation for taking in and caring for abandoned dogs and cats. You would rarely see Deborah without some new waif or stray, or tending to a bedraggled pooch with one or more limbs in a bandage. Almost all her family's own dogs appeared to have been found on rubbish dumps, and whenever anyone raised the possibility of obtaining a pet from anywhere other than a municipal tip she would lecture them severely on their irresponsibility.

Famous as Debs and Manel's family's animal rescue work was becoming, however, what came next took us all by surprise. Manel announced that he was running for the Spanish Senate. At first I thought he was joking – or that it was a wild idea which in the cold light of day would soon be dropped. But no, this was his firm intention and he stuck to it. The election was due in March 2004 and Manel's name had gone forward. His party, PACMA – the Partit Antitaurí Contra el Maltractament Animal (Anti-bullfighting party against cruelty to animals) – were running a national slate of seventeen candidates for the Senate, and Manel was standing for the province of Barcelona.

Extraordinary as this seemed, there was method in Manel's madness. He had not experienced a sudden rush of blood to the head and decided to take a serious crack at becoming a senator. He knew he had no chance of winning. He did not even want to be a senator. 'The gardening and the trees do not leave me

with enough spare time for the Senate,' he pointed out. His was
a token candidature, and a way of promoting his and Debs's great
cause: the abolition of bullfighting.

Manel's family had become deeply involved in the anti-
bullfighting cause after a group of inhabitants of Manlleu had
started a campaign to get a bullring built in the town. To all my
family, including me, there was something provocative about the
idea of spreading bullfighting to places where it had not been the
custom. I was more open than my two sisters to the thought that
where bullfighting is already a local tradition there is a case for
not interfering; but their reaction to the proposal to build a new
bullring – in the twenty-first century – and reintroduce an enter-
tainment that had long fallen out of favour was the same as mine
would have been: strong distaste.

By no means was this a matter of a brood of interfering English
expatriate busybodies trying to spoil the simple pleasures of local
folk. A section of the Manlleu community (including many whose
families had migrated there from Andalucia and the poorer parts
of southern Spain) undoubtedly did support the bullring proposal;
but large numbers of townspeople in Manlleu felt just as my
siblings did. Manel, whose family's roots in Manlleu were long-
established, believed, if anything even more strongly than much of
my own family, that the proposal must be stopped.

For her pains, Belinda was dubbed 'Queen Victoria' on the radio
by Albert Boadella, her co-debater: the fierce, brilliant and subver-
sive director of the *Joglars* theatrical troupe who confused everybody
by embracing the anti-Francoist, neo-anarchist, anti-traditionalist, pro-
bullfighting tendency, of which he was possibly the sole member.

As I write, the proposal for a bullring in Manlleu is in abeyance.
But for Manel and Deborah, supported by her sister, this had been
only the beginning. Their hope is to carry the fight into the heart
of bullfighting Spain.

The prospect may not be fanciful, for Manel's first campaign
went astonishingly well. He went down to Barcelona to give a
speech in the Plaça Catalunya, which was a bit like mounting a
soapbox in Trafalgar Square. Though a studious and crusading

character with encyclopaedic knowledge on a range of unlikely things – an ideal *Mastermind* contestant – Manel was a farmer, with no experience of political campaigning or speechmaking. We all thought it was brave of him. Deborah and their children went down to Barcelona to support him in his campaigning speech. And that, we thought, would be the limit of it: a bit of publicity, a token campaign – and in the end only a handful of votes.

Not so. In the elections to the Senate, Manel received 23,000 votes. This did not make him a senator, but it gave his candidature and his cause a surprise boost. Animal-rights issues – and in particular the bullfighting question – had more resonance among the ordinary voters in Barcelona province than most of us had imagined. It was followed by a decision by the Barcelona city council to designate the city an anti-bullfighting zone, a decision which (like the 'Nuclear-Free Zones' which left-wing councils in Britain used to create) was only declaratory because the council has no power to ban bullfighting, and it continues. But the bullring in Girona is to be demolished: a sign of shifting opinion in Spain, which (it might surprise readers of popular newspapers in Britain) is by a clear margin opposed to the sport nationally, and opposed by a larger margin in Catalunya. Now Lloret de Mar on the Costa Brava has followed Girona.

If anyone had hoped that after Manel's triumphant senatorial campaign the animal-rights elements in my family would rest on their laurels, they were mistaken. Later that year, in the depths of winter, Adam e-mailed me with disturbing news. 'Did you know that Deborah and Manel are in Barcelona? There is an anti-fur-trapping demonstration in the Plaça Catalunya. Hundreds of people are going to take their clothes off and lie naked on the steps, and Deborah' (my heart sank) 'will be one of them.'

The idea, apparently, was to offer onlookers a vivid and memorable demonstration of what it would be like to be skinned. There seemed to me to be various logical problems with the parallels implied, but there is never any point in arguing with Debs once her mind is settled upon a proposition. 'Wish her good luck,' I said.

When the day of the protest dawned, Barcelona was in the

middle of a cold snap. Temperatures hovered around zero. There exists in the media archive a range of press and television pictures of a huddled mass of very cold bodies draped over the stone in the Plaça Catalunya. Photographs were published as far afield as Ecuador. Among the blue-tinged and wobbling buttocks on display, my sister's is one – or rather two.

Later I spoke to her about Spain's 2005 referendum on whether to accept the proposed new European constitution. How would she, an enthusiastic pro-European, be voting, I asked. 'No,' she said. 'Manel and I will both be voting "No", because the draft constitution mentions human rights but has no section on animal rights.'

Some in my family would be happy if l'Avenc were a carnivore-free zone. Quim – an unrepentant carnivore – would not agree at all. His wife, who does not eat meat herself, does not want to prevent others from choosing their own food. I am as convinced as Quim that we should cater to all types. But when a country-hams manufacturer suggested that they use images of l'Avenc as part of their corporate profile and as a marketing strategy – and added that they could not pay but were sure we would welcome the extra publicity it would bring – we were agreed. No.

And with a fair degree of certainty we think we can say that there will never be a bullring at l'Avenc. As I write Deborah's family are off to 'walk for the animals' and protest against the bull-run in Pamplona.

I shall never go as far as my sisters; I cannot even follow Belinda to her conclusion that animals have rights though I share her wish that we should not serve food whose production has involved cruelty. Who knows what animals know, or how much they feel? But they have feelings; of that I'm sure. After Tom was killed, Jerry was never the same. He made a new friend – Nala, Belinda's neurotic boxer with a permanently aghast expression – and they run and bark together. But the spring went from his step the day Tom died and it has never returned. Jerry and Nala howl at the moon but never with the old abandon. My friendship with Jerry and the late Tom has led me to this conclusion at least: if humans have souls, so do animals.

15. A Bottomless Pit

Were I to have my time again, I would have hanged the expense and employed a high-calibre project manager at l'Avenc from the start. That said, if we had hired a project manager, he would probably have resigned within weeks.

We lacked a real foreman with a foreman's authority. Joan Sarsanedas's workmen had been beavering away on parts of the work in his domain (he had too many other projects on the go to be there himself all the time), while Toni Molina's men had been getting on with the holiday cottages at the other end of the site. Andrew had been plodding on alone with his circuitry (cursing various individuals under his breath for sneaking power-hungry appliances into places from which he had tried to ban them), and my brother-in-law himself had been outside on his big earthmover, hacking wildly into a mountainside for reasons best known to himself . . . and there was nobody to draw these threads together, and occasionally bang heads together.

There was one problem we were lucky to be spared. With Sarsanedas's help we were not often or for long critically short of craftsmen. One way or another, stonemasons and carpenters who really understood the traditional building crafts of rural Catalunya always seemed to be found. In Spain as in England there has been for years a wailing chorus of those who cry that the old crafts are dying, that skills are being forgotten, and that soon it will be impossible to find men who can carry on the building traditions of their fathers and grandfathers.

Maybe. I observe only that there are as many skilled drystone-wallers in the Derbyshire Peak District today as there were thirty years ago (my hunch is that there are rather more) and they are by no means wheezing old gaffers on their last legs as another branch of rural folk knowledge dies. Many are young. They are making good money. There is a reason for this. The national park authorities and other government bodies offer subsidies for drystone-walling. The skills and the labour follow. This channelling of public subsidy (and private interest) away from food production and towards 'quality of life' aspects of the rural European economies is unlikely to diminish in the era ahead.

The skills of those Catalan workmen who carved our lintels, built our walls and joined our timbers were prodigious; in no way inferior to the skills of the men who built l'Avenc and maintained it through the centuries. And they were comparatively better paid than their peers of a century ago were likely to have been, and at least as highly regarded. There is money in the rural building crafts, probably more money than there was a generation ago as wealthier people move from the city to the country and work from there; and where there is the demand and the money, the skills will follow and endure.

Skill shortages in the world of craftsmanship are not (as the more mystically inclined among country-lovers sometimes like to sigh) a spiritual problem, nor does the availability or otherwise of carpenters and stonemasons tell us much about the contemporary human condition. It is a matter of economics. In the century ahead the economics of traditional craftsmanship are good, and the prospects better. We are apt to diagnose ills some years (often some decades) after they have set seriously in, and often after they have passed their worst. My guess is that if there has been a crisis of craftsmanship in Europe, its trough occurred about three-quarters of the way through the last century, in an epoch when everybody thought there was no future in the old skills and crafts. There plainly is such a future, and I think we can see it clearly now.

By extension, I would guess that the passing of l'Avenc's point of greatest peril – those years in the late twentieth century when the house was close to ruin, people were still leaving the land in Catalunya, and few were interested in living in the country as a 'lifestyle choice' and working from there – may be seen as a parable for many comparable parts of the European countryside. I reckon that in Spain that low point has just passed – more recently than in Britain – and that the future for rural heritage is good.

I am just glad that we shored up that ridge beam and shored up l'Avenc, at the critical point. We served our purpose when willing spirits were few, and when we are gone it will no longer be diffi-cult to find people who want to carry on the job and ownership.

So I kept repeating to myself the words of my television producer, said in the midst of interminable, morale-sapping nego-tiations to organize the permissions needed for my months on the island of Kerguelen: 'It gets harder, then it gets easier.' In that case it had. Maddening how the most banale of homilies so often turns out to be the truest. 'One step at a time' really was the most useful guide, and there does come a point when, all at once, it strikes you that the list of things still to be sorted out is for the first time noticeably shorter than the list of things already accomplished. Slowly, that became true of the house. This was not a 'corner' we had 'turned' but we were getting there.

First came the stairs and floors. We had started on these while the construction of the holiday cottages was moving towards completion. The three principal elements of this work were oak, stone and lead. Joan Sarsanedas and his assistants were in charge, but as we proceeded we took permanently on to our own payroll a couple of supporting hands, Catalan workmen.

All the floors and the joists supporting them had to be removed. They were of hard, black and very heavy oak (we found almost no pine in the original construction of l'Avenc), and almost all this timber was about 500 years old or more, but about half of it was rotten: centuries of woodworm and rainwater-penetration had taken their toll. For sentimental as well as practical reasons we wanted to reuse as much of the original timbers as we could, so we stacked up all the timber outside next to the wood from the roof and picked from it the pieces which could be returned. The rest would keep us in firewood for years.

Joan Sarsanedas, meanwhile, had ordered in huge quantities of new French oak, which he had been seasoning in preparation for use. This he kept at his own house near Pruit which, ever since he had started bulk-buying oak for the roof timbers, had turned into a wood-yard.

With supplies of rolled lead sheet readily at hand from his own mill, Quim decided that this would be a once-in-a-millennium opportunity to lay down a complete lead skin between each floor and the ceiling beneath it, for the purposes of sound insulation. My brother-in-law's brain was a fertile source of once-in-a-millennium opportunities and this plan was to be neither the last nor the most millennial.

Above the lead sheet, a layer of lightweight, porous cement was to be laid down to insulate and secure the floor. This strange material — slightly soft underfoot when set — arrived in liquid form in mixer-lorries. But how to get 1,000-odd gallons of the stuff up on to the upper floors? It was too high to pump, and too much to labour up the stairs with in buckets. The problem was solved by the arrival of a spindly, livid green machine which looked like a mechanical praying mantis. On an extending telescopic arm like a giant municipal cherry-picker, huge dollops of the cement were lifted in an open drum and poured through the windows on each floor.

Not for the first time I pictured in my mind's eye the dead generations of Catalan *masovers*, generation upon generation for 800 years, men and women for whom l'Avenc had been home since the twelfth century; and the sixteenth-century labourers who built the modern façade of the house, stone by stone, with only mules for transport and their arms, ropes and pulleys to lift. I pictured them as a silent army, ghostly and grey, rank upon rank from every succeeding century, massed around the house like a sea around an island, watching, wordless, as the green machine gesticulates.

If only we could transport ourselves in time to 1300, or 1559, or 1850. If only we could watch as the last poor family left l'Avenc in the 1950s, turning their backs on their old homestead as they trudged towards Tavertet with all the possessions they could carry and load on their mule-carts. If only we could cast ourselves forward 300 years and see the families who may be living there then — what kind of people they are, how they look and speak and dress, what changes they in turn make to the house, just as we are changing it now.

Will the wide vista out over the river valley and Montseny mountains be different? Will it still be wooded? Will there be farms? Will there be a road in the valley? Will the spire of Sant Romà still needle above the lake at low water? Will the planeloads of tourists bound for the Costa Brava still trundle along the eastern sky? Will Catalan still be spoken or become a dead language known only to scholars? Will Catalunya be a nation-state again?

We too, our family, Belinda and Quim, Deborah and Manel, my mother, Theresa, and my increasingly frail father, Leslie, were bound for the grey ranks of l'Avenc's ghosts. A bottomless pit, Dad had warned me the house would become. Might we too, in our turn, stand among the ghosts and stare, and wonder at what time brings?

16. A Parris Enters Politics

Early in 2002 Belinda had asked my thoughts on an idea she was mulling over. Toni was looking for an extra name to add to his slate of council candidates for the village's municipal elections. Tavertet's politics is largely local and not strongly party-led, still less ideological; but there are groupings on the council and Toni leads one of them. He had asked her whether she would like to join as a candidate, though there was no guarantee at all that she would be elected: seats are keenly and properly contested in Tavertet, heaven knows why.

Don't even think about it, was my advice. Either you won't be elected – in which case you'll be disappointed and miserable, and feel the whole village has somehow rejected you personally because you're English – or, far worse, you will be elected. Then you will have to endure years of people moaning at you, complaining about their neighbours, wanting you to do things which are beyond the bounds of possibility, and blaming you when anything goes wrong.

I warmed to my theme. You'll have to sit through endless meetings of hog-whimpering tediousness, I continued, listen to boring people gassing on interminably and pretend to be interested, negotiate with small-minded jobsworth officials in Barcelona, spend your evenings poring over pages of bureaucratic language and preparing for meetings – and get no thanks from anybody for what you're doing.

Anyway, I said, everybody is going to think you're doing it so that you can use your influence to swing planning decisions or grant-applications l'Avenc's way. Every time the council has to deal with any matter which touches on our house, your influence will be suspected. 'Why would this Englishwoman want to be on our council?' people will mutter. 'What's she up to? Who does she think she is?'

The more I spoke, the more passionate became my warning against any entanglement with local politics, or any politics, and certainly democracy in any shape or form. My advice was categorical. Her husband's was identical. Don't do it.

The next we heard was that my sister had allowed her name to be added to Toni's list. 'Don't worry,' she told her husband and me, 'I probably won't be elected and I shan't mind; but I wanted to show a bit of support, anyway.'

That month she was elected as a councillor for Tavertet. She was worried that her role in the l'Avenc project might clash with her responsibilities as councillor, or seem to; or that people might think it was her intention to use her public position to promote her private interest in l'Avenc. But in fact conflicts have rarely arisen and our village seems to have grown used to its English councillor from the big house on the hill.

Even as they did, my father's warnings of a bottomless pit came true more literally – and faster – than even he may have guessed, when my brother-in-law decided that l'Avenc needed a garage. An unexceptional idea, we thought, until he explained what he meant. It would be a garage to house more than forty vehicles. And it would be underground.

Quim's digger-mania had struck again. All of us, even his loyal wife, were nonplussed. What had he in mind? Some kind of vast subterranean cavern? Yes, he replied modestly, something like that. The garage would be about one hundred yards long, some thirty feet high, as wide as a three-lane carriageway, arched in cross-section like a section of tunnel on the London Underground (but much bigger), constructed in reinforced concrete, sunk entirely below ground level and covered over with lawn. Oh – and it would be right in front of l'Avenc.

Our reaction was unanimous: why?

He gestured to the litter of vehicles already scattered across the site: my Land-Rover, his and his wife's Renault Clio, their faithful white Toyota pickup, a digger, three builders' cars, Deborah's van. And this at a time when nothing was happening at the house beyond the usual building work, and we had no guests. A place

with three or four holiday cottages, he said, plus four owners with
their own apartments, the possibility one day of more apartments
or cottages, and the likelihood that there would be regular events
– weddings, conferences, symposia – needed a car-park if it was
not to look like a permanent car-boot sale with vehicles on every
verge or patch of mud or grass.

We agreed that this was true.

Well, he continued, if there was to be a car-park then the only
question was: what kind? An ugly covered garage on a couple of
floors? A quarter-acre gouged out of the hillside and paved, as it
would have to be – and visible for twenty miles in most directions? Or underground where nobody could see it? Surely that
was the least intrusive?

We agreed that this was true.

In that case, he concluded, and given that we had agreed in
principle to the construction of an underground garage, when was
the best time to construct it? Later, when the property had been
landscaped, the area in front of l'Avenc paved in stone, and trees
and grass planted all around – in which case everything would
have to be ripped up again – or now, when the place still looked
like a building site, before anything was laid down?

The logic was hard to resist. But what about the cost? The
construction of a huge reinforced-concrete tunnel was beyond our
skill or daring, and not Joan Sarsanedas's kind of thing at all. Quim
made enquiries and found a company who said they would do it
on a contract, leaving our regular builders free to press on with the
house. I noted wryly to myself that the price was about two-thirds
of what we had paid for the whole property seven years previously.

The plan did make sense. But, quite apart from the cost (and
£100,000 was money we did not have), there was just this heart-
sinking feeling that at the very point when we seemed to be over
the hill, with most of the major construction and reconstruction
work complete – the point where what was left to do, though
onerous and expensive, was basically 'fitting out' internally, connecting up the services and landscaping – the thought of starting up
that ruddy digger again and tearing a great hole in the ground,

as big as l'Avenc itself and right in front of the poor old house, was hard to bear.

Not for Quim. He positively relished the idea. With no great enthusiasm I agreed to it, and Belinda volunteered to make some enquiries about the possibility of getting an environmental grant to help with the cost – to which our reaction was, broadly, 'Yeah, right.'

But she got the grant, though we had to pay the bulk ourselves, and we signed the contract, and work began. Whereupon it emerged that the planning permission we were still awaiting for the whole project at and around l'Avenc would be needed to validate the installation of an underground car-park. We did not need the same permission, however, for a store-room. So a store-room it would have to be, unless (hopefully until) the planning application came through.

I am poor at visualizing from architects' plans the reality as it will be on the ground, or in this case under the ground. But as work proceeded through the summer of 2004, both the ingenuity and the scale of Quim's design were brought home to me.

L'Avenc stands on the gentle rise formed by the lower slope of the shoulder of a hill. The road skirts around the site in a curve, in front of the property: we had moved the road thirty yards down the slope away from the house. Thus the house is on a big mound. The road curves around the mound, in front of the house but some way away. My brother-in-law's idea was to tunnel through the mound from the Tavertet side (where the tunnel left the road) to the Rupit side (where the tunnel rejoined the road). The tunnel would describe a wide curve in a mirror-image of the curve of the road – curving *into* the mound. This allowed it extra length.

The two mouths of the tunnel would be no more than vehicle-sized, but, within, the tunnel would be cavernous, allowing to either side a line of vehicles parked nose-into-the-side. It would be lit by a line of vertical shafts (*avencs*) from the ceiling up to where they broke the surface of the ground above.

The method of construction would be cut-and-cover – the same method as was used to construct the New York subway system, though on a slightly less ambitious scale (only very slightly, it sometimes seemed). So an enormous curved trench, as wide and high as a two-storey house and a hundred yards long, had to be cut into the hillside. And at its closest point it would be much less than a stone's throw from l'Avenc's front door.

This would then be paved in thick concrete (a plastic membrane beneath), and upon it a reinforced concrete shell, semi-circular in cross-section, would be built, section by section, each one precon-structed from thousands of wood planks held up by poles and scaffolding, over which the steel reinforcing rods would be laid, and upon which the liquid concrete would then be poured. As each section set, the next would be built. A substantial staircase and lift-shaft would be constructed next to the garage, on the l'Avenc side, so that we would have access for the elderly and disabled too.

When the whole tunnel and shaft were complete, the exterior would be painted in thick bitumen, it would be covered in a plas-tic membrane, and the earth would be bulldozed back over it. The flat half-acre of ground in front of the house would be restored to its former aspect – but now with a garage beneath it. The whole thing, we were assured, could be more or less complete within the year, before the winter rains arrived.

Well, it took only about twice as long as that, and – as our overruns went – this was not bad going.

As the rain came in November 2004, the view from the upper windows at the front of l'Avenc was of an ocean of wet clay which, like the Red Sea for Moses, had miraculously parted a few yards in front of the front door. An abyss had opened up, seem-ingly almost as deep as the house was high. The clay walls of the abyss were unstable, sections kept falling in, and appalling cracks had opened up in the ground immediately in front of the house. Both my sister and I (and in his darker moments, he later admit-ted, Quim too) honestly feared the whole house might simply fall into the infernal pit. The scene put one in mind of San Francisco in 1906, immediately after the earthquake.

But work proceeded, even through winter, though the water

and clay made it hard. The contractors had bitten off more than they had expected to chew, I suspect, but still the orange cement lorries with their slowly churning silos came lurching up the rutted road from Tavertet. What seemed like hundreds of loads were chuted down into the pit; and the arched shell, as it rose from the bottom, was a truly impressive and strangely beautiful sight.

When, finally, in the spring of 2005, Quim's digger trundled back to work, laboriously returning soil and clay into empty spaces, scoop by scoop, and spreading them over the roof, too, our relief was intense. Soon there was no hole for the house to fall into.

Then came the grass seed – sprayed on in industrial quantities – and the apron of stone slabs outside the big front door, lowered gingerly into place while strung from the bucket of the digger. Deborah, Manel and Adam had already made a lovely wild area with olive trees and shrubs in front of the holiday cottages, and tamed the slopes around the old brick well. They had started planting grass and *alzina* trees, and even the elegant dark pencil of a cypress behind the house.

Abel, a young man with the tireless, slow, solitary, painstaking practical genius of an English drystone-waller, was piecing his way, yard by yard, down the 150-yard cast-concrete retaining wall we had built on the upside of the road skirting l'Avenc to hold back the hill, facing it beautifully with local stone. He built gateposts, too, at the entrances to the garage and to the house. We paid him by the yard, and with his transistor radio, alone and out in all weathers but never in quite the same place twice, he became a familiar sight for nearly a year at l'Avenc.

L'Avenc – dared we say it? – was beginning to look civilized. It was at this point that Quim's thoughts – and a digger trundled never far behind his thoughts – turned to the construction of a swimming pool. As I write, the outer retaining walls are already in place, and the logic is (as it was for the construction of the garage) as impeccable as its conclusion is challenging. If we are going to have a pool at all, now is the time to build it. So onward my brother-in-law ploughs. At least the area behind the house contained nothing already established to be messed up. The steps

I built in that first summer alone in the house had long gone.

He was right to plough on, but there were times when it would have been reasonable to feel we had reached a staging-post where we could tell ourselves that a phase was now complete and there was no pressing need to storm forward into the next stage; and instead, pause, stand back, relax, and admire and enjoy what we had done already. Such staging-posts never seemed to come.

And as all this work around the outside of the house had gathered pace since the year 2000, the importance of protecting the whole property from marauding cattle had grown too. We desperately needed fences. Despairing that walkers and drivers would keep gates shut – and because the public road came across our land – we needed cattle-grids at each entry, too.

Traffic was increasing. Since those early days when the track could not have been called a road at all, the local authority had begun upgrading it. A plan was advanced (before, I had better add, Belinda became a local councillor) to put a permanent surface on the road, which kept washing away. It was to be not tarmac but concrete, and single-track. In 2003 contractors had prepared the surface all the way from Tavertet, past l'Avenc and Rajols, to the main C153 road near Rupit, and put in impressive pre-cast-concrete culverts wherever drainage under the carriageway was needed. Rainstorms had then washed some of this away, but in 2004 the section between the main road and l'Avenc, via Rajols, was concreted. This was important as the uphill stretch through the beechwoods and past Rajols is horribly steep for one short section.

It is possible to be sentimental – and I sometimes am – about rough roads, and the way they bring peace and quiet by isolating you, but we were by now travelling so often to and from l'Avenc that the surfacing of that stretch of road was a huge boon. It did, however, bring extra picnickers and weekend expeditionaries, not unwelcome in themselves, but another reason along with the cows to define and fence our property properly.

I'm pretty admiring in this book of the rural skills and conscientious workmanship of Catalan country people, but their talents do not extend to agricultural fencing. This is makeshift in the

Collsacabra; rotten, rickety poles, never high enough, strung with sagging lengths of loose barbed wire. Throughout Spain it always seems to be a choice between high-security steel fencing of a kind which would serve well enough along the Israeli border – you half-expect searchlights – or broken-down bits of stick and wire.

There are no better rural fencers and wall-builders in Europe than in England, and no better fencers in England than Jim Rushton and his workmate Mark Edge, from a Derbyshire farming family. Mark's only previous experience of going abroad had been a short package holiday, but both of them were up for flying out as independent travellers, pacing-out the land, sizing-up, establishing what could and what could not be obtained in Catalunya, doing the sums and calculations, and returning to Britain to put a major fencing expedition together.

On their return they sought the help of another friend, Ken Buxton, a specialist in fencing materials, whose site is in the hills above the Derbyshire town of Buxton, and who equipped Jim's formidably customized big Toyota Hilux van with everything they would need. Neither had driven on the continent before, but the pair proceeded fearlessly to the English Channel, were thoroughly sick on the overnight ferry, advanced across France, made it through the Pyrenees, and spent a couple of tremendously productive weeks giving l'Avenc proper fences. The work was hard: the soil is thin, hard and rocky, and one fence had to go straight up a hillside at about forty-five degrees; but the strong fences and the effective cattle-grid-and-gating system we now have in place are a monument to their success.

We had scored an important victory in the War of Rajols's Cows. It is good to see the 'Ken Buxton – Agricultural Supplier' plastic tag swinging in the wind, attached to the tensioned wire outside l'Avenc. Whether any Catalan passers-by have been impressed enough to try the Buxton telephone number I doubt: Ken does not include the international dialling code in his publicity.

Jim, Mark and Ken were not the only foreign contractors to work for us at l'Avenc. I think we can claim to have introduced the first Aga into northern Spain.

Most of our heating and cooking is to be done by gas, and before we buried them the cylinders upon which we rely were, as I say, of a size, shape and capacity to attract the attention of US bombers, probably when a wedding party was in full swing. This bulk supply of gas argued for a big, efficient, gas-fired oven, but we wanted something that would look and feel good in the ancient kitchen.

My original plan had been to buy the biggest Aga I could fit into my truck, and drive it from England to Catalunya; but I found that the Aga people and their retailers have to assemble, fit, adjust and test new cookers themselves, on-site. The only Aga agent and distributor I could find in Spain was in Castellón, hundreds of miles down the coast; but there was a French agency near Toulouse, about seventy miles away, so I rang them.

On a wild, wet winter's day in 2004, two rather anxious Frenchmen arrived with our new stove. They had almost been beaten back by the mud on the road. They said it would be good training for the Paris to Dakar rally. But they did the job, and did it well. That Aga – a huge beast, the biggest the company make – has become like a warm heart to the kitchen, and we use it all the time.

For within the main house, things were really moving now. Proper staircases had been made (a huge task), some in wood and some in stone. And beautiful oak-framed windows had been put in.

Choosing these had been a difficult job, for l'Avenc had never, in all the thirty years we had known the house, had proper windows – just rotting, flapping, eyeless shutters – and the whole look of the house as we had come to know it was windowless. Once the frames and panes were in place, it was striking what a difference that made, changing the whole appearance and character. It was a bit of a wrench at first, but the windows were designed (with Joan Sarsanedas's help) to be as much in keeping as possible, and I think we succeeded. Inside, we gave them the wooden shutters that are so much part of Catalan houses. And we even put discreet little panes of glass into the arrow-slits, to stop the wind whistling through.

With the windows came new oak doors, made to reproduce so

far as possible the broken and rotten doors (where there were doors at all) which they replaced. They were magnificent. The great front doors, beneath the arch at the front of the house, were almost kingly.

The oak floors having been laid down, we could go ahead with radiators: a water-circulated system, heated by gas. These proved more effective than I had imagined possible. Being constructed with thick stone walls, and with all the insulation we had laid down, and now that the new doors and windows excluded the gale, l'Avenc turned out to be a surprisingly heatable and cosy house.

I have said little about the climate, supposing, perhaps wrongly, that the reader is well enough aware that at an altitude of more than 3,000 feet in northern Spain, we are not talking Benidorm. In my family we have often tried to give visitors from Britain a picture, before they arrive, of what to expect, but it is difficult.

At the height of summer, l'Avenc can be very, very hot, and sometimes for weeks on end. During blazing Augusts and even Septembers it is easy to believe you are living in Spain. But winters are at least as cold as England and sometimes colder, with the temperature dropping regularly well below freezing. Rarely a winter passes without many days or nights like that. It always snows in winter, but only every few winters do we get the sort of blizzards which leave roads closed and villages cut off for very long. In one such year my parents were cut off for two weeks at l'Hostalot, with snow up to the windows outside; and my father had to improvise snow-shoes from tennis rackets. L'Avenc is often cut off for a morning or so after heavy snow, but, as in England, it soon melts.

In a nutshell, spring arrives about ten days earlier, autumn about two weeks later; the sun in summer is higher and hotter; the temperatures in winter go a little lower and stay down for longer; and overall I would say that the most striking difference is that the weather is more stable; the rain can set in for a week, and the sun can shine for a month; and when the wind rises from across the Pyrenees, it can blow for days. Vic and Manlleu, down on the plain, are beset by dreadful freezing fogs, but l'Avenc almost always rises clear of these, and we look out (as I did on the first page of this book) over a sea of cloud.

The ancient pear tree in front of the house – I noticed it the very first time I came, for it is most unusual, as big as a small oak – struggles during drought, and since buying the house I have started to water it during hot summers. It is wonderful to see the old tree regaining some of its youth and vigour, freed from drought and from the super-concentrates of animal excrement with which the herds of cows who used to shelter from the baking sun beneath its branches used to repay the poor tree. In 2005 it flowered for the first time in memory.

So l'Avenc was used to almost everything the weather could throw at it, except hot, dry central heating in winter when the air anyway lacks moisture. One immediate result was that some of the new oak, though cured, started curling and cracking; but my view was that the worst we could replace or repair, while, for the rest, a few curls and cracks helped the house keep its air of antiquity.

Upstairs, in the upper state room, a stunning new fireplace was built, complete with stone chimney-breast and mantelpiece. Carved into the stone above, we had engraved the new crest we had designed to answer the old crest on the fireplace; the one with an A for Abey and a P for Parris. And while replacing a window on the northern flank of the house we had a lintel carved, likewise, to answer the 'IHS Maria 1559' lintel on the south-facing side.

OK – tell me it was pretentious to have our names carved. We didn't care. In the best sense of the word, l'Avenc is a pretentious house: not uppity, not keeping-up-with-the-Joneses, but a house with a strong sense of the grand gesture. L'Avenc is imposing, and intends to be. The gods of this house will have been pleased to see us adding our initials to the roll of honour.

17. An End and a Beginning

Late in 2004 Francesc, Quim's older brother and a constant, stalwart pillar of strength as partner in our enterprise, asked to withdraw from our consortium. There had never been the least dispute or difference between us and nor was there now. Francesc wanted to concentrate his energies and resources on the family business; he had not been, or wanted to be, as closely or emotionally involved as we were in the twists and turns the project took, but supported us (as Lord Melbourne said of his support for the Church of England) 'like a bulwark rather than a pillar: from the outside', and we knew what we all owed him for that. He felt we could now manage without him, and offered us all the time we needed to stump up the extra cash to buy him out of his share. Henceforward the ownership would be tripartite.

It was a friendly parting. It came at a time when our confidence was growing that now we really had begun to win. Success genuinely did seem within sight. Then, in the spring of 2005, my father died.

It was the middle of May. He had not long celebrated his eighty-second birthday, and he and my mother, Theresa, were ten days short of their fifty-eighth wedding anniversary. But Dad had been struggling with ever greater difficulty against poor lungs and a weakened heart. He and Mum were still living alone together at l'Hostalot, supported by constant family visits, of course, and their faithful friend Núria, who lived at the farm up the lane; but his last year (and ours, and especially my mother's who at seventy-eight was becoming a full-time nurse) had been increasingly overshadowed by his illness, his depression and his frustration.

I flew straight from England and got to the state hospital in Vic just in time. If only the old could expect the same care, kindness and individual attention as my father was receiving there. As he died in the small hours of a cool Saturday morning, Belinda, my mother and I sat by him, holding his hand and talking to him, with rain falling softly outside, dripping from the trees. I am fifty-five, but this was the first time I had lost anyone close.

Death is strange. Not frightening, not particularly painful, not even (for me) 'tragic'. I was not knocked over by grief. Instead I felt disoriented, forgetful, fretful . . . 'distracted' is the word. A world which had always had him in it no longer did; and he had not wanted to go, not at all except when the struggle overwhelmed him. He kept hoping a cure would be found and he would get better. Waves more of depression than of grief would sweep over me quite briefly, then seem to pass.

We had to wait for a couple of hours after he died for an orderly to arrive with papers for my mother to sign, releasing the corneas of his eyes for transplant. All the rest of my poor father was too clapped out to be of any use to medicine. And when I returned to the ward an hour after his death and looked at and touched the corpse, I felt nothing. It was not him at all. He had gone.

But that is not how Catalans deal with death. There followed a short and intensive course in a different culture – a culture, in fact, which has more in common with old-fashioned working-class practice in England.

The first thing the nurse wanted to know was how and when the body was to be displayed for visitors. The custom in the whole Iberian peninsula (it is in fact the Muslim custom) is that the funeral and burial should take place within twenty-four hours, but the nurse understood our wish that there should be two days to arrange the funeral; the display of the body, however, must be on the following day, and for a maximum of six hours, which we would have to designate. Would we like the body moved to a special display room in the nearby funeral parlour, where visitors could walk around and touch the corpse, or would we be content to leave it in the hospital morgue, where visitors could just look through a glass screen?

We opted for the latter. Usually, I learned, the widow and close family would be present, so people could pay their respects to us too; but we all agreed with my mother that she should stay at home to receive visitors there. So on the Sunday afternoon, from noon to six, my two sisters took it in turns to be present by the morgue. I doubted many would want to avail themselves of this facility. I was wrong. There was a continuous stream of people all afternoon. Some fifty in all. Some of them we did not even know.

At home at l'Hostalot, I thought, one or two close friends might call, but the house is twenty miles (or more) away for most of them, up a long and winding road, and I expected most to write or perhaps telephone, as we might in England. Again I was wrong. All through Saturday, Sunday and Monday, cars kept arriving. On the occasions Mum was temporarily out, people went away and came back again later. She and I lost track of the numbers who came, sat with her, sometimes awkwardly, for a while, and then departed – usually as yet another car came down the hill towards us. People she hardly knew – people such as the trade-union convenor from the days Dad had been general manager at the cable factory in Manlleu – turned up with wives and often families. Dad had retired after his heart-attack almost twenty-five years earlier, but still they remembered him, and came.

How everyone knew is a mystery to me. A couple of days later a notice was placed in the local paper, and in the national paper the *Vanguardia*, but the visitors started within hours of my getting home from the hospital. Mum told one person in Rupit, and within half an hour people from miles around all knew, and were calling.

We arranged the funeral at the small, ancient church at Pruit: once the centre of a parish, now just a sentinel on the hill, with a couple of houses attached. My brother Roger's beautiful water-colour painting of the coast near Pals where we have a flat (Dad loved the sea) was printed on the Order of Service, all the family were there, and with icy rain pelting down outside, the priest from Tavertet conducted an eclectic remembrance and funeral (slightly chaotic, typical of my family, with younger members turning tape-recorders on and off, my mother reading poems, and readings in Catalan and Castilian too).

The church was completely packed, with standing-room only.

About 200 people came – again, how they all knew is a mystery to me – including some of the workers at Dad's factory all those years ago, whom nobody else in my family knew, but who seemed to have found their way to the church out in the wilds of the Collsacabra.

Joan Sarsanedas and his family were there, as were all who worked for us at l'Avenc. Some of the mourners were friends and workers whose association was more with l'Avenc than with my father, for he too was now associated with the house.

My family stood at the door of the church when the service was over, every mourner bidding leave of us all as they left. As it is the custom to kiss twice – to left and right – on greeting or leaving, this meant about 400 kisses for each of us and threatened to end in a seriously cricked neck, but the kindness was overwhelming.

By now the rain was coming down in sheets, knocking the May blossom and the new leaves off the trees, and it grew bitterly cold. Dad's coffin – he was to be cremated – departed into the storm. I watched the tail-lights of the hearse as it rocked along the little road which climbs the hill to Pruit.

I remembered a night not long after we had bought l'Avenc, before the house had even had its roof renewed, when I had driven out from England to visit. And I remembered again Dad's chuckled warning: 'pozo sin fondo' – bottomless pit. To return to England I had needed to leave in the early hours of the morning, to catch a ferry from Bilbao. I was in my ancient Land-Rover, which had been proving difficult to start, and whose headlights had been faulty; Dad, who taught me car mechanics, had helped me fix them.

He had woken up and dressed to see me off, and to see the Land-Rover started and check again its lights. It did start, and, waving goodbye to both parents, I set off, climbing in first gear (I was heavily loaded with olive oil, tiles, wine, trees from Deborah and Manel and garden pots) up the long hill at the end of l'Hostalot's drive.

Half-way up the hill I noticed there was a car behind me, keeping its distance and making no attempt to overtake. I recognized my father's headlights. I knew at once that he was following for a while to see that I was all right with the Land-Rover. He followed to the end of the rural road, where it meets the C153 and where my parents' letter-box stands. I turned on to the main road, and he followed still, as far as the hollow past Rupit where the road crosses the bridge over the Rupit stream, and shortly before the turn-off to l'Avenc.

As I crossed the bridge and pulled away up the hill, heading towards Vic, I saw his headlights dwindle in the rear-view mirror. He had stopped, assured that I was OK, and would return to l'Hostalot, and his bed. He did not flash his lights, or hoot, or want any kind of goodbye conversation. The support was wordless, at a distance and without show. It always was, with him.

I was alone now. Continuing on my way through the Catalan night I felt a momentary pang of loneliness that his headlights were no longer with me, and my rear-view mirror was empty and dark. I felt it again outside the church in Pruit. My father had joined l'Avenc's legion of ghosts.

The day after his death Belinda suggested a walk from l'Avenc. To our considerable surprise my brother-in-law had found an entirely new path down through to the foot of the cliffs on which Tavertet stands. The main path I have already described: it is now the GR2, makes its way up from valley of the Ter and was once an important packhorse and *guarà* route from the plain of Vic. But Quim had recently enlisted a footpath-preservation gang who with maps and machetes had been cutting back some of the overgrown byways of the Collsacabra and Guilleries, and they had spent a morning clearing a path previously unknown to all of us. This took a different route down through the rocks, and (he said) followed the cliff's base on reaching it, back towards l'Avenc. You ended up, he said, virtually beneath the house itself.

Following his directions, Belinda, her son Rodger and I found the start of the path not a stone's throw from the Church of Sant Cristòfol, in the middle of Tavertet, right by the house where Toni Molina was born. We followed the newly cleared path. As it tumbled straight down the mountain we soon realized that this too was an ancient pack route: in the steepest parts, small flights of crude rock-hewn steps described curves just wide enough for a laden horse, mule or donkey to get round. In places and precipitously the path followed horizontal ledges across the cliff's face as it wound downward. Finally, at the bottom, it forked, one route leading off across the bottom of the valley towards the river, and another turning sharp left and following the cliff's foot. We took that path. Here, too, Quim's gang had been at work.

Glimpses of the cliff above us were astonishing. It was directly above us. It soared. Half-way up, where the rock's stratum changes from ochre to grey, was a sort of gallery – a continuous ledge, level, about a mile long and dizzyingly narrow yet not too narrow to crawl and clamber along.

'It's called the Iron Way by rock-climbers,' said Rodger, 'because they've put clamps into the rock to cling on to where the ledge is narrowest. But it's been blocked off and forbidden to adventurers because apparently lots of hawks and eagles nest there.' We saw an eagle soar from the cliff. In one place we could see that the rock at the cliff's edge at the top jutted out into a big overhang, so that anyone standing there at the edge would in fact be standing above air. I realized that was the place where I had lain awhile in the sun when I had left the track, thirty years ago, on the way to discovering l'Avenc. I had been twenty-five, Belinda twelve, and Dad had still been general manager at the cable factory down in Manlleu.

We had been following the rock for about half an hour when the cliff changed orientation slightly, curving inward into a sort of wide bowl before curving back out to regain its old, east–west alignment. At the neck of this concave curve there was a nick in the rock at the top, and a discolouring of the rock beneath, in a vertical streak. That, I thought, would be where the Avenc waterfall comes down after rain. I have so many times watched the water flooding over from the top, into thin air.

Among undergrowth for a few minutes we lost sight of the cliff above us, but the path had turned into the bowl, towards the place where the waterfall would hit the cliff's foot.

We got there quite suddenly, unexpectedly. All at once the undergrowth cleared. The cliff towered above us, seemingly miles above us. It was totally sheer, a great, blank, grey-and-ochre wall, 1,000 feet high and twice as wide, in a great, even, shallow curve, like a massive dam wall. I clapped, and the wall clapped back. At our feet were the marks and droppings of wild goats, and boar had disturbed the roots of the bushes. It was sunset and the air was full of butterflies.

We were standing on what was evidently the bed of a shallow lake. At its head were strewn enormous boulders, and from their wear and markings you could see that it was on to these that the cascade fell. All around were reeds. I stood on the rocks and – yes – directly, vertically above me was the lip of the cliff's top. Birds wheeled around in the air currents, calling. If I believed in gods I would have had the strongest sensation that a cliff god lived here.

You could stand under the overhang with your back to the rock, well behind – inside – what would be the curtain of falling water when the stream up there was flowing. Craning my neck upward, I could just see the bushes and small trees clinging to the edge high above, bushes and trees I knew from their other, safe, side. L'Avenc stood just across the sloping meadow behind them. The abyss into which the old house had briefly stared while excavations for the garage were in progress was reproduced here, and magnified five hundredfold, by these cliffs.

All three of us found ourselves spontaneously dispersing, each to stand alone in a separate spot, in silent awe. Then we regrouped and turned back, hurrying up towards Tavertet before the night closed in. The streetlamps were coming on, and Toni's latchkey white husky, Lluna, was waiting to greet us as we scrambled up over the edge and on to the street.

Awaiting us at l'Avenc was a warm house (the gas-fired central heating was at last working well), a pool of light (the solar panels and batteries were doing their job and soon, God and the Ministry of Urbanization willing, the wind would be helping us make power too), the newly installed Aga in which a meal would be cooking, and in the cellar where we had cleared the debris of the earthquakes of 1427 and an oak barrel of red wine. A toast, perhaps, to my father.

How far we had come with our beloved *pozo sin fondo*: from the cliff's top on that sunny, cloud-strewn morning in 1975 when I had been smitten by an enchanted ruin, to the cliff's foot this May evening three decades on, looking up into the sky where an almost restored l'Avenc now stood. This had been a long road with many strange turnings. Who knows where next it may lead?

I think l'Avenc does know. Right at the start of this book I said – and you may have picked up the hint again and again as the tale proceeded – that the house seemed to have a personality of its own, unbound by time, place or even country: a stranger in its own land. I have never thought of l'Avenc, and never found myself describing it, as 'my' or even 'our' house, and nor, I notice, do Quim or Belinda, though Lord knows we have done more to make it ours and deserve that possessive adjective than most people in most homes can boast.

But I do not want l'Avenc to be 'mine', even if I could make it so. I have from the beginning had the strange feeling that the house is watching us as it has watched all its owners, smiling at our labours, unperturbed. So strong is its sense of timelessness and disengagement from its time that nothing we or any of our predecessors have done to it has seemed 'inappropriate' or 'out of keeping' – those favourite words of planners and architectural historians.

I have said earlier that the arrow-slits were almost certainly pointless. The great façade, the thrilling three-wayness of its layout . . . these are, in the most magnificent sense of the word, whimsical. Something in l'Avenc's nature whispers 'Be bold – just do it' to its owners. I said earlier that a rocket-launch pad would not look out of place. When in 2001 I persuaded a helicopter-pilot friend to collect a band of my French friends (met in Kerguelen) and me from a mountaintop in the Pyrenees and helicopter us over the Collsacabra to the flat ground in front of the balcony at l'Avenc, the house greeted us as though it were the most natural way in the world to arrive – as natural as the donkeys, mules, horses and cars which for 800 years it had watched come and go.

Quim's underground garage, though terrifying in its construction, has never seemed wrong for l'Avenc: no more wrong than the arrow-slits, or Joan Sarsanedas's capricious chimneys. The small black square of photovoltaic cells up the hill behind us appears, as will the smooth white turbine of our wind-powered generator above them, as a new venture; just as the white cattle grazing around are the old venture. L'Avenc is not a house for the faint-hearted, never has been, and does not want to be.

And for all the changes we will make, l'Avenc never really changes. It is the same place it was when first we saw it. It has a spirit, and the spirit is immutable.

If I had my time over again, would I have been fainter-hearted? Would I have done things differently? Yes: we made many mistakes.

Would I have wanted different partners? No: Belinda and Quim were the best team I could ever hope to be part of.

Would I have done it at all? Should I, when I rounded the corner and first saw the house on that fateful morning, have shaken my head sorrowfully at l'Avenc's impending ruin, walked on and banished it from my thoughts? Should we have saved our energies for challenges more easily within our reach?

No. Though it has put grey hair on all our heads, a million times no. We accepted a mission which was very close to being beyond us, but it was not beyond us. We rescued a house when nobody else would take the risk. There were good reasons why nobody would take the risk, and I doubt anyone else would have done so. L'Avenc would be in ruins now were it not for us.

L'Avenc is a story. I have told it as well as I can, though partially and imperfectly I know. It was a story which might have ended. My family and I have stopped it ending. We have reopened the book. We have begun our own chapter. We can each of us, at least, know this: we saved l'Avenc. And as this book closes I am prouder of that than I can say.

Beyond that, who knows? Among all now living, visiting or working at l'Avenc there were only ever two who knew without question their place in the picture. Tom and Jerry never doubted their role or questioned their future, and now Tom is gone. Jerry will die there without asking where next, or why. I don't know where next and I've often asked why. L'Avenc knows.